M @ Snyder

The Hub's Metropolis

James C. O'Connell
September 22, 2014

Contents

     The City Spreads Out   69

     Development Impacts in Brookline and Beyond   74

     The Zone of Emergence and the Three-Decker   79

     Streetcar-Driven Growth in Cambridge, Belmont, and Arlington   82

     Controlling Growth   84

     Exploring Streetcar Suburbs   86

6   Metropolitan Parkway Suburbs (1895–1945)   89

     Origins of the Metropolitan Park-and-Parkway System   89

     Debate over Regionalization   97

     Parkways Shape the Suburban Landscape   99

     Country Clubs: Social Stratification in the Suburban Landscape   103

     Suburbs in the 1920s and 1930s   107

     The Suburban House Becomes "Comfortable"   109

     Exploring Metropolitan Parks and Parkways   112

7   Suburban Mill Towns (1820–2012)   115

     Boston's Industrial Suburbs   115

     Company Towns   120

     From Mill Towns to Suburbs   125

     New Uses for Old Factories   130

     Exploring Industrial Sites   133

8   Postwar Automobile Suburbs (1945–1970)   135

     Pent-up Suburban Exodus   135

     Living the American Dream   140

     Route 128 and the Technology Boom   148

     Birth of the Shopping Center   156

     From "Stringtowns" to "Strips"   160

     Shaping the Postwar Suburban Landscape   164

     The Role of Zoning and Land Conservation   170

     Exploring Post–World War II Suburbs   175

Preface

There are two Bostons. The most obvious is the historic hub city of forty-eight square miles. The second is the metropolitan area, which is more difficult to grasp. It varies in size and makeup depending on who is defining it. Some consider it to be the 101 cities and towns around Boston that are covered by the Metropolitan Area Planning Council. The federal government identifies 234 communities in the Boston-Cambridge-Quincy, MA-NH Metropolitan Statistical Area and 385 communities in the Boston-Worcester-Manchester, MA-RI-NH Combined Statistical Area. Geographers, demographers, and marketers each define regional retail, labor, and media markets according to the conventions of their fields.

Because of its rich history, the city of Boston has been the subject of thousands of books and studies. Such iconic landmarks as Boston Common, Quincy Market, Beacon Hill, Back Bay, and Fenway Park define the urban core. Metropolitan Boston, on the other hand, has been studied in fragmentary ways, with few books providing a comprehensive overview. Residents lack a clear perspective of the entire region and how it has developed. People know the communities they live and work in, but their concept of the rest of the region is often vague. Yet, the region provides the socioeconomic and environmental framework for contemporary life. It is essential to understand the regional context to address the challenges of global economic competition, rising energy prices, and climate change. Knowledge about regional development trends informs individual decisions about work, residence, education, and free time.

As an urban historian and planner, I have set out to explain metropolitan Boston's development in a way that helps people understand the landscape they live in and the decisions that are being made to change it. The book's format has been inspired by Yale professor Dolores Hayden's *Building Suburbia: Green Fields and Urban Growth, 1820–2000*. Hayden surveyed the history of American suburbs by creating typologies for seven eras of their development.[1] I thought that I could provide a clear explanation of metropolitan Boston's layered history and geography by identifying nine distinct planning and development practices and arranging them into time sequences. Also included is a chapter on how Boston reversed its decline vis-à-vis the suburbs in the latter twentieth century and reinforced its role as the center of a multinucleated metropolis. Each layer of metropolitan development has distinctive characteristics in relation to transportation, real-estate development patterns, business location, housing styles, and the treatment of open and public space.

With the country's oldest large city and some of the earliest suburbs, Greater Boston has multiple layers of suburban infrastructure, architecture, and institutions, which only New York, Philadelphia, and Baltimore can match. Boston has been a national pacesetter for many features of suburbanization: country estates, railroad suburbs, streetcar suburbs, zoning, open-space conservation, highway beltways, shopping centers, office parks, edge cities, and transit-oriented development. Landscape architecture pioneer Frederick Law Olmsted settled in his ideal garden suburb of Brookline. The Metropolitan District Commission's park-and-parkway system, which was created during the 1890s, was the country's first example of regional planning. The city of Boston is noteworthy for its vibrant central city, which suffered a painful postwar decline,, but, through luck and pluck, it crafted a revival that few American cities can match. Metropolitan Boston is currently pursuing a new development paradigm popularly referred to as *smart growth* as a dialectical response to the low-density, automobile-oriented development pattern that has dominated for decades. This growth promotes more compact development, public transit, and preservation of open spaces.

The Hub's Metropolis focuses on the territory covered by Boston's Metropolitan Area Planning Council (MAPC), which serves the region's core 101 cities and towns inside the Interstate-495 beltway. The suburban communities that have been trendsetters in various eras receive the most attention. For the latter twentieth century, the book expands its focus to include areas that traditionally were on Boston's periphery, such as Cape Cod, the Merrimack Valley, and Southern New Hampshire. Boston's relationship with its suburbs is a major theme. Whereas most suburbanites originally worked in Boston, today they may work anywhere in the region and visit Boston only infrequently. Yet, Boston remains the region's primary business center, a cultural and entertainment mecca, and the symbolic hub.

The idea for this book originated in 2000, when my family was scouting homes to buy in the Boston area. As we were driving along Blue Hill Parkway in Milton, I recognized that this parkway and the surrounding neighborhood were typical of Boston's inner core suburbs. I thought it would be interesting to learn more about how these early twentieth-century suburban communities developed, and this book project developed from there. My favorite avocation is investigating places and writing about where I have lived. I have written three books on Springfield and the Pioneer Valley and a history of Cape Cod tourism. Moving to metropolitan Boston (residence in Newton; workplace in downtown Boston), I set out to understand Boston's metropolitan development.

I first tested my approach to explaining suburban development in a paper presented at Environmental History Seminar of the Massachusetts Historical Society in 2004—"Developing Metropolitan Boston, 1889–1945." I also have written studies, book chapters, and papers that have provided some of the material in this book. These writings include "The Evolution of Twentieth-Century Boston's Metropolitan Landscape," in *A Landscape History of New England*, ed. Blake Harrison and Richard W. Judd (MIT Press, 2011); "How Metropolitan Parks Shaped Greater Boston, 1893–1945," in *Remaking Boston: An Environmental History of the City and Its Surroundings*, ed. Anthony N. Penna and Conrad Edick Wright (University of Pittsburgh Press, 2009); "Buildout: Why Boston and Hopkinton Need Each Other," *Architecture Boston*, March/April 2008; "Ahead or Behind the Curve?: Compact Mixed-Use Development in Suburban Boston" (Lincoln Institute of Land Policy, 2003); "Connecting the Region and Its People: Civic Leadership in Greater Boston," in *Governing Greater Boston: The Politics and Policy of Place*, ed. Charles C. Euchner (Rappaport Institute of Greater Boston, John F. Kennedy School of Government, Harvard University, 2003); "Thinking Like a Region: Greater Boston," in *Governing Greater Boston: Meeting the Needs of the Region's People*, ed. Charles C. Euchner (Rappaport Institute of Greater Boston, John F. Kennedy School of Government, Harvard University, 2002).

This book has drawn on my work as an urban planner. I developed much of the material on smart growth for my planning course in the Sustainable Design Program of the Boston Architectural College. I have learned a lot about contemporary planning from my involvement with the Massachusetts Zoning Reform Working Group. My work with the National Park Service has enabled me to work on projects that interpret the historical development of regions and communities across the Northeast. As a planner for the Frederick Law Olmsted National Historic Site in Brookline,

Massachusetts, I have had the opportunity to delve into the work of Olmsted, his firm, and the field of landscape design. As the best way to learn about a city is to walk it, I have taken countless weekend walks with my wife, Ann Marie, in parks, neighborhoods, waterfronts, and town centers. I also have ridden every commuter rail and subway line and many bus lines.

The Hub's Metropolis combines the perspectives of history and urban-regional planning for both a general audience and for those particularly interested in local history, planning, preservation, development, and environmental protection. This book elucidates the major trends that have affected the development of Boston from a small but vigorous city two centuries ago to a sprawling metropolitan area today.

Exploring the Metropolitan Landscape

The best way to learn about the nine different layers of metropolitan Boston's development is to experience them firsthand. As this book makes clear, all of metropolitan Boston, from Boston Common to the I-495 beltway and beyond is worth exploration. Every building, open space, neighborhood, rail line, shopping center, and highway reflects at least one of the development phases discussed in the book, sometimes several.

In researching this book, my wife and I visited sites of interest across the region. We so enjoyed these tours that I have provided at the end of each chapter a description of sites that exemplify a particular historical practice so that an interested reader can enjoy touring, too. Grab your *Official Arrow Metro Boston/Eastern Massachusetts Street Atlas*, open up Mapquest or Google Maps, hook up your GPS system, and get started. A list at the end of the book cross-references sites by location to assist in creating convenient itineraries.

There are several books that can supplement this one and provide background information on specific landmarks. The most helpful resource is *Buildings of Massachusetts: Metropolitan Boston*, ed. Keith N. Morgan (University of Virginia Press, 2009). It covers exemplary buildings in Boston, Cambridge, and forty surrounding cities and towns. Another important source on the architectural history of Boston and many of its suburbs is Douglas Shand-Tucci's *Built in Boston: City and Suburb, 1800–2000* (University of Massachusetts Press, 2000). For the architecture and planning of central Boston and Cambridge, consult Susan and Michael Southworth's *AIA Guide to Boston*, 3rd edition (GPP Travel, 2008). For landscape architecture in the metropolitan area, see Jack Ahern's *A Guide to the Landscape Architecture of Boston* (Hubbard Educational Trust, 1999). Many cities and towns have published historic walking tours through their historic commissions or historical societies.

Acknowledgments

Many people have helped bring this book project along. Perhaps the leading influence has been the Environmental History Seminar at the Massachusetts Historical Society. Participating in the Environmental History Seminar since the early 2000s, I have learned a lot from its members and have enjoyed their fellowship. Conrad Wright, Karl Haglund, Nancy Seasholes, and Phyllis Andersen have commented on segments of the book or provided helpful leads on various topics. Scholars Sam Bass Warner, Anthony Penna, and Blake Harrison read the manuscript and provided extensive comments. Sam Bass Warner suggested the inclusion of sites to visit, making the book more of a user's manual to metropolitan Boston. My literary agent, Albert LaFarge, has made decisive contributions in getting this book published. Charles V. Ryan IV provided valuable insights along the way. The staff of the Metropolitan Area Planning Council (MAPC) have been extremely helpful in providing maps and data. My wife, Ann Marie, played an important role in this book. She explored metropolitan Boston with me, made many suggestions about the book's content, made careful edits, and provided emotional support.

Metropolitan Boston's Layers of Development

The scale of Greater Boston is enormous. According to one survey, Greater Boston ranks as the world's sixth largest metropolitan area, with 1,736 square miles.[1] According to the US Census Bureau, the Boston-Worcester-Manchester MA-RI-NH Combined Statistical Area (CSA) has a population of 7,427,336 living in 385 communities, which makes it the country's fifth largest CSA. The vast region can be difficult to comprehend.

Boston's metropolitan landscape has been 200 years in the making. This book identifies nine layers of suburban development, each having a distinctive pattern of development:

- Traditional Village Centers and Proto-Suburbs (1800–1860)

- Country Retreats (1820–1920)

- Railroad Suburbs (1840–1920)

- Streetcar Suburbs (1870–1930)

- Metropolitan Parkway Suburbs (1895–1945)

- Suburban Mill Towns (1820–2012)

- Postwar Automobile Suburbs (1945–1970)

- Interstates, Exurbs, and Sprawl (1970–2012)

- Smart Growth Era (1990–2012).

Each layer of suburbanization has created a characteristic approach to real-estate patterns, transportation, housing styles, business location, and open space in shaping the built landscape. Government and private-sector investments in railroads, streetcar lines, and highways structured each phase of suburban development. Those planning transportation improvements had visions for changing life in the region, but the transformations always turned out to be farther reaching than anyone could have imagined. Cultural conceptions of appropriate modes of suburban and city living and the desire to create communities suitable for certain social classes also played paramount roles in shaping each phase of suburban development.

These factors combined to create a vernacular development pattern, which was carried out by thousands of actors over decades. It was not dictated by a premeditated plan but rather evolved organically from adaptations to new transportation infrastructures and modes of living. In reality, planners did not plan much actual development—they created the framework for individuals and businesses to undertake it.

Each model of suburban development has left its imprint on the landscape. In some places, a development template complemented an earlier model and in others replaced it. Because Boston is so old and its suburbs are some of the country's earliest, the metropolitan area incorporates overlays of country towns, railroad and streetcar suburbs, automobile-oriented suburbs and commercial sprawl, urban neighborhoods, and an increasing number of compact, transit-oriented projects. The span of each era does not have clear-cut temporal boundaries. There can be overlap between different suburban paradigms. For instance, country retreats for the wealthy, railroad suburbs, and streetcar suburbs were all developing at the same time.

Until about 1820, Boston had no suburbs. Surrounding towns were engaged in farming and used the port of Boston as their commercial center. After the War of 1812, Boston grew to such a point that the surrounding communities of Cambridge, Charlestown, Roxbury, and Somerville started to become extensions of the city. Development was ad hoc. Market gardens, stockyards, blacksmiths, and small factories opened there to serve Boston. As country roads were the only transportation infrastructure, travel was slow and settlement around Boston was scattered.

The first suburban residents were wealthy families who established country seats to escape from the city. Because horse-drawn travel was slow, country estates were initially located in a close ring around Boston. There was no overarching plan for creating a landscape of country estates, but a clear paradigm evolved for estates, where gentleman farmers created model farms and experimental gardens. By the 1840s, the design of the houses and grounds sought to achieve a pastoral Arcadia, a goal that continues to influence suburbanites of all social classes.

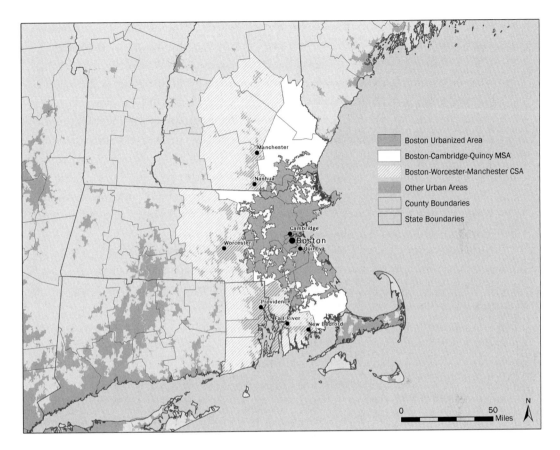

FIGURE 1.1
Map of Boston-Cambridge-Quincy, MA-NH Metropolitan Statistical Area (MSA) and Boston-Worcester-
Manchester MA-RI-NH Combined Statistical Area (CSA). The Boston MSA is the conventional
center-city-based metropolitan area, while the Boston CSA is a combination of the Boston; Worcester;
Providence, RI; and Manchester MSAs. The Federal Office of Management and Budget designates CSAs
when there is a moderate level of commuting between adjoining MSAs.
Source: Metropolitan Area Planning Council.

The first concerted plans for shaping a metropolitan region came from the investors who built the railroads radiating out from Boston in the mid-1830s. They originally expected trains to carry agricultural and industrial freight, but within a decade commuters discovered that the railroad allowed them to live in the country and work in Boston. Speculators spotted opportunities and bought tracts of land near railroad stations, which they divided into house lots. These subdivisions, in Brookline, Newton, and Belmont, were the first planned suburbs. The upper and middle classes developed a template for suburbia that cultivated a country atmosphere and a cocoon for family life, while still taking advantage of the nearby economic and cultural opportunities of one of America's foremost cities. The new suburbs attracted Yankee businessmen and professionals seeking to escape the industry, immigrants, and infections of the teeming city.

Landscape architect and Brookline resident Frederick Law Olmsted helped translate the upper-class suburban development pattern for broader middle-class use. He designed leafy subdivisions in Brookline and beyond and proselytized for suburban communities that had ample tree belts and lawns. Olmsted claimed that the pastoral suburbs represented "the most attractive, the most refined, and the most soundly wholesome forms of domestic life, and the best application of the arts of civilization to which mankind has yet attained."[2]

The coming of the horse-drawn streetcar (1852) and, later, the electrically powered streetcar (1889) transformed how the region was settled. The streetcar companies laid out a web of transit lines with the intention of spurring commuting and the spread of affordable, lower-density housing, creating "streetcar suburbs." Horse-drawn streetcars pushed the city's effective radius out four miles, and the electric streetcar created a development zone that stretched nine miles from downtown. The leading streetcar developer was Henry Whitney, who built Boston's first electric streetcar line, on Beacon Street in Brookline, while buying up large tracts along the street to sell for housing lots. Frederick Law Olmsted was responsible for designing Whitney's streetcar boulevard, which eventually became lined by upscale apartment blocks. All over metropolitan Boston, small-scale land investors and home builders incrementally developed neighborhoods along streetcar lines. The houses, built on smaller lots than the railroad suburbs, ranged from single- to three-family homes, housing middle-class and lower-middle-class families.

As Greater Boston grew in the post–Civil War era, so did the burdens of planning. In order to obtain the urban infrastructure of roads, water supply, sewers, schools, street lighting, parks, and other services, the surrounding municipalities of

Dorchester, Roxbury, West Roxbury, Charlestown, and Brighton voted to become part of Boston. In 1874, Brookline voted to reject annexation and provide its own municipal services. This provided a precedent for other suburban communities to maintain their autonomy.

Nevertheless, suburbs experienced difficulty providing public services and turned to metropolitan planning. In 1889, the state legislature established the Metropolitan Sewerage Commission to build sewerage collection facilities for Boston and surrounding suburbs. In 1895, the state created the Metropolitan Water Board to provide a regional water supply. The most influential regional entity was the Metropolitan Park Commission, which was established in 1893 to conserve natural beauty spots and provide recreational opportunities in a Metropolitan District initially made up of Boston and thirty-five neighboring communities. Landscape architect Charles Eliot's metropolitan parks created a framework of green spaces for a suburban land pattern that featured single-family and some two-family houses built in relatively compact neighborhoods. The leafy parkways set the stage for automobiles to become the leading mode of commuting and the adjoining countryside to be suburbanized. The metropolitan park system, which was a signature Progressive Era initiative, prioritized the creation of public space as did no other era of development.

By 1910, Boston was the fourth largest metropolitan area in the country, trailing only New York, Chicago, and Philadelphia. Metropolitan Boston had a population of 1,520,470 living across 414 square miles. *A Handbook of New England* (1917) observed: "This great concentrated population, equipped with the intensive transportation facilities of a huge metropolis, is what invariably astonishes the stranger who, with census figures in mind, expects to find Boston a city of the St. Louis, Cleveland, or Baltimore type, rather than one comparing with Chicago and Philadelphia."[3]

In the metropolitan landscape, there were also mill towns, which represented a different sort of development pattern. In Lowell, Lawrence, and many smaller manufacturing communities, the factory owners built massive factories as well as tenements and boardinghouses for workers. These paternalistic communities were relatively self-contained. With the demise of the textile and shoe industries and the increased accessibility provided by the highways after World War II, mill towns like Brockton and Haverhill began to blend into the rest of the metropolis, even taking on some of the physical and socioeconomic attributes of suburbia. During the 1970s and the rise of historic preservation, New Englanders discovered that aging factories could be recycled for housing, commercial uses, and museums, creating a new paradigm for urban redevelopment.

In the residential suburbs, the biggest challenge was protecting the verdant community character and commensurate real estate values. During the late nineteenth century, upscale subdivisions utilized property covenants to insure that houses maintained a certain size and design. In the 1920s, zoning emerged as a municipal tool to formalize land-use patterns. Twenty-eight communities in Greater Boston created zones that separated residential, commercial, and industrial uses. Zoning also restricted multi-family dwellings from being located in the same areas as single-family homes. After World War II, zoning became ubiquitous. The other major instrument for preserving the pastoral quality of suburbs was land conservation.

By the 1930s, the leading catalyst to suburban growth was the state's highway system. The most prominent highway was Route 128 (the main stretch opened in 1951), the limited access, four-lane highway that encircled Boston's Metropolitan District suburbs a dozen miles from downtown. The postwar spurt of highway construction was the outcome of the 1948 *State Highway Master Plan*, which called for a statewide network of highways. They ultimately included Boston's Central Artery, Massachusetts Turnpike, Southeast Expressway, Route 3, and Interstate 93. The state's highway program was complemented by funding for the Federal Interstate Highway System, which completed an extensive highway network by 1970.

Route 128, the country's first outer beltway, was called America's Technology Highway because it attracted many of the first office and research parks. Though incubated at Massachusetts Institute of Technology (MIT), tech businesses migrated to the suburbs during the 1950s and 1960s. Some state highways, especially Route 1 and Route 9, evolved into commercial strips. On Route 9, Framingham's Shoppers' World (1951) was the first regional shopping center on the East Coast.

The highway system drew thousands of families out of the cities into emerging suburbs after World War II. In upscale country suburbs like Lincoln, Weston, Sudbury, Dover, and Sherborn, builders constructed single-family houses on large lots in wooded settings, creating a model for housing development that spread far and wide. Subdivisions of mass-produced ranch and split-level houses became middle-class havens, from Weymouth to Westwood to Wakefield. Just as the federal government played a critical role in funding interstate highways, it also spurred suburban residential development through Federal Housing Administration (FHA) and Veterans Administration (VA) mortgages. The postwar era saw the most concerted efforts on the part of government—federal and state—to promote planning and suburban growth. Meanwhile, this was the period of the greatest divide between the city and the suburbs. Boston, Cambridge, and smaller industrial cities like Brockton and Lawrence declined, as white middle-class families left for the suburbs.

The completion of Greater Boston's highway system in the early 1970s accelerated the sprawl development patterns that emerged after World War II. As in other parts of New England, highways expanded potential commuting distances, encouraged low-density housing, and fostered strips of shopping malls, big box stores, and office buildings clustered near highway exits. The shopping strips, which originally were lined with local businesses, became dominated by Wall Street-capitalized corporate chains.

Like Route 128 before it, I-495 encircled the metropolitan area at a distance of almost thirty miles from downtown Boston. I-495 (which opened in the late 1960s) encouraged further spread-out business development, much of which accommodated the campuses of high-tech corporations like Digital Equipment, Wang Labs, EMC, and Bristol-Myers Squibb. With the ability to build far from the city, residential lots consumed increasingly more open space. Large developers played a key role in building subdivisions for both McMansions and less pretentious houses. Low-density land-use patterns reflected a desire to maintain the rural landscape and protect the social status quo.

The interstate highways spun off growth beyond conventional suburbs. In rural areas, second homes spurred low-scale suburbanization and commercial strips. Analysts refer to this automobile-oriented development pattern as "sprawl," "exurbia," or the "edgeless," "endless," or "limitless" city. Urban historian Robert Fishman observed that low-density suburbanization was a culturally embedded "deep structure" of development that could not be easily altered by planners, politicians, or developers.[4]

As Greater Boston spread into a vast hinterland, open developable land became scarce within the I-495 beltway. The region became "built out" under existing zoning. The spread of auto-oriented development degraded the natural environment and pastoral qualities of suburbs. Traffic congestion, concerns about greenhouse gas emissions, and a desire to maintain viable city and town centers have inspired a return to compact development patterns that are oriented to transit, biking, and walking. Personal-vehicle motor transportation is not about to lose its dominance any time soon, but the development patterns it has spawned are changing. The "smart growth" movement is reviving land-use patterns originally put in place by the railroad and streetcar suburbs of the nineteenth century.

The key to promoting compact development is the public transit system of the Massachusetts Bay Transportation Authority (MBTA). In recent decades, the MBTA has extended its services and ridership. With about 120 commuter rail stations and dozens of subway and bus lines in the suburbs, the region has a public transit infrastructure that, despite physical and fiscal deficiencies that need to be addressed, provides a true alternative to the automobile. The compact, mixed-use development pattern has been reasserted in town centers and near commuter rail stations in Abington, Canton, Medford, Newton, Norwood, Salem, Waltham, Westborough, and many other suburbs.

The vision statement for the new planning paradigm is Boston's Metropolitan Area Planning Council's (MAPC) *MetroFuture* plan (2008). MAPC prepared *MetroFuture* as an advisory plan for 101 Greater Boston cities and towns to determine how best to accommodate 465,000 people who are estimated to be added to the region's population by 2030. The planning process determined that recent sprawl trends would be unsustainable. *MetroFuture* proposed a growth scenario that would intensify development in existing urban neighborhoods and town centers and consume significantly less open land. The template for compact, mixed-use developments tends to be located near railroad and transit stations. Its intent is to reduce carbon emissions and mitigate the effects of climate change. The *MetroFuture* plan also called for complementing compact development with the preservation of remaining open land and the creation of greenways to encourage biking and walking.

Like earlier regional and city plans, the *MetroFuture* plan offers a narrative that describes the predicaments and aspirations of Greater Boston communities and how they intend to address them. MAPC's plan reflects a significant shift in urban-suburban development policies, which is referred to as "smart growth," "New Urbanism," "sustainable development," or "walkable urbanism." These movements are national trends, and *MetroFuture* is a strategy for their pursuit in Greater Boston.

The resuscitation of compact mixed-development has been led by the cities of Boston and Cambridge, which have undergone a remarkable renaissance. This planning template has spread to suburban centers that once clustered around town greens and railroad stations. As with many things related to suburban development, Greater Boston seems to be ahead of the curve. Although often derided for fusty traditionalism, Boston has been as an innovator in metropolitan development.

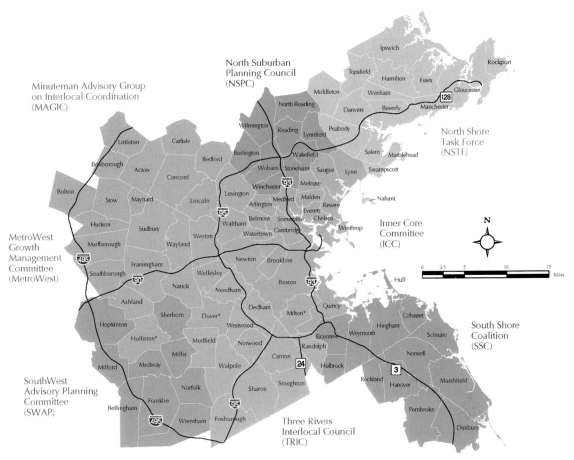

FIGURE 1.2
Metropolitan Area Planning Council communities by subregion. The Metropolitan Area Planning Council (MAPC) plans for 101 cities and towns of metropolitan Boston.
Note: *Communities in more than one subregion: Dover is in TRIC and SWAP, and Milton is in the Inner Core and TRIC.
Source: Metropolitan Area Planning Council.

BOX 1.1
Boston's Metropolitan Area Planning Council's subregions
Metropolitan Area Planning Council (MAPC) divides its 101 cities and towns into eight subregions (communities are indicated on MAPC map and will be written out for each subregion). The eight subregions start at the Inner Core and circle around from the North Shore to the west and ending on the South Shore.[5]

INNER CORE
Arlington
Belmont
Boston
Brookline
Cambridge
Chelsea
Everett
Lynn
Malden
Medford
Melrose
Milton
Newton
Quincy
Revere
Saugus
Somerville
Waltham
Watertown
Winthrop

NORTH SHORE
Beverly
Danvers
Essex
Gloucester
Hamilton
Ipswich
Manchester
Marblehead
Middleton
Peabody
Rockport
Salem
Swampscott
Topsfield
Wenham

NORTH SUBURBAN
Burlington
Lynnfield
North Reading
Reading
Stoneham
Wakefield
Wilmington
Winchester
Woburn

MINUTEMAN
Acton
Bedford
Bolton
Boxborough
Carlisle
Concord
Hudson
Lexington
Lincoln
Littleton
Maynard
Stow
Sudbury

METROWEST
Ashland
Framingham
Holliston
Marlborough
Natick
Southborough
Wayland
Wellesley
Weston

SOUTHWEST
Bellingham
Franklin
Hopkinton
Medway
Milford
Millis
Norfolk
Sherborn
Wrentham

THREE RIVERS
Canton
Dedham
Dover
Foxborough
Medfield
Needham
Norwood
Randolph
Sharon
Stoughton
Walpole
Westwood

SOUTH SHORE
Braintree
Cohasset
Duxbury
Hanover
Hingham
Holbrook
Marshfield
Norwell
Pembroke
Rockland
Scituate
Weymouth

Source: Metropolitan Area Planning Council.

2

Prelude to Suburbia: Traditional Village Centers and Proto-Suburbs (1800–1860)

In 1800, there were no suburbs around Boston. The surrounding communities of Cambridge, Dorchester, Roxbury, and Concord were independent towns that traded and interacted politically with Boston but did not fulfill commercial or residential functions that were an urban extension of Boston. Towns of eastern Massachusetts were engaged in farming and maintained limited trade with the port city of Boston. They were a hinterland but were in no way suburban.

Because there was so little trade and manufacturing during the colonial era, New England farm towns lacked active centers. The town center was the meetinghouse, as townships were established as religious communities. The meetinghouse was the spiritual, political, and geographical focus of the community. Besides religious services, it was used for town meeting and other public assemblies. At first, farmhouses clustered near the meetinghouse, but gradually they spread out. Adjacent to the meetinghouse was the meetinghouse lot, which usually included a militia training field, stocks and gallows, and a common area for collecting livestock for grazing on the settlement's outskirts. As the common was trampled by livestock, it tended to be muddy and was a far cry from a "green." There were few businesses in town except for taverns, which played an important social function.[1]

In the post-Revolutionary era, town centers, which are now recognized as New England icons, started to appear. This era produced the town common surrounded by a white meetinghouse, other public buildings, and stately houses. These centers were brought about by a shift from subsistence farming to the production of special-ized crops and livestock for a market economy. With a growing market economy, shops, blacksmiths, and attorney's offices grew up around the traditional New Eng-land meetinghouses. According to Joseph S. Wood's history of *The New England Village*, the emerging capitalistic society created a "landscape of commercial places where meetinghouses had long stood alone."[2] Framingham provides an illustrative example of an emerging town center. Between 1790 and 1805, Framingham's village center attracted a new tavern, a store, an academy, two blacksmiths, a hatter, cord-wainer, tanner, lawyer, carpenter, doctor, saddler, and a mason.[3] Turnpikes and improved roads promoted trade and reinforced the importance of town centers.

With the development of village centers, urban amenities came to the country. Village centers advertised their importance by building elaborate meetinghouses,

FIGURE 2.1
Brighton cattle market, 1839. This engraving by John Warner Barber depicts the Brighton cattle market and stockyards, which were examples of the industrial activity that developed in towns surrounding Boston during the first half of the nineteenth century.
Source: John Warner Barber, *Historical Collections, Being a General Collection of Interesting Facts, Traditions, Biographical Sketches, Anecdotes, &c., Relating to the History and Antiquities of Every Town in Massachusetts, with Geographical Descriptions* (Worcester: Dorr Howland & Co., 1839). Print from author's collection.

which were often painted white and decorated with columns, pediments, and soaring steeples in the Federal and Greek Revival styles. The beautified town common or green began to appear at this time, as livestock were banished from the town center. (Boston Common banned livestock in 1830 and became America's first public park.) Originally, these village centers epitomized the traditional self-sustaining New England town. By the twentieth century, they provided a design motif for suburbs seeking to project a historic aura.

As activity intensified in village centers, communities surrounding Boston experienced widespread development. Cambridge, Charlestown, and Somerville became extensions of the city by developing goods and services for it. According to Henry C. Binford's *The First Suburbs: Residential Communities on the Boston Periphery, 1815–1860*, the nearby towns mingled "scattered residences and small farms with storage and marketing facilities, noxious industries, dumps, prisons and similar institutions, cemeteries, and other land-intensive, city-related but often city-rejected phenomena."[4] Farms and stockyards at Brighton and Cambridge served the growing Boston market. Charlestown's Milk Row collected the region's dairy products for distribution to city-dwellers. Shoemakers, tanners, and tradesmen living on the outskirts brought their products to the urban marketplace. Small business and land speculators found many opportunities in scattered villages. This was organic development that did not follow a clearly defined planning model. It was driven by myriad individual investment decisions.

A growing network of transportation arteries spurred small business opportunities. Bridges between Boston and Charlestown (1786) and Cambridge (1793 and 1809) eased connections with the north side of the harbor and the Charles River. The twenty-seven-mile Middlesex Canal (1802) linked Lowell and the Merrimack River to Charlestown. A spate of turnpikes made it easier to transport goods into Boston. They included the Salem Turnpike (1802), Medford Turnpike (1802), Newburyport Turnpike (1805), Cambridge & Concord Turnpike (1806), Norfolk & Dedham Turnpike (1806), and Worcester Turnpike (1810).

Villages near Boston, in the early nineteenth century, began to grow together along well-traveled roadways creating "ribbon villages," where residents tended to be involved in commercial occupations. Yale President Timothy Dwight observed: "From Weymouth the country may with little extravagance be considered one continued village, raised up by the commerce of Boston, and forming a kind of suburb to that capital."[5] The combined population of Boston's neighbors Cambridge and Charlestown tripled to 20,000 between 1810 and 1840.

FIGURE 2.2
Lexington Green, Lexington. This iconic green was the site where the "shot heard 'round the world"
launched the American Revolution. The Revolutionary War Monument (1799) marks the site where
slain Lexington militia were buried.
Source: Andrew McFarland.

At first, the fringe towns were not suburbs in the sense that people lived there
and traveled into Boston for work. There was no public transport to facilitate travel
between the city and surrounding communities until the railroad and the omnibus
were introduced in 1834. It took more than a decade for transit to catch on and city
dwellers to begin moving to the suburbs. By the 1840s, *The New England Gazetteer*
reported: "It must be considered that the neighboring towns of Quincy, Dorchester,
Milton, Roxbury, Brookline, Brighton, Watertown, Cambridge, Charlestown, Medford, Malden, and Chelsea, although not included in the city charter, are component
parts of the city, and are as much associated with it in all its commercial, manufacturing, literary, and social relations and feelings, as Greenwich, Manhattanville, and
Harlem are with the city of New York; or Southwark and the Northern Liberties
with Philadelphia."[6]

Exploring Traditional Village Centers and Early Suburbs

The best way to learn about the different layers of metropolitan Boston's development is to explore them firsthand. Each chapter suggests several sites that are mentioned in the text and that can be easily visited. A list at the end of the book cross-references sites by location to assist in creating convenient itineraries.

Town Greens/Commons

Most towns in Greater Boston have a town common or green. In more densely settled communities near Boston, the common tends to be a smaller open space or may not even exist. Smaller town commons are located in Cambridge, Concord, Norwood, Waltham, and Woburn. Farther from the city, where rural towns were able to maintain their distinctiveness longer, there are more likely to be large commons with impressive historical buildings ranged around them. Some larger commons are located in Cohasset, Dedham, East Bridgewater, Foxborough, Reading, Wakefield, and Wrentham.

Lexington Green, Massachusetts Avenue at Bedford Street and Harrington Road

Lexington Green is quintessentially historic. Also called Battle Green, it is the site of the first military engagement of the American Revolution. In the Revolutionary era, it was used for grazing livestock and the militia training ground. During the nineteenth century, it became a commemorative site and was beautified. The statue of the Minuteman (1898) was sculpted by Henry Hudson Kitson. Lexington Green is surrounded by historic structures dating from the late eighteenth and nineteenth centuries. Under the influence of the Colonial Revival, property owners, in 1917, made Lexington one of the first communities in the country to adopt preservation covenants. The deed covenants prohibited commercial uses and prescribed a uniform setback around the green.[7] The most evocative day of the year to visit Lexington Green is the morning of Patriot's Day, when the 1775 skirmish between British soldiers and the Lexington militia is reenacted.

Weston Town Green, Boston Post Road at School and Church Streets, Weston

Weston Town Green (1912) is a fine example of a Colonial Revival creation of a town green. It reflects the affluent suburban template that Joseph S. Wood discussed in *The New England Village*. Arthur Shurcliff designed the green in a bowl shape that accommodates summer concerts and winter sledding. Sited around the green are the Town House (1917), two churches, the former library, a fire station, and the Josiah Smith Tavern (1757).

Brighton Cattle Market, Market and Washington Streets, Brighton

It is difficult to get a sense of what proto-suburbs looked like because so much development has occurred since the early nineteenth century. Sometimes a historical marker is the only evidence of Boston's early suburban development. In this case it is a marker for the Brighton Cattle Market at the corner of Washington and Market Streets in Brighton. A cattle yard flourished in Brighton Center during the nineteenth century; more than forty small slaughterhouses operated in the area. As the streetcar opened up Brighton to residential development in the late nineteenth century, the cattle market moved down Market Street and was replaced by streets of houses.

North Cambridge Cattle Market, Porter Square, 1815 Massachusetts Avenue, Cambridge

The suburbs of the 1820s and 1830s, most notably Cambridge, have been almost entirely built over. The former North Cambridge Cattle Market thrived during the nineteenth century at Porter Square. It developed here because the Great Road (today's Massachusetts Avenue) brought livestock into this area, where the cattle were sold and slaughtered for the Boston market. Other small-scale manufacturing enterprises grew up along the Great Road. The most notable landmark was the Porter House Hotel, established by Zacariah Porter in the 1830s. An interpretive marker near to the Porter Square Red Line station, on the building at 1853 Massachusetts Avenue, tells the history of the cattle yards.

3

Country Retreats (1820–1920)

Escaping to the Country

The first people to establish suburban residences were wealthy Bostonians seeking respite from the crowded city. Maintaining their house in Boston, they developed second-home estates in the pastoral countryside, where they created carefully manicured landscapes. There was no concerted planning involved in establishing rural retreats. They were the individual initiatives of wealthy families pursuing leisure interests. The villa owner was entirely responsible for developing the country estate and maintaining the open space that surrounded it. Local government played a scant role in providing infrastructure or shaping land uses until later in the century. Country estates had a permanent effect on Greater Boston's landscape, establishing a paradigm for cultivated suburban living in socially homogeneous communities, a pattern subsequently followed by the middle classes.

The first country homes of the wealthy were close to Boston because the city was geographically compact and attractive countryside existed nearby. Jamaica Plain, Milton, and Brookline were the early locations for country estates. Even before the American Revolution, the Boston elite were building second homes outside the city. Royal Governors William Shirley, Francis Bernard, and Thomas Hutchinson built country seats respectively at Roxbury, Jamaica Pond, and Milton. Samuel Adams built an estate on Jamaica Pond. Milton Hill had estates belonging to the Forbes family and Oliver Peabody, of the Kidder Peabody investment house. In South Brookline, merchant Thomas Handasyd Perkins initiated that community's appeal as a suburban retreat when he bought a farm in 1800. The Gardner family soon built a summer home on Brookline's Green Hill, which was subsequently inhabited by Jack and Isabella Stewart Gardner.[1]

Gradually, estates began to form residential enclaves, where wealthy families associated with their own sort. At Chestnut Hill, straddling Brookline and Newton, Francis Lee started a Brahmin enclave when he turned an old family farm into a gracious estate in the early 1850s. Lee, whose family hailed from Beverly, attracted other socially prominent families with North Shore roots, including the Lowells, Cabots, Lawrences, and Saltonstalls. Chestnut Hill became known as the "Essex Colony." Chestnut Hill evolved from a seasonal resort into a year-round suburb after the opening of the Highland Branch commuter railroad service in 1886.[2]

FIGURE 3.1
Lyman Estate, Waltham. In 1793, merchant Theodore Lyman built a country estate he called "The Vale." Such country seats launched the development of suburban Boston.
Source: Courtesy of Historic New England.

The country estate played an important role in Boston Brahmin society. In John P. Marquand's novel *The Late George Apley* (1936), the Apley family's summer estate, Hillcrest, was in Milton. Hillcrest was "a considerable distance from town, a large estate with driveways under arching elms, with a rambling house dating from the forties."[3] Marquand's Henry Pulham, in *H. M. Pulham, Esquire* (1941), had a Brookline summer home in the early twentieth century.

Wealthy country estates dotted the outskirts of Boston in the midst of working farms and old country villages. In 1870, this zone was three-and-a-half to ten miles from Boston City Hall. By 1900, the zone of countryside estates reached between five and fifteen miles from downtown Boston. Sam Bass Warner, in *Streetcar Suburbs: The Process of Growth in Boston, 1870–1900*, estimated that five percent of Boston's population in the latter nineteenth century was wealthy enough to afford a country seat.[4]

The gentlemen's estates were located in the "borderland" between the country and the city, representing the opening phase of suburbanization examined by John Stilgoe in *Borderland: Origins of the American Suburb, 1820–1939*. As Stilgoe points out, the "borderland" was a zone of creative invention, a dynamic place where the form and meaning of suburbs were constantly being explored. The country seats had symbolic importance as habitations of the elite and examples for middle-class families to emulate.[5]

Wealthy people moving to estates on the urban periphery thought that they were living in the "country." The term "suburb" originally indicated the areas outside the city where industry and poorer working people were located. It was a derogatory term. Estate owners only adopted the name "suburb" in the 1850s, when it had become a distinct type of place that combined the best of rural and city life.[6]

As the gentry moved into the countryside, they practiced model agriculture and horticulture. Landscape gardening was a favorite pastime for those making their fortunes in commerce and industry. Gardening was both a form of patriotic moral reform and personal therapy. Horticulture and model farming were politically safe activities for antebellum Yankee capitalists, as they assumed the pose of a Jeffersonian yeoman farmer. Estates were supposed to be productive, not be an example of conspicuous consumption.[7]

The country estates of the antebellum era transformed the appearance of the countryside, where working farms had a ramshackle quality. Farms were supposed to be productive, not necessarily good-looking. Gentleman farmers and horticulturists designed estates to look attractive. They had the wealth and the moral drive to do so. Growing orchards, flower beds, and decorative shrubbery transformed the countryside

TABLE 3.1
Location of prominent country estates surrounding Boston prior to 1860

Owner	Town
Timothy Bigelow	Medford
James Brown	Watertown
Benjamin Bussey	Jamaica Plain
John Codman	Lincoln
Zebedee Cook	Dorchester
Henry Alexander Scannell Dearborn	Roxbury
Aaron Dexter	Chelsea
Samuel Downer	Dorchester
Nathaniel Goddard	Brighton
John Chipman Gay	Cambridge
Nathaniel Ingersoll	Brookline
James Jackson	Waltham
Cheever Newhall	Dorchester
Francis Parkman	Jamaica Plain
John Prince	Roxbury
Josiah Stickney	Watertown
John Collins Warren	Roxbury
John Welles	Dorchester

Note: Most of these antebellum estates have disappeared, primarily because these country places were located in areas that are today neighborhoods of Boston and other urbanized communities.
Source: Tamara Plakins Thornton, *Cultivating Gentlemen: The Meaning of Country Life among the Boston Elite, 1785–1860* (New Haven, Conn.: Yale University Press, 1989).

into a "sub-urban" park-like landscape with woods, gardens, walks, ponds, and streams.[8] Gentleman gardeners invited the public to inspect their plants on open days, inspiring others to build suburban homes of their own.

The heyday of this landscape gardening, between 1820 and 1860, saw scores of gentleman gardeners trying to outdo each other. They competed in fruit and vegetable-growing contests sponsored by the Massachusetts Horticultural Society (1829). The elaborate efforts were exemplified by Benjamin Bussey's Woodland Hills in Jamaica Plain, which ultimately became the site of Harvard's Bussey Institute and the Arnold Arboretum. Estate owners endowed their properties with romantic pastoral names, which working farms usually lacked. A sampling of estate names in the late nineteenth-century Lexington, for example, included Beechwood, Cedarcroft, Cedarcrest, Maywood, Meadowview, Sunnyslope, and Wild Acre Farm.[9] Interest in gardening declined by the end of the nineteenth century, when affluent gentlemen took up golf, polo, and yachting.

Many aspiring country gentleman used Robert Morris Copeland's *Country Life: A Handbook of Agriculture, Horticulture, and Landscape Gardening* (1859) as a guide for cultivating an estate. Copeland, a landscape gardener whose home still stands in Beaver Brook Reservation in Belmont, offered plans for a model estate of sixty acres with a large house, farm, flower garden, kitchen garden, fruit orchard, and various lawns, woods, and ponds. As a planner who helped design Boston's Commonwealth Avenue and proposed a metropolitan park system for Boston, Copeland recommended that "decayed and sterile towns" should develop their economic base by attracting estates and resorts. Copeland maintained:

> Every year we see men of wealth leaving the cities in summer to buy houses in the country; however wrapt in money making they are not insensible to rural beauty. Country towns properly improved will become exceedingly attractive; their lanes and by-ways through woods and along water courses, will make drives of uncommon beauty; the places will draw summer residents whose money will give employment to many persons, and will contribute to the permanent enrichment of the little community. The more the number of such persons who visit a town, the more land increases in value.[10]

Belmont demonstrates how Copeland's suggestion about promoting estates in decaying rural districts could spur suburbanization. In 1840, John P. Cushing, a China Trade tycoon, built a fifty-room summer home called "Bellmont" on a hill in Watertown. Designed by Asher Benjamin, the mansion had fifty marble fireplaces, an immense garden, and large greenhouses. As the area around Cushing's estate, which included parts of Watertown, Waltham, and West Cambridge (Arlington), attracted development, the residents pushed for establishment of a new municipality. In 1859, "Belmont" became a town, with Cushing bearing the incorporation costs. Businessmen Samuel R. Payson and Colonel Everett Chamberlain Benton subsequently owned the mansion before it burned down in 1927. After that the property was subdivided for houses.

The core of Wellesley, which originally was the western part of Needham, was also an estate—banker H. H. Hunnewell's 1851 mansion. Hunnewell named it "Wellesley," after his wife's family name "Welles." Hunnewell's grounds, which were

FIGURE 3.2
"Bellmont," Belmont, 1922. In 1840, merchant John P. Cushing built a 50-room mansion called "Bellmont" in Watertown. When parts of Watertown, Waltham, and West Cambridge (Arlington) broke off in 1859 to form a new town in the area of the estate, Cushing paid the incorporation expenses and the town assumed the name of "Belmont."
Source: Courtesy of Historic New England.

open to the genteel public, included a renowned arboretum, the first rhododendrons, and the first topiary garden in the United States. On his 500-acre estate, Hunnewell built mansions for seven of his eight children and their families during the latter part of the nineteenth century. Much of the Hunnewell holdings still exist.

"Wellesley" gave its name to the college opened in 1875 across Lake Waban on Attorney Henry Fowle Durant's 300-acre "Homestead" estate. In 1881, Wellesley was established as a separate town, which was evolving into an exclusive railroad suburb. Hunnewell not only gave the town its name but also donated the French Chateau-style town hall and library. Seeking to create a model suburb, Hunnewell purchased and demolished a factory near the town hall, laid out streets, and installed street lights, concrete sidewalks, and a water system.

Many other "gentleman gardeners" welcomed guests to show off their accomplishments. One of the most conspicuous examples was that of sewing machine magnate William Emerson Baker, who owned Ridge Hill Farms on the Needham-Wellesley border. Baker turned the 755-acre summer estate into a public pleasure ground. After the 1876 Philadelphia Centennial Exposition, he bought the Chile and Peru Pavilions and a hotel and moved them to Ridge Hill Farms. The pavilions housed exhibits, and the hotel became the 160-room Hotel Wellesley. Baker offered boating on Sabrina Lake and the Charles River, decorative gardens, a zoo, fountains, a camera obscura, a 100-foot lookout tower, and facilities for picnics and parties. Most eccentric were the stuffed horses that mechanically nodded their heads. The estate was open on weekends and charged 10 cents for admission.[11] After Baker's death in 1888, the estate was subdivided for smaller estates, which were subdivided further in the 1930s.

The Design of Country Villas

"Bellmont" and "Wellesley" were some of the most ostentatious examples of country estates. Most estates were more modest and tasteful. Cleveland Amory, in *The Proper Bostonians*, explained:

> The merchants who moved to the country did not go in for show places. Generally speaking they built practical, durable, comfortable homes, and this has been the keynote of Proper Bostonian suburban architecture ever since. There are country estates in a few places around Boston, particularly on the North Shore and in Wellesley, which could hardly be classed as simple, but at the same time there is scarcely a home in the chief First Family theatres of operation—in Brookline, Milton or Dedham—which would bear comparison with the truly lush Society estates of Long Island, Lake Forest or Beverly Hills.[12]

Many antebellum estate owners and early suburbanites followed the house designs proposed in Andrew Jackson Downing's handbook *The Architecture of Country Houses* (1850). Andrew Jackson Downing was a great tastemaker in America during the 1840s and 1850s. He was a pioneer in the field of landscape design for suburban and rural homes, writing *A Treatise on the Theory and Practice of Landscape Gardening, Adapted to North America* (1841). Downing sought to achieve a picturesque effect, namely a landscape that made a good picture. This entailed a variety of trees, shrubs, and flowers, as well as irregular sight lines. Houses were supposed to blend into their natural surroundings. Downing's ideal pastoral suburb was Brookline. He wrote: "The whole of this neighborhood of Brookline is a kind of landscape garden, and there is nothing in America, of the sort, so inexpressibly charming as the lanes which lead from one cottage to another."[13]

Andrew Jackson Downing's *Architecture of Country Homes* (1850), which was reprinted numerous times, provides a vivid sense of antebellum houses. Downing's book suggested house designs for cottages, farmhouses, and villas in the belief that every class should be able live comfortably in a natural environment, surrounded by greenery and fresh air. Villas were intended for the upper and upper-middle classes. They were supposed to be "a private house, where beauty, taste, and moral culture are at home." Villas were intended to be the height of civilized living and had a number of specialized rooms. On the main floor, the model villa had a greeting hall, a drawing room for "social intercourse," a dining room, a library for "intellectual culture," an office for the master of the household, and a kitchen. The second floor would have bedrooms, a lady's boudoir or dressing room, a bathing room, and a water closet. At the rear of the house, there would be back stairs for the servants. The front of the villa often had a veranda to increase exposure to the surrounding country.[14]

Downing also provided cottage designs for laborers and workingmen as well as middle-class families. Cottages were small but tasteful, having a single floor with at least a living room, kitchen, bedroom, and possibly a parlor, a pantry, or another bedroom.[15] Though situated on compact lots, they, also, were surrounded by plantings and trees.

This being the mid-Victorian era, a wide range of ornate historical styles was deemed appropriate for villas—Italianate, Norman, Rural Gothic, Romanesque, Classical, and Bracketed. Downing believed that villas should "manifest individuality," thus such a range of architectural styles. Yankee Boston tended to favor Italianate villas with their flat roofs and exaggerated eaves supported by decorative brackets, sometimes with a cupola or widow's walk. Downing also advocated a switch from the conservative white paint that had characterized the Federal and Greek Revival styles to a range of color paints that would heighten the picturesque quality of the villa.

Most antebellum Boston suburban villas have been lost because they were demolished for new houses or subdivided for residential neighborhoods. Yet examples survive in Roxbury, Dorchester, Chestnut Hill, Newton Corner, South Brookline, Milton, and Waltham. After the Civil War era, fortunes grew and the countryside near Boston became built up. Wealthy families started building summer estates in rural communities farther from Boston—in Weston, Lincoln, and Dover.

Weston and Lincoln: Communities of Country Seats

As wealthy families scouted for estate locations outside the city, they found much inexpensive farm land. The New England agricultural economy was declining in comparison with the Midwest farm belt, and farmers were eager to sell. Dairy farms, which flourished in eastern Massachusetts after the Civil War, became uncompetitive with northern New England by the early twentieth century. The replacement of the horse by the automobile accelerated farm abandonment because the hay farms provided was no longer needed for horses.[16]

The *Boston Evening Transcript* observed of wealthy families building country estates: "They usually buy a farm boasting an attractive Colonial type of house and make it over after the manner persistently illustrated and exploited in the popular magazines." Rural communities outside Boston attracted the wealthy with their pastoral scenery, healthy air, and short train rides to the city. Instead of the antebellum pattern of living in estates scattered around Boston's perimeter, wealthy families settled in a select group of communities that included Lincoln and Weston. Of the upper-class western suburban belt, the *Boston Evening Transcript* observed: "This is the district that is drawing away from Brookline those who are fussy enough to continue to demand the comfort, freedom and exclusiveness which caused them to go to Brookline years ago."[17] As the countryside close to Boston filled in with railroad and streetcar suburbs, wealthy families initiated a trend toward migration in search of spatial seclusion and social exclusion.

Weston was the foremost of the wealthy country suburbs. It was called the "Lenox of the East" for the mansions that dotted its landscape in a fashion like that Berkshire Hills resort town. Most mansions were built between 1890 and World War I.[18] During the 1890s alone, thirty-five mansions were built in Weston. The popular season was the early fall, when the eastern Massachusetts countryside could be enjoyed at its scenic best. Many Weston Social Register families lived in Boston in the winter, at a summer resort like the North Shore in summer, and in Weston during the fall. Rural enclaves like Weston tended to remain seasonal until the coming of the automobile because rural roads were not well plowed in winter.

The great estate owners in Weston made their fortunes in the booming industrial economy of the Gilded Age, and magnates flaunted their wealth by building elaborate mansions. Civil War general and industrial investor Charles Jackson Paine, owner of a 758-acre estate, was called "the modern discoverer of Weston."[19] Businessman Horace Sears, whose Italianate mansion was Weston's most ostentatious estate, became the town's biggest benefactor by providing funds for the First Church, town common, library, fire station, and schools. Robert Winsor, the representative of the J. P. Morgan banking interests in New England, built the Tudor-style Chestnut Farm in 1902. Francis Blake, inventor of a voice amplifier used in Bell's telephone, built Keewaydin, which was designed by Charles Follen McKim with gardens inspired by Hampton Court. Several dozen magnates like them settled in Weston prior to World War I.

During the 1890s, Weston adopted a two-pronged strategy for attracting wealthy families—providing the latest infrastructure improvements while keeping tax rates low. Paving roads, erecting street lights, and planting trees were considered necessary for creating a desirable community. The Village Improvement Association took an active role in promoting such endeavors. Weston emulated the romantic New England village ideal by redesigning the town center to embody the image of a traditional New England town.[20] This reinforced the sense that Weston was an independent, historically rooted enclave (which was only a fifteen-mile commute from Boston). In 1912, landscape architect Arthur Shurcliff (he changed his named from "Shurtleff" to adopt the Old English spelling in 1930) laid out a spacious town green, which was surrounded by the First Church, the town library, and a new town hall.[21] On the Weston Town Green, Shurcliff created a model Colonial Revival landscape that inspired his later work at Colonial Williamsburg and Old Sturbridge Village.

Despite also building a new high school, fire station, and water system, Weston's tax rates were among the lowest in Greater Boston. This made the maintenance of extensive estates affordable so that property owners were not driven to subdivide and produce modestly priced housing.[22] Keeping out the middle class maintained Weston's exclusivity and minimized the demand for public services.

In this vein, Weston town meeting voted not to join the Metropolitan Park System and successfully fought off several attempts to build a trolley line at the turn of the century. A broadside opposing the trolley sounded much like the NIMBYism (Not in My Back Yard) that Westonites voiced in opposing a trans-town bike trail in the early twenty-first century:

> The more frequent service and ready communication with Waltham; agreeable Sunday and holiday travel; the expense for the town and the danger to our citizens; the obstruction to travel, and the piling up of snow beside the track in winter; the possible benefit to small holdings of land immediately on the railway; the destruction for the market for the large holdings and for land off the line; that is, the loss of the character of the place and of the distinction which our town has for attractive residence free from the annoyances electric roads bring.[23]

Neighboring Dover, Lincoln, Sherborn, and Sudbury similarly vetoed trolley service, avoiding concomitant development pressures and maintaining a rural upper-class atmosphere.

Weston used its planning board (1922) and zoning regulations (1928) to limit residential development primarily to single-family homes and to exclude industrial and strip commercial uses by severely restricting business zones. Similar zoning methods for protecting the community's character were gradually adopted by other affluent towns.

Lincoln, situated just north of Weston, turned into a comparable suburb of country estates. By 1900, many prominent Bostonians owned second homes in Lincoln. They included Julian deCordova, whose home later became the deCordova Art Museum, and Louise Gordon Hathaway, whose Gordon Hall subsequently became the headquarters of the Massachusetts Audubon Society. Fairhaven, a 300-acre, Olmsted-landscaped estate, was purchased by Charles F. Adams, Jr., a descendent of Presidents John and John Quincy Adams. Adams was the first chairman of the Metropolitan Park Commission and the partner of Henry Whitney in developing the streetcar line on Beacon Street in Brookline that would end the days of rural estates in that community and push the elite farther out into the country. Adams became so disturbed by the urbanization of his family's hometown of Quincy that he abandoned it for Lincoln in the 1890s.

General Motors financier and unsuccessful Boston mayoral candidate James Storrow lived in Lincoln most of the year and stayed in Boston only between Thanksgiving and Easter.[24] Alexander Henry Higginson, who owned Middlesex Meadows Farm, established the Middlesex Hunt Club (1904) to organize fox hunts through the woods and fields of Lincoln. The fox hunts ended a decade later, when increasing auto traffic made it difficult for the hounds and hunters to cross the roads.[25]

In 1904, there were fifty daily commuters taking the train from Lincoln to Boston, and the number grew as more Bostonians migrated out.[26] The quiet countryside was a strong lure. The *Boston Herald* reported:

> He [a new resident from Boston] is one of a considerable number of men who hear the roar of Boston all day long and when night falls each desires to retire to some quiet place where electric lights shall not dazzle his eyes nor electric cars [streetcars] irritate his nerves. Lincoln meets his desires to perfection.[27]

Though located only fifteen miles from Boston, Lincoln remained a rural community. The town never established a substantial town center or attracted industry. In 1900, when a streetcar company proposed to build a line through Lincoln and create "places of amusement" on Walden and Sandy Ponds, the wealthy estate owners said they did not want "rowdies" visiting their town. Although local farmers favored streetcars to improve access to the rest of the metropolitan area, the wealthy home-owners successfully opposed them. Two years later, town meeting did approve a streetcar line through North Lincoln, where the elite did not reside; but the line was never built.[28]

Well-to-do country suburbs like Weston and Lincoln reinforced their elite status by curbing modern incursions and maintaining the appearance of a classic New England village center. The iconic village centers conjured associations with the virtuous Puritan and Revolutionary past as a response to the immigrant inflow and noxious industries of the growing cities. According to Joseph S. Wood, the idealized village proclaimed the "inherited ideals of stable Puritan community and democratic society" and asserted the primacy of the Anglo-Saxon race, New England culture, and pastoral community.[29] The tradition of the independent New England township embodied in the postcard village center shaped suburbs that have been jealous of their political autonomy, protective of the interests of their socioeconomic niche, and skeptical toward regional cooperation.

This traditional New England town ideology inspired communities like Weston and Lincoln, as well as Concord, Lexington, Reading, Sudbury, Wakefield, and Winchester, to beautify their village centers and decorate greens with trees, shrubs, statuary, fountains, and bandstands. The late nineteenth and early twentieth centuries marked the heyday of the Village Improvement Societies, which vied for producing the most attractive village center. The Colonial Revival architectural style was adopted to reinforce connections to the Revolutionary and Federal periods. Historic preservation became a method of protecting community character. The historic village centers became magnets for the affluent and aspirational models for middle-class residential suburbs.

The age of the great estates in Weston, Lincoln, and other elite suburbs came to a close during the 1920s and 1930s. The cost of maintenance and servants rose, and income and taxes and the Depression diminished disposable wealth. Heirs to the great estates could not afford them and often lost interest in owning them altogether. The only people who could afford the estates were wealthy self-made men. People like that wanted to build their own trophy homes, not buy one built decades earlier by another self-made man.

Some estate owners started subdividing their properties to create neighborhoods for congenial upper-income families. During the early 1920s, Charles W. Hubbard

CHILTERN HUNDREDS

HILTERN HUNDREDS is part of a group of large family estates on the border line of Wellesley and Weston, overlooking the Charles River valley. The owners of these estates are developing a tract of about 150 acres as a beautiful residential section, under certain social and building restrictions.

A FAMILY ESTATE

CHILTERN HUNDREDS is separated from the congested suburban districts by these large estates and by the Charles River Reservation of the Metropolitan Park, a river valley a mile and a half long.

EDGEWOOD   THE KNOLL   RIDGEWAYS

SOME OF THE HOUSES ON THE ESTATE

VALLEY OF THE CHARLES RIVER AND THE METROPOLITAN PARK

Wellesley Farms Station, on the B. & A. R.R. four track main line, has twenty trains a day each way, with numerous expresses, twenty-five minutes to South Station. All lots within half a mile of the station have gas, electricity and water, with frequent fire hydrants.

FIGURE 3.3

Chiltern Hundreds, Weston, 1926. This promotional brochure for the Chiltern Hundreds subdivision depicted the rural charms that appealed to upper-middle-class families. Estate owner and developer Charles W. Hubbard required that each new house should be located on a one-quarter-acre or a one-half-acre lot and should cost at least $10,000.

Source: Courtesy Weston Historical Society.

hired landscape architect Arthur Shurcliff to lay out the Chiltern Hundreds subdivi-
sion on part of his Ridgehurst estate. Robert Winsor hired Frederick Law Olmsted,
Jr., to lay out an exclusive subdivision on his property. He relocated the Weston
Country Club and Meadowbrook School to the subdivision and created highly desirable house lots for prosperous WASP families (required by property covenants to be
Protestant), including executives in his brokerage firm Kidder Peabody. After Winsor
died, his mansion was demolished and additional residential parcels were created.
Horace Sears's "Hialewa" suffered a similar fate. Sears's Italianate villa was demolished in 1950, and a one-story ranch house replaced it. The Swiedler Development
Corporation demolished Francis Blake's Keewaydin in 1965 to create a subdivision
of twenty houses. Other portions of Blake's estate along the Charles River were taken
to build Route 128 and the Massachusetts Turnpike. Naturally, Westonites vocally
opposed highway construction through their town, but to no avail.[30]

The construction of the two major highways and the subdivision of estates
spurred much development after World War II. Between 1950 and 1970, Weston
permitted fifty subdivisions, and the number of dwellings more than doubled from
1,186 to 2,763. The new housing attracted professionals working on the Route 128
beltway as well as in downtown Boston.[31] To maintain its exclusive status as the highest per-capita-income community in the state, Weston aggressively purchased open
land for conservation and zoned out smaller houses (in 1972, it was only one of
twelve communities in Greater Boston to prohibit two-family homes).

The remaining "big houses" sprinkled across Boston's outskirts were no longer
gentlemen's semi-rural estates. Many were hemmed in by residential subdivisions.
Estates in Arlington, Belmont, Brookline, Newton, Somerville, Winchester, and virtually every other close-in Boston suburb were carved up into several building lots to
the acre, at a nearly urban density. Some estates burned, and others were donated to
nonprofit institutions. These suburbs were evolving into upper-middle-class bedroom communities rather than country seats for the wealthy.

Perhaps the most lasting legacy of the country estates is the land-use pattern of
the single-family house situated in a country suburb. In this development pattern, the
home owner builds his own house on a parcel that is set back from the road in a
wooded or meadow setting. It is not part of a mass-built subdivision. The parcel may
not be more than an acre or two, but it is separated from the surrounding houses. To
maintain the country atmosphere, sidewalks are not built and street lights are few. It
does not feel like a neighborhood and seems rural. These country suburbs are found
today outside the Route 128 beltway in such towns as Carlisle, Medfield, Stow,

Sudbury, Wayland, and North Shore towns such as Essex, Ipswich, and Topsfield. The country suburb also forms the template for contemporary exurban communities beyond the metropolitan area.

From Summer Resorts to Suburbs: North Shore, South Shore, and Countryside

Seaside resorts, particularly on the North Shore, became enclaves for the wealthy. Instead of being country seats, the estates were seaside cottages. In the 1820s, Nahant became Boston's first seaside resort. Within two decades, vacationers bought homes in Beverly and Manchester, along the rocky, breezy coast. After the Civil War, the Brahmin elite created social enclaves in Marblehead, Beverly Farms, Prides Crossing in Beverly, Manchester-by-the Sea, and the Magnolia and Eastern Point sections of Gloucester. Yachting became a prominent pastime. Just inland, Hamilton, Topsfield, and Wenham developed as country-estate towns, with a strong emphasis on equestrian sports and golf.

Such notables as Presidents William Howard Taft and Calvin Coolidge and steel magnate Henry Clay Frick summered on the North Shore. During the first decades of the twentieth century, the majority of Washington-based foreign ambassadors stayed on the North Shore. In 1941, Franklin D. Roosevelt stayed at Swampscott's New Ocean House when meeting with Winston Churchill to discuss the "Atlantic Charter" on a ship offshore.[32] Despite the big names that visited North Shore, most summer residents came from the Boston area. Owners of the imposing so-called cottages were often successful local businessmen seeking to proclaim their worldly success.

The coastline was ripe for development, with rocky points and wetland border areas that were inhospitable to farming. The first summer homes were comfortable, not ostentatious. By the 1890s, great fortunes were being made, and the tycoons started to build more elaborate mansions. On the Gold Coast, several hundred magnificent estates were built in the first decades of the twentieth century, when mind-boggling fortunes went virtually untaxed. The North Shore estates mimicked England's stately homes. Along the coast, the lots might run to fifty or sixty acres, but in Hamilton and Wenham, estates ranged from 100 to 3,000 acres, some of which are still preserved.

Such well-known architects as McKim, Mead & White, Carrere & Hastings, Guy Lowell, Peabody & Stearns, and Shepley, Rutan & Coolidge designed Colonial

Revival mansions, Tudor manors, neoclassical palaces, Italian villas, and French châ-
teaus. The Olmsted firm designed the landscapes for several estates. Many Boston
Brahmins favored the more modest Colonial Revival or Shingle styles. Out-of-town-
ers like Henry Clay Frick preferred the more pretentious European styles. Frick's
Eagle Rock (1906), a 104-room neoclassical palazzo designed by the Boston firm of
Little & Browne, was called "the grandest mansion north of Newport." (Frick's
daughter Helen downsized Eagle Rock in 1938 and demolished it in 1969 to avoid
the exorbitant cost of upkeep.)[33]

One of the favorite recreational activities on the North Shore was yachting, and
Marblehead was its center. The Boston area's first yacht club—the Eastern Yacht
Club—was established there in 1870. Between 1885 and 1887, the defenders of the
America's Cup sailed out of the Eastern Yacht Club. Well into the twentieth century,

FIGURE 3.4
Tupper Manor, Endicott College, Beverly. Tupper Manor (1904) is an example of the way elaborate
mansions have been saved by institutional reuse. The Italianate seaside estate designed by architect Guy
Lowell is now the Wylie Inn and Conference Center at Endicott College.
Source: Endicott College.

Marblehead skippers and boat designers were successful at winning the America's Cup and other prestigious yacht races. The Boston Yacht Club, Corinthian Yacht Club, Marblehead Yacht Club, Dolphin Yacht Club, and Pleon Yacht Club also established themselves on the historic harbor. *The WPA Guide to Massachusetts* (1937) observed: "Summer estates line the once bleak shore of the neck and overlook the harbor where hundreds of sleek-hulled craft ride at anchor."[34]

By 1930s, many families were ready to sell off estates. Some had lost interest, others wanted to vacation farther from Boston, and others could not afford the upkeep. The elaborate gardens declined, as longtime gardeners retired and commercial services were unable to maintain high standards. There were few buyers, especially as many of the homes were unfashionable Victorian piles. Some families sold to colleges and religious orders, while others demolished the houses and subdivided them into smaller lots. Both Endicott College in Beverly and Gordon College in Wenham started their campuses by occupying mansions. Several estates, including the magnificent 2,100-acre Crane Estate in Ipswich, were donated as public amenities to the Trustees of Reservations and comparable preservation organizations.[35]

In Swampscott, former stockbroker John Blodgett organized several of the real-estate trusts that transformed estates into subdivisions. Blodgett, who was careful to promote quality development, allowed no multifamily housing and instituted property covenants that required new houses should cost at least $10,000. Swampscott evolved into a suburb, as most of the new homes attracted year-round residents commuting into the city.[36]

Until the 1920s, the North Shore was mainly a seasonal resort, not a bedroom suburb. These communities became an integral part of the metropolitan area only with the coming of the automobile. North Shore historian Joseph Garland claims that the completion of Route 1 (1930s), Sumner Tunnel (1934), Tobin Bridge (1950), and Route 128 (1956) opened up the North Shore to motorists from the city, eroding the exclusiveness of the Gold Coast.[37] The effects were most felt inland from the shore, where farmland was easily converted into middle-class subdivisions. Although there remained pockets of wealth along the North Shore, many neighborhoods were middle-class, with residents moving out from Cambridge, Lynn, Salem, and Saugus. Italians, who made their first homes in Boston's North End, subsequently moved to Revere and Winthrop, before moving farther up the North Shore.

Despite postwar suburban development, the North Shore maintained much of its historic character. The traditional ports of Essex, Gloucester, Ipswich, Marblehead, Newburyport, Rockport, and Salem, retained their urban qualities and their nineteenth-century architecture, converting the area into new commercial and residential resort uses for the post-maritime consumer society. The extensive coastal marshlands between Essex and Newburyport precluded development and helped maintain the rural landscape. Even though highways brought the maritime and rural North Shore communities into Boston's metropolitan orbit, these communities have avoided many of the manifestations of sprawl and maintained their traditional small-town character

The South Shore was not as fashionable, nor did it boast sizable ports. The South Shore, which stretches from Quincy to Plymouth, is flat and has extensive marshlands along the coast, except at the granite ledges of Cohasset. With few harbors, it never developed port towns like those on the North Shore.

Hull, with the sandy stretch of Nantasket Beach and regular boat service to downtown Boston, became a late-nineteenth-century vacation getaway for many Bostonians. In the William Dean Howells novel *The Rise of Silas Lapham* (1885), businessman Silas Lapham and his family spent the summer at Nantasket. Mayor John "Honey Fitz" Fitzgerald, father of Rose Fitzgerald Kennedy, regularly took a cottage at Nantasket. Hull followed the classic suburban trajectory of many resort towns. First, there were hotels to accommodate vacationers. Then, developers built rental cottages. The vacationers became so enamored that they bought their own cottages. After a while, they converted the cottages into year-round homes. This cycle of development was repeated all the way down the South Shore through Plymouth and onto Cape Cod.

Some towns became attractive for their quaintness. Bostonians moved to communities like Hingham because of historical character that did not appear to be "suburban." Elizabeth Coatsworth, resident of Hingham during the 1920s and 1930s, wrote that Hingham

> has grown so slowly that it still maintains for the most part its eighteenth century appearance. True, we have our morning trains stamping through the village with a ringing of bells, carrying people to Boston, and our afternoon trains which bring them home. We have our First National Store and our A. & P., but our small downtown has a pleasantly antiquated appearance grouped as it is around the railroad station.[38]

Cohasset's stately summer homes offered long vistas over land and sea, particularly along the coastal Jerusalem Road. The Cohasset Improvement Association (established in 1917) raised private funds to preserve green spaces and landscape the grounds of public buildings. Property owners chafed against a proposal to adopt zoning in the 1920s, waiting until 1955 and the onslaught of suburbanization to do so. Cohasset cultivated a WASPy aloofness. Famously, during the mid-1920s, the Cohasset Country Club denied Joseph Kennedy membership, so he bought a summer home in Hyannisport, where the local golf club welcomed him.

The South Shore became nicknamed the "Irish Riviera" during the post–World War II period, as the sons and daughters of immigrants living in Dorchester, Jamaica Plain, and South Boston bought vacation homes and later year-round homes. According to the 2000 census, one-third of the South Shore is of Irish descent. The twenty Massachusetts communities with the largest proportions of Irish Americans are all located along the South Shore, led by Milton, Braintree, Marshfield, and Scituate. In Marshfield, popular summer colonies included Brant Rock, Fieldston, Green Harbor, and Ocean Bluff. In Scituate, Humarock and Minot started as seasonal resorts and evolved into year-round neighborhoods for those enjoying proximity to the beach.

A middle-class version of the countryside experience was provided by resort hotels in country towns west of Boston. These hotels gave urbanites a taste for "borderland" living. Prior to World War I, many outlying towns had resort hotels that were reached by railroad or streetcar. Tastes in vacations were modest. During much of the nineteenth century, there was a resort hotel at Fresh Pond in Cambridge. Boasting the clear air of Arlington Heights were the Robbins Spring Hotel and Outlook Spa Hotel ("Noted for Ozone"). Lexington's Russell House was called the "Doorway to Lexington" because many vacationers later made the town their residence. The Massachusetts House, which had been built as the Massachusetts Pavilion for the 1876 Centennial Exposition in Philadelphia, was moved to Lexington and opened as a hotel in 1878 (it became an asylum for alcoholics fourteen years later).

The Drabbington Lodge, operating in Weston between 1897 and 1935, provided quiet country-style getaways. The lodge featured a seven-hole golf course, tennis, horseback riding and indoor activities like card games and lectures. Wellesley's Elm Park Hotel hosted both vacationers those hoping to convalesce from tuberculosis. Sharon's Lake Massapoag, with its vaunted pure water and high ozone count, was a popular resort in the days when city-dwellers vacationed close to home. The Massapoag Lake House (1880–1955) had 100 rooms, and several smaller Sharon hotels also attracted vacationers.

Even Newton had a resort hotel. The Woodland Park Hotel, on Washington Street near Auburndale, served visitors from 1882 until World War I. *King's Handbook of Newton, Massachusetts* compared Woodland Park's clear air and protection from chilly coastal winds to the French Riviera and claimed that "several of the best physicians of the New-England metropolis have been in the habit of advising their patients to go to Florida or Auburndale, during the inclement seasons of the year."[39]

After World War I, the widespread use of the automobile allowed vacationers to visit Cape Cod, the Maine Coast, and more remote destinations, and the suburban Boston resort hotels closed down. The work of the resort hotels had been accomplished. Middle-class urbanites had been introduced to the country towns surrounding Boston.

FIGURE 3.5
Glen House Hotel, Weston, ca. 1900. The Glen House Hotel, opened in 1875, was typical of late nineteenth-century rural hotels outside Boston, which inspired middle-class families to seek out suburban homes.
Source: Courtesy Weston Historical Society.

Exploring Country Retreats

Shirley-Eustis House, 33 Shirley Street, Roxbury

Royal Governor William Shirley completed this country house in 1751. The Georgian mansion was designed by Peter Harrison, considered America's first professional architect. The house passed through many hands, including those of Massachusetts Governor William Eustis (1823–1825). During the nineteenth century, urbanization transformed the Roxbury neighborhood. In 1867, most of the estate was subdivided into fifty-three house lots. Soon thereafter, the house itself was divided up to house ten families. It deteriorated and later was abandoned. The Shirley-Eustis House Association, one of the country's earliest preservation initiatives, was established in 1913 to preserve the historic house. Efforts to move the house out of Roxbury in the late 1960s were rebuffed and restoration eventually took place. Today, the historic mansion is open to the public.

Gore Place, 52 Gore Street, Waltham

It is noteworthy that three of the best surviving nineteenth-century country estates are located within a mile of each other in urban Waltham. Gore Place was the country home of Governor and US Senator Christopher Gore, who built it in 1806, after an earlier house burned down. Like many gentleman farmers, Governor Gore promoted model agriculture on his estate. The historic house is furnished and offers tours to the public seasonally.

Lyman Estate/The Vale, 185 Lyman Street, Waltham

When the Vale was built in 1793, it was decidedly a country home and remained one through the nineteenth century. Designed by Samuel McIntyre, the Federal-style house has attractive grounds and the region's oldest greenhouses. Managed by Historic New England, the Vale's interior is open only for weddings and functions.

Robert Treat Paine House/Stonehurst, 577 Beaver Street, Waltham

Adjacent to the Lyman Estate, the Paine House (built for social reformer Robert Treat Paine, Jr., who was married to Lydia Lyman) was expanded in 1884 to 1886 by H. H. Richardson, with spacious living areas and glacial boulders accenting the exterior. With grounds designed by Frederick Law Olmsted, Stonehurst is considered an architectural masterpiece. It is open to the public.

Captain Forbes House, 215 Adams Street, Milton

Milton was another location of early country estates. The Forbes House (1833), built by China Trade merchant Robert Bennett Forbes, is an outstanding example. The interior is full of furnishings related to China and is open to the public. The surrounding Milton Hill Historic District, which spreads along Adams Street and Randolph and Canton Avenues, has numerous historic estates from the nineteenth and early twentieth centuries. Across the street from the Forbes House is Governor Hutchinson's Field, where the last royal governor of Massachusetts owned an estate in the 1770s. The house was demolished in 1870, but the site still offers terrific views of Boston's harbor and skyline. It is owned by The Trustees of Reservations, which was the world's first regional land trust.

Henderson House, 99 Westcliff Road, Weston

This Tudor Revival manor harkens back to the era when similar estates dominated Weston. Rebuilt after a fire by Edward Pierce in 1926, it is considered the last great mansion to be built in town before the Great Depression. At one time, the estate owned 300 acres, most of which were subdivided for upper-middle-class homes in the 1960s. Henderson House currently is a conference center managed by Northeastern University. The vast majority of country estates like Henderson House have been lost. Those that remain have usually been reused by an educational or religious institution.

Hunnewell Estate, 845 Washington Street, Wellesley

The Hunnewell Estates Historic District, which incorporates several Hunnewell family estates (originally a dozen), is off Washington Street and Pond Road in Wellesley. The estates are closed to the public, but visitors can amble around the shore of Lake Waban from Wellesley College and view the 150-year-old Italian topiary garden and other plantings. Wellesley College, with one of the country's most attractive campuses, was named for the original estate of H. H. Hunnewell, a highly successful investor who sought to create the most dazzling gardens.

Larz Anderson Auto Museum, 15 Newton Street, Brookline

Only the carriage house of the Larz Anderson estate, "Weld," still survives. Containing what it calls "America's oldest car collection," the museum is located in a copy of the Château de Chaumont-sur-Loire in France. If this is the carriage house, one can only imagine what the actual mansion was like before it was demolished in 1955. The estate was built by Isabel Weld Perkins and her husband, American diplomat Larz Anderson, who served as ambassador to Japan. Isabel's grandfather was William Fletcher Weld, owner of the Black Horse Flag fleet of clipper ships. When he died, he left his granddaughter a fortune of $17 million, making her the wealthiest woman in the world. Her home was designed to resemble Lulworth Hall, the Weld ancestral home in Britain. Charles Platt designed the Italian gardens, which were also destroyed after Isabel died; and she bequeathed her estate to the Town of Brookline. The sixty-four-acre estate is now a public park with a superb view of downtown Boston to go along with the auto museum.

Crane Estate at Castle Hill, 290 Argilla Road, Ipswich

Many of the classic North Shore mansions of the late nineteenth and early twentieth centuries have either been demolished or are still private and hidden from view. You can get a sense of the Gold Coast by driving up Route 127 through Beverly and Manchester-by-the-Sea. The best opportunity to view a classic seaside mansion is at the Crane Estate at Castle Hill, which is owned by The Trustees of Reservations. The original Crane Estate (1912) was modeled on an Italian Renaissance villa; but Mrs. Crane did not like it, and her husband replaced it with a manor in the seventeenth-century English style (1928). The most spectacular element of the estate is the half-mile-long Grand Allee lawn stretching from the manor to the sea, which was designed by Arthur Shurcliff. The Great House is available for tours and private functions.

Endicott College, 376 Hale Street (Route 127), Beverly

The Endicott College campus provides a remarkable window on historic North Shore estates. Endicott demonstrates how many mansions were acquired by institutions when their owners could maintain them no longer. Endicott College uses seven historic estates for administrative and residential space (and owns numerous contemporary buildings as well). Several of the estates look directly over the ocean. Two of the most spectacular are the Italianate Tupper Manor (1904) and Tudor Revival College Hall (1916). Tupper Manor, designed by Guy Lowell, was built for the Allan family, owners of Canada's Allan Shipping Lines. The manse was originally named "Allandale" and was renamed for the founder of Endicott College. Obtain a walking tour brochure at the Campus Safety office at the college's main entrance.

Gordon College, 255 Grapevine Road, Wenham

Near Endicott College is Wenham's Gordon College, which is situated on Frederick H. Prince's 1,000-acre estate Princemere (1911). Prince, who was son of the founder of the Myopia Hunt Club, was an avid fan of polo, fox hunting, and the steeple-chase. He made a fortune as chairman of Chicago's Union Stockyards and Armour & Company and was profiled on the cover of *Time Magazine* in 1933 as Boston's wealthiest man. As with many North Shore estates, he sold it for a nominal sum so that Gordon College might move from Boston to a spacious landscaped campus. His mansion is used as the Gordon College administration building, Frost Hall.

Glen House Hotel, 247 Glen Road, Weston

The Glen House Hotel started operation in 1875, when Willard Jennings took summer guests into his large farmhouse. By the early twentieth century, the Glen House Hotel had forty rooms and five cottages. It hosted parents of Wellesley College students and those seeking a close railroad connection to Boston. The rambling Victorian structure eventually burned, but four guest cottages still stand. The house at 247 Glen Road is a private home.

Railroad Suburbs (1840–1920)

On April 7, 1834, the first railroad train ever to depart Boston headed out on the Boston & Worcester Railroad line. The directors of the new railroad took along several dozen local notables to experience the transportation novelty. The train terminated its journey at West Newton, where the tracks ended. The makeshift station was Seth Davis's Tavern, a brick building that still stands and houses Sweet Tomatoes Pizza.

West Newton, called Squash End at the time, was an unlikely railroad stop. The company's investors had wanted to route the rail line through Watertown and Waltham, which boasted a flourishing textile industry, but those communities rejected the proposal. Newton, which was a rural community, welcomed the newfangled iron horse and set itself on a course toward becoming one of Boston's first and most prestigious suburbs. Congressman William Jackson (1783–1855), a leading Newton businessman, helped the railroad acquire the right-of-way through his town.

Boston investors quickly built railroads to Providence, Worcester, and Lowell (1835), Salem (1838), Newburyport (1840), and Plymouth, Fitchburg, and Fall River (1845). These train lines, which are spokes emanating from the hub, still serve as the commuter lines of the Massachusetts Bay Transportation Authority. The terminals for each line trace an arc forming the perimeter of today's metropolitan area.

The railroad development plans had a mix of private and public involvement. While the company management and capital were private, the companies were chartered by the legislature and granted the right to buy land for their routes. Government in the nineteenth century did not play a major role in financing or managing transportation infrastructure, but it did provide institutional and legal backing.

The railroad entrepreneurs built their trains to transport freight. Little did they realize their infrastructure would spur the development of a new type of built landscape—railroad suburbs. It took the railroad companies a few years to figure out there was a potential commuter market living on the outskirts of Boston. The Eastern Railroad, which operated between East Boston and Newburyport, introduced the first season tickets in 1839. The Boston & Worcester Railroad started offering reduced commuter fares and scheduling rush-hour trains—the "Newton Special"— four years later. The term *commuter* originated with the "commuted" price reduction.[1]

By 1849 there were fifty-nine commuter trains coming into Boston every weekday from less than fifteen miles away, and another forty-five trains traveled from longer distances. According to the *Boston Directory*, the number of suburbanites commuting into the city grew from 1,600 in 1845 to over 10,000 by 1860. By that year, Boston had a larger proportion of suburban commuters than any other American city, and over half of Boston's attorneys lived in the suburbs. The *Boston Evening Transcript* identified a dozen railroad suburbs: Brighton, Dedham, Dorchester, Malden, Medford, Melrose, Milton, Newton, Quincy, Somerville, West Cambridge (Arlington), and Winchester.[2]

The railroad opened up land near railroad stations for suburban development. Speculators laid out subdivisions and street arrangements that optimized development opportunities—there was no municipal planning or land-use regulation in the nineteenth century. Closer to Boston, houses were clustered on one-half to three-acre lots in suburban villages, while farther from the city lots could be larger. Country estates could take up at least ten acres in a landscape interspersed with farms and woodlands, while middle-class houses in railroad suburbs were clustered on half-acre to three-acre lots.[3] The railroad suburbs were more directly connected to city life than country estates, both through the transportation infrastructure and denser land-use patterns.

The first wave of suburbanization was spurred by the enormous influx of poor Irish immigrants into Boston. Between 1845 and 1855, 230,000 immigrants arrived in Boston fleeing the Potato Famine. One-third of them settled permanently, creating teeming slums near the city's harbor. Middle-class businessmen and professionals

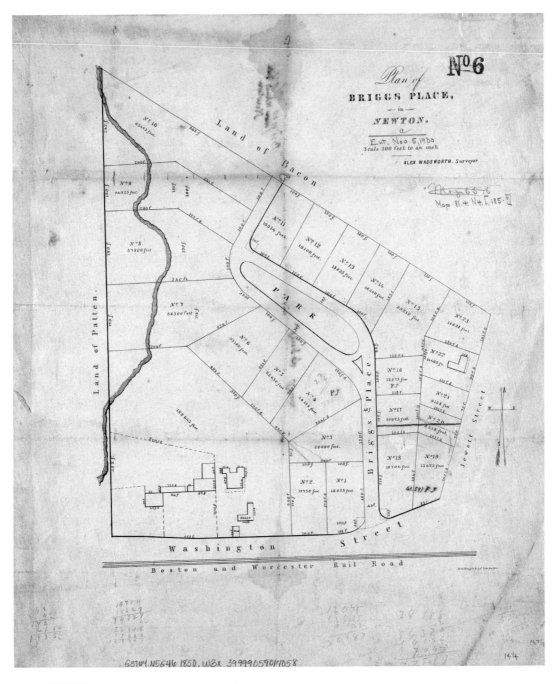

FIGURE 4.1

Plan of Briggs Place/Walnut Park, Newton, 1850. Following the introduction of commuter fares on the Boston & Worcester Railroad in 1843, landowner William Jackson laid out on his farm Newton's first residential subdivision—Briggs Place (subsequently referred to as Walnut Park).

Source: Map reproduction courtesy of the Norman B. Leventhal Map Center at the Boston Public Library.

started to seek a suburban outlet to escape the emerging slums, as they would do right through the twentieth century. Oscar Handlin wrote in *Boston's Immigrants*: "Primarily, this centrifugal movement winnowed the well-to-do from the impoverished."[4] As the decades wore on and the Irish solidified their presence and ethnic tensions intensified, middle-class Yankees continued to escape the city and avoid the political dominance of the Irish.

After the Civil War, railroad companies built out the train network to its maximum extent. By 1871, an average of 28,000 passengers, a large proportion being commuters, entered Boston daily by rail. Ridership grew to a peak of 87,000 inbound passengers in 1893, and then declined by fifteen percent by 1901 because of competition from electric streetcars.[5] The railroad extended suburban living from a belt five to twenty-five miles from the city.

Boston's preeminent railroad suburb was Newton, with its collection of thirteen "villages," most of which grew up around railroad stops. Four of the largest villages developed on the Boston & Albany Railroad line—Newton Corner, Newtonville, West Newton, and Auburndale. Except for Newton Corner, there was scant population in these places before the railroad line was opened. After the commuter service was introduced in 1843, several new residential areas appeared. Railroad advocate William Jackson, whose Jackson Homestead near Newton Corner currently houses the Newton Historical Society, saw the development potential created by the Boston & Worcester Railroad. Emulating the creation of house lots undertaken on Beacon Hill, Jackson created Newton's first residential subdivision in 1844 on fourteen acres of his farm. He hired Alexander Wadsworth, the engineer who had helped design Mount Auburn Cemetery, to lay out the house lots, streets, and green space of Walnut Park (also referred to as Briggs Place). Jackson and Wadsworth went on to develop Waban Park in Newton Corner two years later. Wadsworth also laid out Kenrick Park (turned into a residential subdivision on part of William Kenrick's nursery) at Newton Corner as well as Webster Park and Sylvan Heights in West Newton.

The most notable collaboration between Jackson and Wadsworth was establishing Auburndale in 1847. The new suburb, named after Mount Auburn Cemetery, adapted many of the picturesque landscape elements of the "garden cemetery" to create a "garden suburb."[6] Jackson's North Auburn Dale Land Company subdivided 120 acres into eighty-four lots north of the Boston & Albany Railroad tracks. Jackson wrote "puffing" articles in Boston newspapers over different signatures and ran a free train from Boston to a land auction that attracted more than 200 Boston businessmen.[7]

The green oval at Islington Park near the Charles River attracted homes of the well-to-do. House lots near the railroad station accommodated middle- and working-class families. In 1851, Jackson partnered in development around the Auburndale Female Seminary (today's Lasell College), creating a community that attracted retired clergy and was nicknamed "Saints Rest." Auburndale's population grew to 698 by 1865, 1,258 in 1878, and almost 2,000 people by 1889.[8]

The house lots laid out by William Jackson and Alexander Wadsworth helped create a standard, salable real-estate commodity that suburbs would use to facilitate large-scale development. Although houses were not mass-produced until the mid-twentieth century—for decades, they were erected by homeowners and individual builders—they tended to follow standard housing styles. These fit popular tastes and made suburban housing worthwhile investments. Each era has had characteristic housing styles that were copied thousands of times over because of their replicability and predictability as investments. This cycle consistently happened in suburbs that emerged from railroads, streetcars, parkways, and highways.

Development was often haphazard in the early suburbs, even when there were subdivisions. "Newtonville" first appeared in town records in 1847, when a railroad stop was established. Because of its central location, the village of Newtonville became the site of the first town high school. During the boom between the end of the Civil War and the Panic of 1873, Newtonville experienced substantial construction activity. By 1889, *King's Handbook of Newton, Massachusetts* reported: "It has four comfortable little churches, a dozen or more shops, and several score of pleasant and quiet homes, strewn fortuitously about in a region of trees and lawns and rural streets."[9]

On the south side of Newton, Chestnut Hill, Newton Centre, and Upper and Lower Falls were also growing. Newton Centre, the location of Andover Newton Theological Seminary, presented a sedate sylvan tone. One of the nation's earliest village improvement associations, the Newton Centre Tree Club (1852), sought to beautify the community by planting trees. A successor organization, the Newton Centre Improvement Association (1879), graded and adorned the village common and improved the shores of Crystal Lake, earning Newton the sobriquet "Garden City."[10] The villages of Newton Highlands and Waban experienced rapid development after passenger service was introduced on the Circuit Railroad/Highland Branch (today's Green Line Riverside D train) in 1886.

Newton Corner, Newton's closest train stop to Boston, was the largest and most fashionable of its villages. *King's Handbook of Newton, Massachusetts* depicted dozens of handsome Queen Anne-style mansions arrayed south of the Newton Corner station.

King's Handbook portrayed Newton as a model bedroom suburb: "At morning, a dozen trains bear eastward the working force of the place, the merchants, clerks, and what not; and at evening they come backward to their homes hereaway, tired with the anxieties and efforts of the day, and ready for their tranquil joys amid the suburban domiciles amid the trees and flowers."[11]

The railroad lines made Newton a commuter bedroom suburb, with clusters of development around each train station. By 1864, one-third of Newton residents commuted to Boston.[12] The town's population, which was a meager 3,351 in 1840, soared to 24,379 by 1890. Newton commuters had a choice of thirty trains per day on the Boston & Albany main line and another twenty trains by the Circuit Railroad/Highland Branch.[13]

As Newton was developing into a suburb, so was Brookline. After the American Revolution, many of Boston's leading families built seasonal homes in Brookline, particularly in the southern part of town. Prominent estate owners included names like Amory, Boylston, Cabot, Gardner, Higginson, Ingersoll, Lee, Perkins, Sargent, Sullivan, and Weld. At first the homes were relatively modest, but they became larger and more ornate in the late nineteenth century.

The first planned residential subdivision was The Lindens, established by Thomas Aspinwall Davis near Brookline Village in 1843. Davis hired engineer Alexander Wadsworth to lay out the streets, twenty-seven house lots, and Linden Park. Davis then auctioned off house lots with property covenants requiring solely residential construction and mandatory street setbacks. Six years later, wealthy Boston merchant David Sears II planned the more ambitious Longwood "garden suburb" nearby, laying out four squares, planting thousands of trees on new streets, and selling building lots to fellow Boston patricians. Sears had been acquiring the property for over two decades and only decided to sell plots to others after the opening of Longwood station of the Brookline branch of the Boston & Worcester Railroad in 1847.

Amos A. and William Lawrence, leading textile magnates and founders of the eponymous Merrimack Valley mill town, secured a romantically landscaped family compound at Cottage Farm in 1850, purchasing 200 acres from David Sears. Alexander Wadsworth, once again, was hired to lay out the house lots. At first, the houses were built for family members, but Cottage Farm lots were later sold to other members of Boston's upper class, after Amos A. Lawrence died. Interest in this and other Brookline developments was heightened by the construction of Beacon Street from the Mill Dam in Boston through Brookline in 1851.

FIGURE 4.2
Sears House, Longwood, Brookline, 1933. In 1849, after railroad service was introduced to Brookline, landowner David Sears II laid out the Longwood subdivision. Architect Arthur Gilman designed this home for the Sears family in 1858. It was demolished in the mid-twentieth century.
Source: Brookline Preservation Commission.

As Brookline grew into a prominent suburb, pressure mounted for merging with the central city. Prior to 1866, communities could annex neighbors with state legislative approval, but, from then on, a local referendum was required. In order to obtain Boston's street, water, sewer, and educational services, Roxbury (1868), Dorchester (1870), Brighton, Charlestown, and West Roxbury (1874) each voted to be annexed by the city. Boosters thought a bigger city would be better for business and bragging rights. Brookline town meeting, faced with a similar vote in 1874, opposed annexation. Wealthy property owners opposed the idea, while local businessmen and workers supported it. The opponents were satisfied with the infrastructure, which they felt was appropriate for a country suburb. They also feared higher taxes and meddling in their way of life by urban politicians. Supporters of annexation favored urban growth and the economic opportunities that accompanied it. The Brookline battle continued until 1880, when town meeting defeated annexation for the final time.[14] The elite that controlled Brookline town government were able to maintain its pastoral atmosphere, while providing such urban services as water, sewer, road construction, and even snow clearance. In an era prior to zoning, when developers submitted plans for large lots and houses, the town agreed to provide the required services, but when an investor submitted plans for small houses on compact lots, the town refused to provide roads and utilities. The town also encouraged large estates by routinely assessing them at low real estate values.[15] Brookline represented a social winnowing that took place as each suburb established its socioeconomic niche. Even as Back Bay flourished as Boston's most prominent neighborhood, Brookline was establishing a suburban alternative that eventually drained the Back Bay of many of its first families.

The Brookline annexation vote was portentous for Boston's relations with its surrounding communities. Suburban communities grew to fear the immigrants, machine politics, messy industrialization, and rising taxes. Middle-class families living in outlying communities favored small-town life, with its participatory town meeting, low public expenditures, and social homogeneity. Cambridge, Newton, and Somerville, where factions favored annexation, voted to maintain their autonomy. Except for Hyde Park (1912), no other suburb voted to merge with Boston, thereby enshrining the supremacy of home rule and political fragmentation in the region. This ensured that the city of Boston would remain relatively small in area and in population. New York, Philadelphia, and Chicago, on the other hand, pursued extensive annexation throughout the nineteenth century and created much larger central cities.

Instead of merging with the central city, many communities opted to split into even more autonomous municipalities. The growth pressures in metropolitan Boston during the nineteenth century caused twenty communities to divide. The coming of the railroad played a crucial role in facilitating both residential and industrial development. When towns split, it usually reflected different land use emphases in each community. Some strove to remain agricultural, others were urbanizing and developing industry, while another category of town wanted to have a suburban residential character. Belmont, Melrose, Nahant, Swampscott, Wellesley, Winchester, and Winthrop sought to protect their predominantly residential character. Municipalities such as Everett, Peabody, Revere, and Somerville wanted to develop their industrial base.

Michael Rawson's *Eden on the Charles: The Making of Boston*, in its account of how rural West Roxbury separated from urban Roxbury in 1851, argues that urbanizing communities desired a full range of public services, including water, sewer, gas

TABLE 4.1
Incorporation of new suburbs from existing municipalities

Municipality	Parent Municipality	Year of Incorporation
Somerville	Charlestown	1842
Revere	Chelsea	1846
Melrose	Malden	1850
Winchester	Woburn	1850
Swampscott	Lynn	1852
Winthrop	Revere	1852
Nahant	Lynn	1853
Peabody (South Danvers)	Danvers	1855
Belmont	Arlington, Waltham, Watertown	1859
Everett	Malden	1870
Wellesley	Needham	1888

Source: Municipal websites.

street lights, good streets, sidewalks, police and protection, ash removal, and decent public schools. Pastoral suburbs, such as West Roxbury, originally sought to maintain rural charm, keep taxes low, and minimize urban services, but after the Civil War homeowners came to believe such qualities were necessities. Real-estate speculators, home builders, and laborers supported the provision of urban-style services because it made property more valuable and work opportunities more abundant.[16]

An impetus to establishing new towns came from philanthropists who bequeathed a town hall or library, sometimes with the stipulation that the community be named after him or his home. This occurred in Belmont, Holbrook, Peabody, Wakefield, and Winchester. Perhaps the most notable example was Peabody, named for George Peabody, a South Danvers–born, London-based financier who has been called the "father of modern philanthropy."[17] Peabody not only funded Salem's Peabody Museum, museums at Harvard and Yale, and a charitable trust for the poor in London, but he also funded the Peabody Institute Library in South Danvers, which renamed itself "Peabody" in his honor in 1868. Another example is Holbrook, which separated from Randolph in 1872 and was named after local businessman Elisha N. Holbrook, who donated the funds for a town hall and a library. By 1900, municipalities had sorted themselves out in dealing with urbanization and industrialization, and the practice of splitting townships virtually ended.

Several growing communities took the step of incorporating as cities. The city form of government with a mayor and city council streamlined local authority and spurred the development of schools and infrastructure. This confirmed their autonomy and avoided the need to merge with Boston. Some of the suburban communities that incorporated as cities were Cambridge (1846), Lynn (1850), Chelsea (1857), Somerville (1872), Newton (1873), Malden (1882), and Waltham (1884). Municipal incorporation ended up stimulating further growth, with the new cities achieving urban densities that could equal Boston's. This ended up fragmenting the metropolitan area into a mosaic of urban and suburban communities that jealously guarded their home rule powers.

Frederick Law Olmsted and the Suburban Ideal

One of the most influential shapers of American suburbia during the railroad era lived in Brookline. He was Frederick Law Olmsted, designer of Central Park in New York and Boston's Emerald Necklace parks. He is less known for his contributions to suburban form, but they were part of his overall program to reform the chaotic nineteenth-century American city. Olmsted pronounced: "No great town can long exist without great suburbs."[18] Olmsted helped codify a planned approach to upper- and middle-class suburban subdivisions that included tree belts, spacious front yards, and uniform house setbacks. The land-use form was less dense and greener than in the city but was unlike the agrarian countryside.

From the 1850s through the 1870s, Olmsted mostly lived in New York City. The pace and politics of America's most dynamic city wore him out. After conflict with intransigent political powers and a bout of depression, Olmsted summered in Cambridge and Brookline between 1878 and 1880. He lived full-time in a rented Brookline house in 1881 and 1882. His friend and collaborator architect H. H. Richardson invited Olmsted to settle near him in the sylvan suburb of Brookline. Olmsted was particularly impressed by life in Brookline when he witnessed the town's horse-drawn vehicles clearing snow from the roads in wintertime. In 1883, Olmsted purchased an old farmhouse and renovated it as a family home and office, which he named Fairsted.

Brookline was a perfect spot for Olmsted—it was much easier on his nerves than New York. "Beautiful Brookline" had the ideal pastoral landscape that Olmsted believed the best suburbs should have. The location allowed him to supervise the

FIGURE 4.3
Frederick Law Olmsted. Besides
designing parks and campuses,
Frederic Law Olmsted (1822-1903)
designed many suburban subdivisions,
including Fisher Hill in Brookline.
He maintained that "No great town
can long exist without great suburbs."
Source: Frederick Law Olmsted
National Historic Site.

development of Boston's Emerald Necklace parks, and he could mix easily with Boston's intelligentsia. Considered "the richest town in the world," it had a supportive clientele for Olmsted's services, both at private estates and public parks.[19]

Living only a few minutes from Richardson, he collaborated with the architect on such projects as the public buildings at North Easton, Quincy's Public Library grounds, Robert Treat Paine's Stonehurst estate in Waltham, and the landscaping for fourteen Boston & Albany Railroad stations. Another neighbor was Arnold Arboretum Director Charles Sprague Sargent, with whom Olmsted designed the Arboretum.

South Brookline was a semirural, wooded, hilly suburb only five miles from downtown Boston. As Olmsted did with his parks, he landscaped his two-acre home to fit the natural topography. Fairsted combined outcroppings of puddingstone, wooded glades, a naturalistic sunken garden called the "Hollow," and a meadow sloping around a spreading elm tree. To add to the naturalistic look, Olmsted erected a wire grid on south and east walls of his house and grew Chinese wisteria to cover the house, allowing the architecture to blend with the landscape. Fairsted was an example of his thinking about landscape and domestic life, which the National Park Service has preserved for today's public as the Frederick Law Olmsted National Historic Site.

Olmsted considered suburbs to be one of the fundamental solutions to the problems of the nineteenth-century industrial city. Just as Olmsted designed parks for the public to experience the outdoors in the middle of the city and parkways to create efficient and verdant thoroughfares, he also planned leafy suburban neighborhoods to house the upper and middle classes. He believed that suburbs provided essential contact with nature while providing urban services. He foresaw that suburbia would expand as it came within economic and geographic reach of more people: "It is practically certain that the Boston of today is the mere nucleus of the Boston that is to be. It is practically certain that it is to extend over many miles of country now thoroughly rural in character."[20]

Olmsted developed many of his ideas about suburbs at the Chicago suburb of Riverside, Illinois (1869), and refined them at three subdivisions he designed in Brookline. Riverside, which was the first American suburb planned on such a scale, demonstrated that suburbs could be cohesive and attractive and not simply a random collection of individual houses or, as Olmsted called them, "rude over-dressed villages, or fragmentary half-made towns."[21] Olmsted sought to combine "urban conveniences" with "the special charms and substantial advantages of rural conditions of life." Advantages of country life included "purity of air, umbrageousness, facilities for quiet out-of-door recreation and distance from the jar, noise, confusion, and bustle of commercial thoroughfares."[22]

Olmsted incorporated these qualities in Riverside by emphasizing the features of the area's topography and building winding, shaded roads instead of simply extending Chicago's urban grid. He created house lots of varied sizes with ample yards. Olmsted believed it was important to have a green space with various planting around houses, not only to create a natural setting that provided privacy for family life but also to protect against airborne disease that was thought to be communicated in dense residential conditions. (Before the bacteria theory of disease was promulgated in the 1890s, many Americans believed the miasma theory that poisonous air carried diseases.)[23]

Olmsted was a prominent advocate of the notion that suburbs were private family-oriented places, which should be separated from the teeming commercial and social life of the central city. He maintained that the suburb represented "the most attractive, the most refined, and the most soundly wholesome forms of domestic life."[24] Under this scenario, the suburban home became the domain of women, children, and extended family members like grandparents and unmarried relatives. It was the antithesis of the rough-and-tumble, money-grubbing city, which was the arena of men's work. Surrounded by lawns, trees, shrubs, and fences, suburban homes provided the family a sense of privacy. At his own home, Fairsted, Olmsted deeply appreciated his family life and decided to maintain his landscape architecture office there.

One of Olmsted's major contributions to suburban design was a setback of houses from the sidewalk. This led to the creation of a continuous strip of lawns, creating a broad swath of semipublic green space in addition to the tree belt. Landscape historian John Brinckerhoff Jackson called this "lawn culture," in which families did not tend to use front yards but maintained them as green space, creating the image of a park.[25] This approach to open space relied on private ownership to provide to the public the benefit of a leafy community.

Olmsted believed that commodious yards obviated the need for suburbs to have large parks, as big cities had. When asked at the Brookline Club "whether the town ought to acquire something for a park, . . . he thought not."[26] Because of the suburban neighborhood designs that Olmsted developed for Riverside and other communities, New York city planner Alexander Garvin has written: "American's suburban subdivisions, like urban neighborhoods, vary in size and quality. But they look very much alike because virtually all of them are imbued with the design philosophy of one man: Frederick Law Olmsted, Sr."[27]

Olmsted himself designed only forty-seven suburban neighborhoods, and the successor firm managed by his sons, John Charles Olmsted (1852–1920) and Frederick Law Olmsted, Jr. (1870–1957), designed about 400 subdivisions and new communities across the country. In addition, former Olmsted firm employees and students designed thousands of subdivisions, while imitators designed many more.

Olmsted and his firm made a strong impression on Brookline by designing several upscale residential neighborhoods. His most important projects included Aspinwall Hill (1880, with Ernest Bowditch), Fisher Hill (1884), and the Philbrick subdivision of Pill Hill (1889). Architectural historian Keith Morgan argues that the Olmsted firm's varied Brookline projects, though they were designed at different times and were geographically separate, formed templates for connecting adjacent suburban developments. He suggested that one could "comprehend the model of parallel rivers flowing into an organic whole" by walking down from Fisher Hill to the Brookline Hills railroad station and the grounds of Brookline High School, continuously passing through Olmsted-designed landscapes.[28] Although Olmsted and his successor firm never designed an entire residential suburb in Greater Boston, their ideas were influential throughout the 1880 to 1930 period.

FIGURE 4.4
Fairsted, 99 Warren Street, Brookline. In 1883, Frederick Law Olmsted bought an old farmhouse in South Brookline, which he converted into his home and office and called "Fairsted." His landscape architecture firm and its successor operated out of Fairsted until 1979.
Source: Frederick Law Olmsted National Historic Site.

Victorian Houses in the Suburban Setting

The ultimate purpose of the suburbs was to provide attractive and secure places in which to live. Suburban houses not only provided necessary shelter but also reflected what society considered the best way to live. As Frederick Law Olmsted maintained, suburban homes were the highest expression of domestic civilization. Before the Civil War, the villas of the rich and the middle class were tasteful but seldom ostentatious. Railroad suburbs also had homes of tradesmen and workers, who lived in modest cottages and vernacular two-story homes.

During the post–Civil War boom, the housing styles of the upper and middle classes became more ostentatious. Businessmen and professionals, many of them new to wealth, proclaimed their status with elaborately ornamented houses. The obsessive money-making Gilded Age witnessed America's greatest extremes of income inequality. Affluent families started making Belmont, Brookline, Newton, and Winchester their year-round residences. Manufacturers produced a proliferation of furnishings. Water, sewer, gas, and, later in the century, electric service facilitated the growth of a wide range of appliances for the kitchen and bathroom. Home buyers demanded significantly larger houses. They accommodated extended families, including grandparents, in-laws, and unmarried uncles and aunts. The key to maintaining the sprawling Victorian houses were servants, who were plentiful in the wake of Irish immigration. Upper- and upper-middle-class homes could have several servants, undertaking specialized tasks such as cleaning, cooking, taking care of the children, maintaining the grounds, and caring for horses and carriages. Even middle-class families could afford "help."

Domestic architecture was at its most exuberant during this era. The Second Empire homes, with their mansard roofs and looming towers, and the Queen Anne and Shingle-style homes, with their asymmetrical forms and wrap-around porches, exemplified a culture that believed each house detail "revealed both the personality of a particular family . . . and the virtues of family life as an institution."[29] Pattern books and architectural magazines inspired Americans to take advantage of the endless variety of precut spindle work and decorative details that could provide their home's distinctiveness. The invention of inexpensive plate glass allowed for the installation of bay windows. Queen Anne houses, in particular, were painted in a wider variety of colors than virtually any other style in American history.

A profusion of rooms accompanied a profusion of decoration. The first floor contained public rooms. The parlor was for entertaining and for showcasing the

FIGURE 4.5
Colonial Revival house, 146 Naples Road, Brookline, 1937. This 1895 Colonial Revival house, built by developer Donald McKay in North Brookline, embodies the scale of upper-middle-class homes of the late nineteenth century.
Source: Brookline Preservation Commission.

family possessions. Victorian homes were crowded with furniture, china, artwork, sculpture, wall hangings, decorative screens, and potted plants. Mantelpieces were heaped with bric-a-brac and souvenirs that testified to the taste and travels of the residents. As the formal room, the parlor was also the scene of weddings, funerals, and formal calls. The main hall, often featuring a dramatic staircase, could also be a place of display. The dining room reached the height of importance during this era. It was where the lady of the house held sway in the domestic life of the family and where she entertained guests at multicourse meals. Dining rooms had long tables, carved chairs, and ornate sideboards and cabinets. An astonishing array of silver tableware, which were among the first mass-produced consumer goods, included serving dishes, tureens, candlesticks, fruit baskets, entrée dishes, vases, and special serving utensils. The first floor might also have a sitting room, music room, and a library, which was usually private space for the man of the house.

The kitchen was at the back of the house and was a work area, not a place for dining. Not only were elaborate meals produced there three times a day but also clothes were usually washed there. Newfangled appliances, such as cooking ranges and iceboxes, filled the kitchen, and a bewildering collection of cooking utensils and gadgets filled the pantry.

The upstairs was private family space. Bedrooms could be large enough to have sitting areas, where women and children spent time with family members and friends. Closets were introduced to hold the growing wardrobes. As the average American family had five children in 1870, middle-class families needed several bedrooms. Small sewing rooms were added for the women, and nooks and crannies were added to provide private spaces for children. Bathrooms started to have flush toilets, porcelain sinks, and zinc-covered bath tubs, taking advantage of flowing hot water.[30] There were also bedrooms for servants, usually in the attic. The Victorian-era houses marked the arrival of consumer culture in America.

Neighborhoods of Victorian houses can be found both in Boston and inner-ring suburbs. Urban core neighborhoods tend to have row houses or apartment buildings, but farther out urban neighborhoods have single- or two- and three-family houses. Virtually every community inside Route 128 has neighborhoods with impressive Victorian homes.

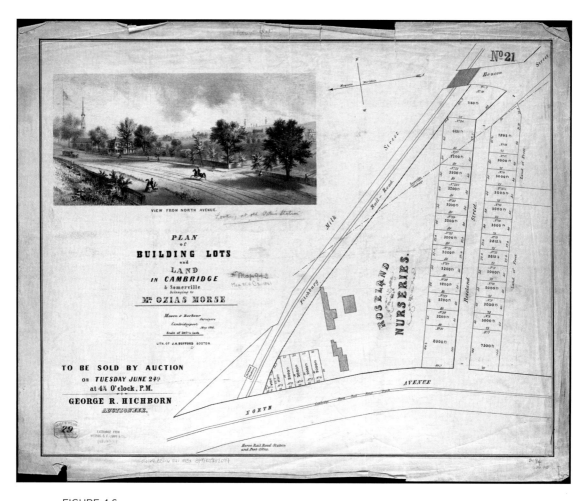

FIGURE 4.6
Plan of lots of Ozias Morse, near Porter Square, Cambridge, 1860. This plan for a subdivision off North Avenue (Massachusetts Avenue) depicts the sylvan quality that people expected in suburbs. Note how the plan indicates proximity to the Fitchburg Railroad and the picture shows a horsecar.
Source: Map reproduction courtesy of the Norman B. Leventhal Map Center at the Boston Public Library.

Railroad Suburbs Come of Age

The railroad suburb pattern of development, where houses clustered near train stations, appeared across the inner ring around Boston in Belmont, Cambridge, Dedham, Medford, Melrose, and Winchester. Cambridge exemplified how a farming community evolved into a railroad suburb and then into a city. During much of the nineteenth century, large parts of Cambridge would be considered suburban, but intense development pressures and industrialization made it mostly urban by 1900.

The northwest section of Cambridge provides a good example of the development process of railroad suburbs. After the Fitchburg Railroad opened a station at Porter Square in 1843, the area's first residential subdivision was created on farm land along North Avenue (today's Massachusetts Avenue). Horse-drawn streetcar service (1856) encouraged further development along North Avenue from Harvard Square. The closing of the cattle yards at Porter Square in 1868 (the porterhouse steak allegedly was named for the hotel that served the stockyards) provided more open land for development.[31]

The Cambridge subdivisions created house lots on small colonial-era farms of approximately ten acres. Farmers often sold off the outer fields but maintained the farmhouse and a market garden or nursery. Surveyors promoted maximum use of the land by making house lots virtually identical in size. An upper-middle-class house lot had approximately 15,000 square feet; a two-family worker house lot had 10,000 square feet; a middle-class single-family house had 5,000 square feet. The narrow side of the lot faced the street, with a ten- or twenty-foot setback. Every house had a backyard. These were fairly dense neighborhoods.[32]

The town just north of Cambridge—Arlington—underwent similar railroad-induced suburban development after the Lexington & West Cambridge Railroad, a branch of the Fitchburg Railroad, reached town in 1846. Suburban and summer homes appeared along Mystic Street on the Mystic Lakes. In the 1870s, Arlington Heights and Crescent Hill became suburban enclaves. The Arlington Land Company created these neighborhoods by subdividing several hundred acres on a rocky hill, which was less valuable than farms on flat land.[33]

In Belmont, the railroad led to the establishment of an independent municipality. The Fitchburg Railroad was built through the northern section of Watertown in 1843. Twelve years later, the Waverley Land Company laid out a subdivision near the station called Plympton's Crossing, soon renamed Waverley, after Sir Walter Scott's romantic novel. The company platted 180 lots of 20,000 to 30,000 square feet, creating a capacious and prestigious neighborhood. The development of Waverley as a railroad suburb gave impetus to the 1859 incorporation of the autonomous municipality of Belmont (sections of Waltham and Arlington were added as well).[34] Belmont Center developed around the turn of the century, with the construction of the railroad station, town hall, school, library, churches, and commercial buildings.

Winchester took a different path to becoming a garden suburb. When it separated from Woburn to become an independent municipality in 1850, Winchester was a tanning, woodworking, and machine-making town, shipping goods on the Middlesex Canal and the Boston & Lowell Railroad. Most industry and workers were located on the northwest side of town, where Irish and blacks lived in a dense neighborhood.

On the other side of the railroad line, wealthy families built summer estates, which became anchors of upscale neighborhoods. In 1875, for example, lumber magnate David Skillings started developing Rangeley Road as a private residential park, with his estate and houses for relatives and wealthy friends. After the turn of the century, Edward Ginn acquired some of the Skillings property and continued to sell to wealthy families. Ginn's son-in-law, Elisha Bangs, president of the Boston Stock Exchange, built some houses and enclosed the enclave with a stone wall to keep out traffic. The planned aspect of the upscale subdivision created a cohesive, self-contained feeling. Other West Winchester upper-class subdivisions were started north of Church Street (1891) and on Glengarry and Grassmere Roads (1896).[35]

The growing number of wealthy suburbanites sought to create a prestigious residential enclave. To establish a traditional image, Winchester created a town common in 1867. During these years, the Winchester Village Improvement Association planted trees and shrubs, built fountains and sidewalks, and encouraged well-maintained lawns. The town built a reservoir to provide a public water supply, adopted a modern public school curriculum, bought a steam fire engine, and hired a police chief. In the 1880s, Winchester reflected a progressive civic spirit by introducing electric street lights, sewers, and horsecars. In 1888, Winchester opened a handsome town hall and library, funded by Colonel William P. Winchester's 1850 bequest.[36]

In the 1890s, wealthy residents sought to remove the tannery, coal yard, lumber yard, railroad freight yard, and worker tenements from the town center. They convinced the town to replace the industry with a park, playground, and new high school. Winchester persuaded the fledgling Metropolitan Park Commission in 1893 to extend the Mystic Valley Parkway from the lakes along the Aberjona River into the heart of town.[37]

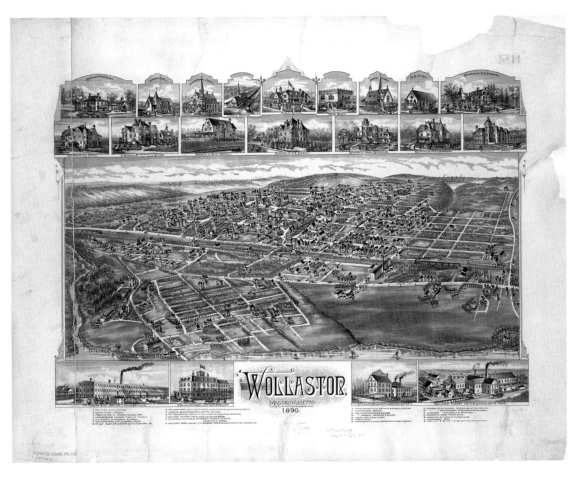

FIGURE 4.7
Bird's eye view of Wollaston, Quincy, 1890. This view of the Wollaston area of Quincy depicts how a middle-class suburb appeared in late nineteenth century.
Source: Print by O. H. Bailey. Map reproduction courtesy of the Norman B. Leventhal Map Center at the Boston Public Library.

Suburban living became quite fashionable in the 1890s, and the spate of public improvements in Winchester reinforced its popularity. Charles F. Adams, Jr., when asked to recommend where to live in suburban Boston, responded: "'In Winchester. Quite apart from the attractiveness of the town and its surroundings, you will find in the community a very unusual civic spirit. The people of that town take an intelligent interest in the management of its affairs and in its continual improvement and beautification.'"[38]

An example of a middle-class railroad suburb was Wollaston Park, in North Quincy along Quincy Shore Drive. The subdivision was carved out of the historic Quincy estate (currently the site of Eastern Nazarene College). The real-estate developer recognized that, to sell the parcels quickly, he needed to provide roads, sidewalks, gas, electricity, and water service, while the community provided public schools. The *Boston Globe* reported: "Many persons came on trains and electric cars to look at the park and select lots. Everything showed signs of life and push that are not to be seen in the old method of building suburbs. It does not now require half a century to build a town."[39] To encourage buyers, the developer gave them a one-year Old Colony Railroad commuter pass to ride to downtown.

The *Globe* also discussed the property covenants that restricted development to certain types of houses and owners: "No lots are sold to persons who cannot give satisfactory reference as to character; no cheap or inferior class of houses are allowed to be built."[40] Property covenants, which were private agreements between a subdivider or builder and a homebuyer, were a forerunner of zoning, which was introduced during the 1920s. Property covenants indicated the controls that were increasingly employed to insure that suburban communities maintained social homogeneity. Under this development regime, developers did not build the houses, as they would in the post–World War II era, but left it up to the homeowner and individual builders.

Farther from Boston, suburbanization came more slowly. Lexington, which was located on hilly terrain northwest of the city, was appreciated for its fresh, healthful air. As early as the 1870s, it attracted hotels and summer homes. By the 1890s, an early cluster of commuters built houses on Meriam Hill near Center Depot Station. The Lexington Land Company developed the upper-class Munroe Hill subdivision in 1891 with deed restrictions requiring house setbacks and minimum house cost of $3,500. A failed Lexington development called Meagherville was illustrative of the follies that could occur when suburban development efforts were premature. In 1891, speculator Mark Meagher subdivided Elm Hill Farm (near today's Route 128) into

1,500 one-sixteenth of an acre (2,722 square feet) lots. Meagher tried to sell the lots by chartering special trains from Boston. The lots were ridiculously small, especially for a country town, so few were ever purchased. In 1951, the town purchased the vacant parcels for conservation land.[41] Residential growth in Lexington did not really take off until the popularization of the automobile.

TABLE 4.2
Population growth in commuter rail suburbs

Municipality	1840	1860	1870	1880	1890
Brookline	1,365	5,164	6,650	8,057	12,103
Dorchester	4,875	9,769	12,259	Part of Boston	Part of Boston
Newton	3,351	5,258	12,825	16,995	24,379
Winchester	—	1,937	2,645	3,802	4,861

Note: These communities grew as commuter rail suburbs. Dorchester, which became part of Boston in 1869, had many of the attributes of a suburb before annexation.
Source: US Census Bureau.

Concord: A Satellite, Not a Suburb

To understand the nature of nineteenth-century railroad suburbs, it is worth examining towns that had railroad service but did not become bedroom communities. They were satellites of the city. A good example is Concord, which is sixteen miles from Boston. The Fitchburg Railroad, which connected the two places in 1844, permitted Concord to flourish as a market town and a literary colony. One of the earliest mentions of the Fitchburg Railroad was in Henry David Thoreau's *Walden*. Thoreau, who lived in a cabin by Walden Pond between 1845 and 1847, wrote that the railroad "touches the pond about a hundred rods south of where I dwell." (You can still see this train pass at the far end of Walden Pond.) We tend to think of Thoreau's stay at Walden as an exile in the wilderness, but the newfangled railroad was an integral part of his life. Thoreau wrote: "The whistle of the locomotive penetrates my woods summer and winter, sounding like the scream of a hawk sailing over some farmer's yard, informing me that many restless city merchants are arriving within the circle of the town."[42] Though he wrote about the transformations the railroad wrought on Concord, he distrusted its effects and avoided riding on it as much as possible.

Emerson, Hawthorne, Bronson Alcott, and Louis May Alcott, who each were attached to the country life of Concord, used the railroad to make the trip to Boston. It allowed them to live in a rural town while participating in the life of the "Athens of America." Emerson frequently commuted to Boston, particularly to attend the literary clubs: the Saturday Club, Town and Country Club, and the Atlantic Club. He delivered many lecture series in Boston, which he then took to lyceums across the country. Even though he preferred the rural atmosphere of Concord and disdained the commercialism of Boston, the city was essential to his life. He, Hawthorne, and others discussed ideas and promoted their writings with publisher James T. Fields at the Old Corner Bookstore. The experience of the Concord writers demonstrates how the railroad was truly a two-way street. Just as suburbs, literary colonies, and resorts were enabled by public transportation, Boston itself flourished because so many people were able to pursue their interests there.[43]

The aura conveyed by the Concord literati and the town's status as the birthplace of the American Revolution attracted people seeking to live amid history and culture. A perfect example is Daniel and Harriet Lothrop's purchase in the 1880s of The Wayside, where both the Alcotts and Hawthorne had lived. Daniel was a Boston publisher and Harriet was a children's book writer known by the pen name Margaret Sidney. Her *Five Little Peppers* books were children's classics. The Lothrops bought The Wayside to preserve it for posterity. In the 1920s, it became a museum and became part of Minute Man National Historical Park in the 1960s. Despite the historical attractions of Concord, it was too far from Boston to become a railroad suburb. Only with the automobile era did Concord become a full-fledged commuter suburb, with most workers commuting to jobs along the Route 128 corridor.

Exploring Railroad Suburbs

Jackson Homestead, 527 Washington Street, Newton

The Jackson Homestead (1809), which is the home of the Newton Historical Society, represents both the eras of country estates and early railroad suburbs. Congressman William Jackson encouraged the Boston & Worcester Railroad to be routed past his property and created the first Newton suburban subdivisions behind his home at Walnut Park (1844) and Waban Park (1846). Victorian houses can be found on these streets today.

Kenrick Park, between Church and Franklin Streets, Newton Corner

Urban renewal in the 1960s and the Massachusetts Turnpike gutted Newton Corner (the railroad station does not even survive), one of the first railroad suburbs in Greater Boston. Nevertheless, historic residential subdivisions can be found around the edges. Perhaps the most intact is Kenrick Park (1846), which was laid out by engineer Alexander Wadsworth. Houses of various styles date from the second half of the nineteenth century. They have the picturesque quality that early railroad suburbs were seeking. A couple blocks away, Farlow Park (1883) is a large green space surrounded by Victorian houses and several churches.

Linden Park, Linden Place, off Harvard Street, Brookline

It may seem difficult to believe, but Linden Park (1843) was supposed to be a suburban residential setting, not the urbanized area it is today. Linden Park was the first suburban subdivision in Brookline and Greater Boston. It was laid out by Alexander Wadsworth, who planned similar developments elsewhere in Brookline and Newton. The square is lined by Greek Revival and Gothic Revival dwellings.

Longwood, Bounded by Kent, Chapel, St. Mary's, and Monmouth Streets, Brookline

Businessman and philanthropist David Sears II developed Longwood (1849). The most striking element is Longwood Mall, which has a number of rare 170-year-old beech trees. Sears commissioned architect Arthur Gilman to build a nondenominational church, Christ's Church (1860), at 70 Colchester Street. Many of the houses in the neighborhood date from the early twentieth century.

Cottage Farm, Bounded by Amory, Dummer, St. Mary's, and Freeman Streets, Brookline

Entrepreneur Amos A. Lawrence purchased property in the section of Brookline closest to Boston to establish a country retreat he named Cottage Farm (1850). Lawrence's stone Gothic Revival house at 135 Ivy Street and his daughter's house at 156 Ivy Street still stand. Lawrence also built rental houses on Ivy and Carlton Street. A number of handsome mansions were added to the neighborhood before World War I. It seems amazing that this little slice of exclusive suburbia sits only a block from Boston University and Commonwealth Avenue.

Frederick Law Olmsted National Historic Site—Fairsted, 99 Warren Street, Brookline

Frederick Law Olmsted moved into Fairsted in 1883 to supervise development of Boston's Emerald Necklace park system. The Olmsted firm, which was later managed by his sons, John Charles and Frederick, Jr., operated in the office wing until it became a National Park site in 1979. The public is welcome to visit the house, office wing, and Olmsted-designed grounds and learn the story of the Olmsteds and how they influenced the development of Brookline, Boston, and communities across North America. It should be noted that Frederick Law Olmsted, Jr., the first chairman of the Brookline Planning Board, was the foremost leader of urban planning in early twentieth-century America. The Olmsted National Historic Site is noteworthy for its archives, which contain the plans and drawings developed by Olmsted and his firm for over 6,000 projects between 1857 and 1980.

Abutting Fairsted is the Green Hill Historic District, which has twenty-four of "the more historically and architecturally distinguished single family homes in Brookline," according to the National Register of Historic Places. The area is named for the 1806 house, which was a country estate for Jack and Isabella Stewart Gardner. The Olmsted firm helped design estate grounds in the neighborhood.

Fisher Hill Historic District, Bounded by Clinton and Sumner Roads, Boylston Street, and Chestnut Hill Avenue, Brookline

Fisher Hill (1886), which lies between Route 9 and Beacon Street, is the most extensive residential neighborhood designed by Frederick Law Olmsted, Sr., in metropolitan Boston. Fisher Avenue, Clinton Road, Buckminster Road, and Dean Road are four of the major thoroughfares, which follow the curve of Fisher Hill. Most of the houses were built between 1890 and 1920. The Newbury College campus was created from Fisher Hill mansions.

Fisher Hill provides an interesting contrast with Green Hill in that it is a planned neighborhood with compact lots and uniform setbacks. This was the model of suburbia that attracted the upper-middle class. For yet another template of suburban development, head down Chestnut Hill Avenue to Beacon Street. This streetcar boulevard is lined by apartment buildings and townhouses that are oriented to mass transit.

Rangeley Park, Rangeley Road, Winchester

David Nelson Skillings divided up his twenty-five-acre estate and built houses that he leased to relatives and friends. The perimeter wall, curvilinear streets, and profuse plantings give the neighborhood a garden aspect. See the houses at 2, 3, 4, 37, and 38 Rangeley Road. This subdivision was close enough to the Winchester railroad station to attract wealthy businessmen wishing to commute to Boston.

Newton Centre Green Line MBTA Station, 70 Union Street, Newton Centre

The best-preserved nineteenth-century suburban railroad station is the Newton Centre Green Line Riverside (D) Branch station. Designed in 1890 by H. H. Richardson's successor firm Shepley, Rutan, and Coolidge, the Newton Centre station is characteristic of suburban stations designed by Richardson and his successors along this rail line. It is rough-finished granite with a steeply pitched roof with wide overhanging eaves. The Newton Centre station has accommodated various eateries.

Victorian Houses in Dorchester, Brookline, Cambridge, Newton

Dorchester has many streets with single-family Victorians, including Melville Avenue, Welles Avenue, and parts of Ashmont and Jones Hill. Wellesley Park has an attractive green oval with an impressive collection of Queen Anne houses. A couple blocks away, Ocean Street, on Ashmont Hill, has some of the area's most varied Victorian houses. Jamaica Plain has handsome Second Empire and Queen Anne houses on Elm Street, Parley Vale, and Robinwood Avenue. In Cambridge, many Queen Anne and Colonial Revival houses can be found on streets off of Brattle Street and Oxford Street. Brookline is full of Victorians, with concentrations on Pill Hill and in the Graffam-McKay neighborhood, where John F. Kennedy grew up.

The differences between upper- and working-class houses can be seen in Newton Corner and West Newton. The Queen Anne estates are located south of the railroad tracks (and the Massachusetts Turnpike), while the functional worker houses, some in the Italianate or Mansard style, are on the other side of the tracks. The search for Victorian houses can be highly rewarding, as they are located in virtually every community in metropolitan Boston.

Streetcar Suburbs (1870–1930)

The City Spreads Out

Many middle- and lower-middle-families gained their entrée to suburban life via streetcars. The horsecar and the electric streetcar opened up large swaths of land to development on the edge of the city, helping to reduce the cost of land and, subsequently, housing. An array of single-, two-, and three-family houses on relatively small lots clustered near transit lines. Streetcar suburbs became vehicles for social mobility. Immigrant groups moved from the inner city into the two- and three-deckers. Emerging middle-class families moved to streets with single-family homes. Streetcar suburb neighborhoods like Dorchester and Cambridge became way stations between the inner city and the outer suburbs.

The development of streetcar suburbs started slowly. Streetcar service was preceded by the omnibus, which was like an elongated stagecoach making regular stops in the city. The first omnibus ran between Harvard College and Boston in 1834. The omnibus, however, was too expensive for most people to ride to work and had a small effect on development patterns. Public transportation took off with the introduction of the first Boston streetcars in 1856 (New York initiated horse-drawn streetcars in 1852). They were drawn by horses along rails laid in the streets. The rails enabled horses to draw more passengers while increasing speed and comfort. The first horsecar line ran from Central Square in Cambridge to Bowdoin Square in downtown Boston.

FIGURE 5.1
Horsecar, Cambridge-Boston, 1880s. Boston's first horsecar line opened in 1856, connecting Harvard Square with Boston's Bowdoin Square. It opened up a broad swath of Cambridge for development. *Source:* Courtesy of the Boston Public Library, Print Department.

Sam Bass Warner, in *Streetcar Suburbs,* explained how the horsecar transformed Boston from a walking city to a streetcar city. The walking city had a two-mile radius of development radiating from the State House. This marked the traditional limit to commuting time, which has been forty-five minutes up to the present day, whether walking, taking public transit, or driving a car. Horsecars, traveling seven or eight miles per hour, pushed the commuting radius to two-and a-half miles by the 1870s and to four miles by the 1880s. Since the fare ranged from two-and-half to twelve cents and additional fare payments were required when transferring lines, it was affordable for the middle class but too expensive for workingmen.[1]

The streetcar system facilitated Boston's greatest growth spurt, between 1850 and 1920. The city grew from a population of 136,881 in 1850 to 560,892 in 1900 to 748,060 in 1920. The streetcar suburbs were mostly the products of two building booms, one in 1865–1873 and another in 1885–1895.[2] The first streetcar suburbs were in communities that had been independent until being annexed to Boston following the Civil War—Brighton, Charlestown, Dorchester, Roxbury, and West Roxbury (between 1868 and 1874 Boston annexed these independent towns). Cambridge, Somerville, and other communities close to Boston also grew because of expanded streetcar service. Prior to horsecars, these communities had been occupied by farms and rural retreats for wealthy Bostonians.

Streetcar suburbs attracted a range of social classes. During the 1870s and 1880s, Dorchester, Roxbury, and West Roxbury became prime locations for professionals and businessmen who might not have been able to afford or gain social entry to Brookline or Newton. They were seeking to escape the poor immigrants, disease, and pollution of the central city for the comfort, open air, and privacy originally attained by gentlemen's country estates. They lived in fairly large single-family homes in neighborhoods that attracted the upwardly mobile ethnic middle class, such as Irish and Jews. From the 1920s on, streetcar neighborhoods increasingly became home to working-class families.

In the Boston neighborhoods of West Roxbury and Dorchester, city government allowed streetcar companies, speculators, and builders to lay out streets and house lots, creating fairly dense neighborhoods. In turn, the city provided public services. Boston's Board of Survey started laying out streets in 1891. Development was incremental, undertaken by individual home buyers and builders. Even though these neighborhoods were located within the city limits of Boston, they were suburban in style, being primarily residential and less crowded than the inner city.

The suburbanization that occurred along horsecar lines was far eclipsed by development spurred by the introduction of the electric streetcar. The effects of the electric streetcar, whose heyday lasted from 1889 until 1920, were felt across Boston and forty or so communities surrounding it. It is ironic that the scene of the electric streetcar breakthrough was Brookline, which had been Boston's premier upper-class country retreat, called the "town of millionaires."[3]

Frederick Law Olmsted, who had moved to Brookline in 1883 for its pastoral beauty, helped undo some of the town's exclusive pastoral character with his 1886 plan for widening Beacon Street to accommodate the streetcar line of Henry C. Whitney's West End Street Railway Company. Olmsted provided a plan to widen Beacon Street from 50 to 200 feet (ultimately it was widened to only 160 feet). The European-style boulevard created a green ribbon for the streetcar tracks and lanes for other vehicles (the automobile was still to come a decade later). Early twentieth-century city planner Charles Mulford Robinson wrote: "It has been said that Frederick Law Olmsted was the first one frankly to accept the car tracks as a permanent feature of the avenue and one that could and should be turned to decorative purpose. On the Beacon Street Boulevard, Boston, he arranged that the tracks should be thrown into a separate turf-planted strip at the road's border, where only the gleaming lines of steel would show upon the greensward."[4]

Olmsted designed Beacon Street as a residential extension of Commonwealth Avenue from the preeminent Back Bay residential district into Brookline. He expected the Beacon Street homes to be mansions, not apartment buildings. Olmsted was also responsible for designing the streetcar boulevard of Commonwealth Avenue from Kenmore Square (Governor's Square prior to 1932) through Allston and Brighton to the Newton line. Commonwealth Avenue eventually was lined by Boston University and many apartment buildings.

As the Beacon Street streetcar boulevard was being constructed, Henry Whitney's West End Railway Company bought out its five rival horsecar companies in an effort to create a consolidated transit system serving all of Boston and surrounding

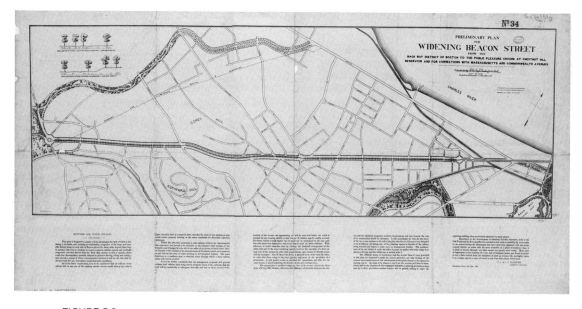

FIGURE 5.2
Preliminary plan for Beacon Street, Brookline, 1886. In 1886, Frederick Law Olmsted planned a wide boulevard along Beacon Street in Brookline to provide a streetcar route. Olmsted also designed the extension of Commonwealth Avenue in Brighton to carry a streetcar line.
Source: Map reproduction courtesy of the Norman B. Leventhal Map Center at the Boston Public Library.

communities. The West End Railway Company, for a time the world's largest transit company, had almost 1,500 streetcars drawn by 7,700 horses. Annually, the company transported 100 million passengers.[5] The great number of horses, however, created public health problems, not to mention the costs of stabling and feeding them. Whitney was desperate to find an alternative means of locomotion and originally considered installing a cable car system like San Francisco's.

Whitney ended up adopting the electric streetcar system introduced by an associate of Thomas Edison's, Frank J. Sprague, in Richmond, Virginia (1888). A pivotal innovation was Sprague's trolley pole, which allowed streetcars to receive electricity from overhead wires. Henry Whitney recognized that the electric streetcar would be much faster and cleaner (no horses or horse manure) and introduced the new technology to link Beacon Street in Brookline with downtown Boston in 1889. (The Green Line's C Branch, which runs along Beacon Street, is the oldest operating electric streetcar line in the country, since the Richmond line has been taken out of service.) Within seven years, Boston had completely phased out the horse-drawn streetcars, eliminating the ubiquitous horse manure from the streets and the need to care for thousands of horses.[6]

The electrification of streetcars quickly extended the zone of development out six miles from downtown Boston and expanded the suburban zone to a nine-mile radius by 1903.[7] With the expansion of streetcar trackage in the state from 157 miles in 1890 to 2,621 miles in 1903, suburban development boomed. The electric streetcar was twice as fast as the horsecar, traveling at thirteen to fifteen miles per hour. The 1897 opening of the subway in downtown Boston, the country's first, eased travel to and from the central city. Each car could carry up to ninety people with some hanging on running boards. The cars were well heated and lighted. The universal fare was five cents, which was affordable for most people.

The streetcar lines exemplified private-sector planning. If investors thought they could make a profit providing streetcar service, they applied to the state legislature for a franchise to operate on certain routes. The companies built the tracks and installed the cars, just as the railroad and canal companies did. After numerous streetcar companies were chartered, they gave way to consolidation by Henry Whitney's West End Railway Company. But the challenges to providing economical and efficient service to the booming metropolis were daunting, and the state legislature created the Rapid Transit Commission in 1891 to come up with a metropolitan transit plan for Boston and twenty-three surrounding communities. The plan recommended establishment of a private company, the Boston Elevated Railway, to expand transit service on elevated and subway lines. Boston Elevated effectively subsumed the West End Railway in 1897, so metropolitan Boston had a private transit monopoly operating under the regulation of the Boston Transit Commission. The arrangement worked until 1918, when the state placed the Boston Elevated Railway under the management of public trustees, while still paying shareholders a dividend.

In 1947, the legislature made transit service public, when it established the Metropolitan Transit Authority to operate the old Boston Elevated system in fourteen communities. It ultimately took over the Highland commuter rail line of the Boston & Albany Railroad, which ran through Brookline and Newton, and established the Green Line D Branch service to Riverside in 1959. Five years later, the state expanded the transit system to seventy-eight Greater Boston communities to be operated by a new entity called the Massachusetts Bay Transit Authority (MBTA). By the 1970s, the MBTA effectively took over the remaining commuter rail service that had formerly been provided by private companies. Thus, public transit evolved from a private-sector operation to being managed and subsidized under the aegis of state government. The government assumed control over public transportation, as well as highways, airports, and harbors, because transportation infrastructure was essential to the workings of modern society.

Development Impacts in Brookline and Beyond

The streetcar encouraged people to build houses and businesses along the route, creating new neighborhoods based on the streetcar suburb template. Henry Whitney expected the Beacon Street electric streetcar to spur development of the 115 acres of Brookline property that he had accumulated.[8] At first, many fine homes and some extraordinary luxury apartments were built along Beacon Street. However, as development pressures and streetcar ridership increased—the *Boston Evening Transcript* reported "The street cars are crowded, often almost to suffocation"—wealthy homeowners moved out and subdivided their property for smaller homes and apartment buildings.[9] Since there were few deed restrictions and no zoning regulations (the first zoning controls were enacted in 1922), there was little to prevent the wholesale construction of apartment buildings during the first decades of the twentieth century. Some of the first Beacon Street apartments were built at nodes near St. Mary's Street and Washington Street. At Coolidge Corner, the town's leading commercial district developed, and the S. S. Pierce building became the foremost landmark. Although

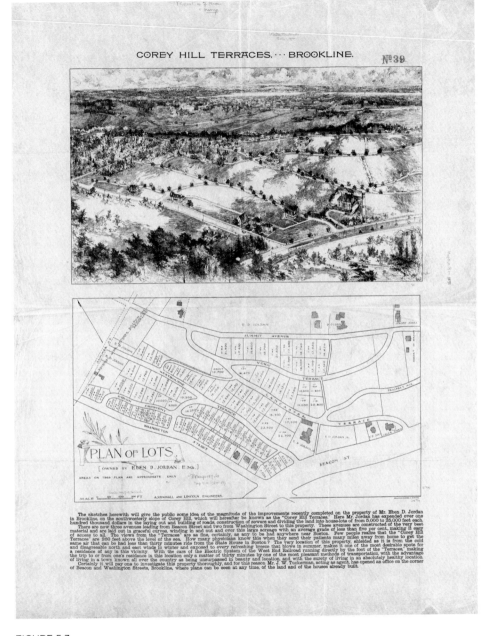

FIGURE 5.3

Corey Hill Terraces, Brookline, 1891. Department store magnate Eben D. Jordan (of Jordan Marsh) created this subdivision on his land after the electric streetcar started service on nearby Beacon Street. Jordan's brochure proclaimed Corey Hill Terraces was "only a matter of thirty minutes by one of the most pleasant methods of transportation" from downtown Boston.

Source: Map reproduction courtesy of the Norman B. Leventhal Map Center at the Boston Public Library.

wealthy estate owners were moving to the countryside, the Brookline apartments, with their "fancy rents," found a market among the "select" who were seeking an urbane address. The *Boston Evening Transcript* announced that the Beacon Street apartments "are perhaps as good as the best."[10]

In 1914, four blocks north of Beacon Street, newlyweds Joseph and Rose Kennedy moved into a center-hall Colonial Revival house at 83 Beals Street. This middle-class suburban street drew the Kennedy couple out of Boston, where Rose's father, John "Honey Fitz" Fitzgerald, had been mayor. President John Fitzgerald Kennedy was born in this house three years later. Since the modest home, situated on a small 0.1-acre lot, had only three bedrooms, the growing Kennedy family moved to a larger house at nearby 51 Abbottsford Road. In 1927, the Kennedys moved to New York, as neither Boston nor North Brookline offered sufficient economic opportunity or social status for the ambitious Joseph P. Kennedy.

By the 1920s, the Beacon Street corridor was urbanized. Between the introduction of the electric streetcar and 1920, Brookline's population tripled from 12,103 to 37,748. As a 1933 history of Brookline observed, "What Boston could not accomplish politically in the 'seventies [annexation of Brookline] has, in large measure, come about physically in the last thirty years."[11] *The WPA Guide to Massachusetts* (1937) observed of Brookline: "Half of Brookline still remains the closed citadel of wealth and leisure; the other half has become a modern residential hive for the better paid of the busy workers of Boston."[12]

The coming of the Beacon Street streetcar alarmed wealthy residents elsewhere in Brookline. When a streetcar line was proposed for Boylston Street (today's Route 9) in 1896, Henry Lee, who owned a summer estate on Fisher Hill, stirred up opposition to the streetcar. Lee considered this stretch of Boylston Street to be a country road, which should not carry public transit.[13] His efforts were dilatory, since the Boston & Worcester Street Railway received approval to operate along Boylston Street and the old Worcester Turnpike seven years later. Overlooking Boylston Street, the elite Fisher Hill neighborhood protected itself against the incursion of multifamily housing through restrictive property covenants.

Brookline resisted other new developments that might attract the masses. In 1902, town meeting vetoed efforts of the Metropolitan Park Commission to acquire the Boylston Street Reservoir for parkland and build connecting parkways to Jamaica Pond and the Chestnut Hill Reservoir. The *Boston Globe* reported that Brookline "doesn't want any beautifully planned parkway running across her chest to be the artery for a stream of red-blooded plebian recreationists."[14]

In less exclusive communities, the streetcar was welcomed. This was true in many communities north of Boston—Chelsea, Everett, Malden, Medford, Somerville, and Watertown. In Medford, streetcars spurred growth, as population grew from 11,079 to 39,038 between 1890 and 1920. The population of Watertown grew from 5,426 to 21,457 during the same period, booming after the opening of the Harvard Square subway station in 1912. Of Malden, *The WPA Guide to Massachusetts* observed: "Inevitably with the years, its suburban identity tends to be swallowed up in the overflowing tide from the greater city. Yet there are not many apartment houses, and if there are no pretentiously wealthy districts, neither is there shabby poverty."[15] By 1910, the thirty-seven municipalities in the Boston Metropolitan District had virtually doubled in population—to 1,970,000—over two decades. This era was Boston's greatest period of growth, and it was facilitated by the electric streetcars.

The transformative impact of streetcars on metropolitan Boston can be surmised from ridership data. In 1890, 164,873,846 passengers rode streetcars in the state (the great majority were in Greater Boston). In 1900, the annual number of passengers had risen to 395,027,198. The peak year for streetcar use was 1920, just before the automobile began to make serious inroads into ridership—there were 837,167,716 passengers.[16]

Historian Edward Mason observed that "the expansion of the street railway network was probably more rapid, more extensive and more reckless in Massachusetts than elsewhere."[17] With more than two dozen streetcar and railroad lines connecting to downtown, Boston was the hub of a burgeoning metropolitan area—if not the "Hub of the Solar System," as Oliver Wendell Holmes, Sr., had facetiously claimed. Boston's vast streetcar network reinforced the region's orientation to downtown for work, shopping, and entertainment. In fact, Boston's downtown attracted a greater proportion of the city's retail business than almost any other American city.[18]

TABLE 5.1
Passengers carried on street railways in Massachusetts

Year	No. of Passengers	Average No. Rides per Inhabitant
1890	164,873,846	73
1900	395,027,198	141
1910	625,774,376	186
1920	837,167,716	217
1930	560,052,338	132

Source: Edward S. Mason, *The Street Railway in Massachusetts: The Rise and Decline of an Industry* (Cambridge, Mass.: Harvard University Press, 1932).

The dramatic increase in streetcar usage between 1890 and 1920 also opened up countryside to public access, at first for recreation and later for settlement. In the country, "streetcars" were called "trolleys" or "interurban railroads." "Joy-riding" in the open streetcars was a popular summer pastime. The metropolitan parks that were being established during the 1890s became easily accessible by trolley, which created a large constituency for Revere Beach, Middlesex Fells, and the Blue Hills.

The streetcar also encouraged the development of amusement parks. Streetcar companies (across the country) built amusement parks at the far end of their lines from the city to encourage ridership on weekends when workers were not commuting. Sundays became the busiest day of the week for streetcar companies. By 1902, streetcar companies owned thirty-one "pleasure parks" in Massachusetts, mainly on cheap land outside the cities.[19] The popular amusement rides at Revere Beach, Nantasket Beach, and Canobie Lake Park all opened during this era.

The connection between a streetcar line, a pleasure park, and residential development is demonstrated by the development of Commonwealth Avenue in Newton. In 1893, City Engineer Alfred F. Noyes laid out a new boulevard to carry a streetcar line and a dual carriageway for horse-drawn vehicles. Owners of estates along the new boulevard donated land for the right-of-way to enhance their property values and create opportunities for new residential development. The Newton Boulevard Syndicate speculated on land between the Boston line and Centre Street, developing an area of Newton that had hitherto been neglected because of its distance from the commuter rail lines. At the end of the streetcar line, Commonwealth Avenue Street Railway Company opened Norumbega Park, which featured canoeing, a carousel, a zoo, and picnic grove. The theater became one of New England's foremost ballrooms, the Totem Pole Ballroom.[20]

Until about 1915, streetcars drove development and dominated traffic on the streets because there were relatively few horse-drawn vehicles and automobile traffic was meager. As automobile traffic increased, streetcars had to slow down. During the 1920s, the percentage of suburbanites commuting by auto increased and the proportion using transit declined.[21] In 1922, the Boston Elevated Railway Company introduced its first motor buses, which were considered more flexible and efficient than streetcars. In most cases, buses followed routes initially laid out for streetcar lines. By 1930, streetcar lines were in broad decline, as evidenced by the closing of the Commonwealth Avenue route in Newton. Yet, despite the elimination of most streetcar routes, streetcars, subways, and buses continued to serve the metropolitan area.

The Zone of Emergence and the Three-Decker

Most streetcar suburbs, except perhaps for Brookline, were inhabited by the lower-middle class and upper-working class. Lower middle-class families were likely to live in single-family houses and working-class families would live in two- and three-family houses. In many respects the streetcar suburbs were really urban neighborhoods, except greener and more salubrious than the inner-city areas people were leaving.

Streetcar suburbs were called the "zone of emergence" for immigrants by South End settlement house workers Robert A. Woods and Albert J. Kennedy in their book *The Zone of Emergence: Observations of the Lower Middle and Upper Working Class Communities of Boston, 1905–1914*. The neighborhoods of this zone offered immigrants the next rung up from the slums of the inner city. In these neighborhoods, people had jobs and maintained their property, in contrast to the blighted and impoverished urban slums. Woods and Kennedy observed that about half the properties in these neighborhoods were owned by families of recent immigrant stock. They wrote: "The zone of emergence is the great Irish belt of the city. They entered the zone on the wake of the industries which drove out the American population. The departing Americans sold their property to the newcomers, who, at a single stroke, often secured living accommodations that represented a decided advance over any they had dreamt of previously."[22]

Woods and Kennedy wrote that the quality of the streetcar suburbs was "distinctly more habitable" than the inner-city tenements. "The air is brighter, cleaner, and more vibrant; sunshine falls in floods rather than in narrow shafts; there is not so much dust and smoke; the streets are quieter; there is less congestion and more evident freedom of movement."[23] Whether houses were in "streetcar suburbs" or more affluent "railroad suburbs," by the 1870s, they had central heating, gas lighting, tap water, and water closets (electric power was not introduced until the 1890s and early 1900s), all expected elements of the middle-class suburban standard of living.[24] Two- and three-family houses became practicable at this time because utility services made it possible to provide heat, water, and light to upper floors. The two- and three-family houses allowed a household to share a dwelling, often with family members, making suburban housing affordable for the lower-middle class. Such houses were often rental properties owned by small investors.

The heyday of Boston's three-deckers (also called triple-deckers or three-families) occurred between 1870 and 1925, with the majority being built between 1900 and 1918. In Boston's outer neighborhoods, over 16,000 three-deckers were built (over

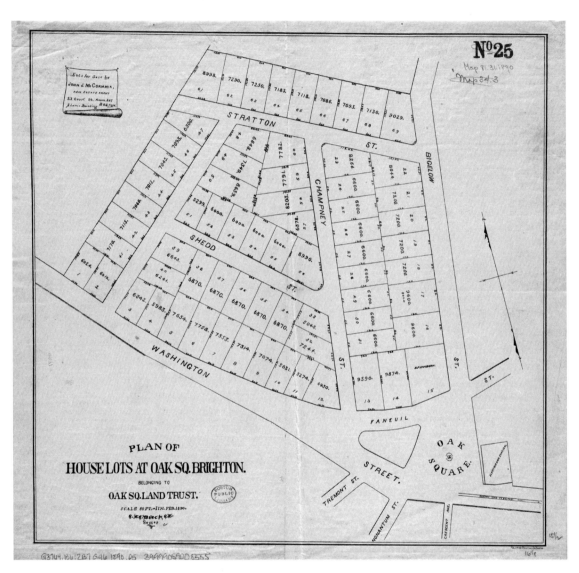

FIGURE 5.4

Plan of lots, Oak Square, Brighton, 1890. This subdivision plan shows the compact lots that were typical of streetcar suburbs. Today, this is a dense neighborhood of two- and three-family homes.

Source: Map reproduction courtesy of the Norman B. Leventhal Map Center at the Boston Public Library.

FIGURE 5.5
Ashmont streetcar station, Dorchester, ca. 1929. Dense neighborhoods of two- and three-family houses
and apartments developed around major streetcar stations like Ashmont.
Source: Courtesy of the Boston Public Library, Print Department.

twenty percent of the city's housing stock today).[25] They marked a clear break from
the crowded, unsanitary tenements of the North End and West End, which were fire
traps, had little ventilation, and featured backyard privies.

The three-decker was a housing type unique to New England. Woods and Kennedy reported that each three-decker unit, which rented from $20 to $25 per month,
included "a parlor, dining room, kitchen with set tubs, cook stove with gas stove and
water heater attached, two bedrooms, front and back piazza, hot air furnace, electricity, and hardwood floors. Such a home, so located and fitted out, is well calculated to
appeal to the ambitious clerk, mechanic and the like whose weekly wage averages in
the neighborhood of twenty-five dollars."[26] The cost of housing was kept relatively
low by stacking three units onto one small parcel of land. There are two basic types of

three-deckers: those with flat roofs, favored in South Boston, and those with pitched roofs, favored in Dorchester.[27] Most had bowed bays that carried up three stories. The higher quality three-deckers had front porches, called "piazzas," while the less expensive units lacked them. Three-deckers kept construction costs down by using mass-produced window sashes, doors, plumbing fixtures, and precut ornamentation like balustrades and Greek columns.

Three-deckers had small front yards and larger yards in back to provide an element of privacy. They were a step up from urban tenements that had no open space, but they lacked enough green space to create a truly suburban ambience. Their boxy forms blocked views. When speculators built whole streets of three-deckers, middle-class people frowned with disfavor. The last three-decker in Boston was permitted in 1928, as two-family homes replaced them.[28] They still cover blocks of Brighton, Dorchester, East Boston, Roxbury, South Boston, Cambridge, Malden, Revere, and Somerville. Today, two- and three-deckers may be considered dowdy, superseded housing templates, but they are suggestive for those considering ways to build semiattached housing and create greater density near transit service.

Streetcar-Driven Growth in Cambridge, Belmont, and Arlington

The electric streetcar radically transformed many communities outside Boston. Cambridge evolved from a suburban to an urban landscape. Prestigious houses were built along North Street north of Harvard Square until about 1890, when the electric streetcar appeared. That year the street was widened and renamed Massachusetts Avenue, and the Harvard/Massachusetts Avenue Bridge was opened across the Charles River to Boston. With increasing traffic and noise, no single-family homes were built on Massachusetts Avenue north of Harvard Square after 1895. Some houses were converted to offices, funeral parlors, clubs, and rooming houses. After 1910, the house lawns on Massachusetts Avenue started to fill in with stores, which obscured the houses behind them. By 1923, all the colonial farmhouses on Massachusetts Avenue had been demolished. The side streets filled in with tightly packed homes, many of them two-deckers. Developers erected a row of apartment buildings and one-story commercial blocks along Massachusetts Avenue between 1900 and World War II.[29] By the 1920s, the automobile made Massachusetts Avenue into a major traffic corridor, and gas stations and diners appeared on street corners.

Electric streetcars spurred comparable growth in Arlington and Belmont, which boomed during the streetcar era. Arlington grew from 5,629 in 1890 to 18,665 in 1920. Two-family homes lined the streets of East Arlington. Belmont expanded from a sleepy semirural town with 2,098 people in 1890 to an established suburb of 15,256 by 1925. The town reached virtual buildout by 1950 with 27,381 people (the 2010 population was 24,729). *The WPA Guide to Massachusetts* observed of Belmont: "Improved transportation facilitates a change in the town's interests. . . . Today the fields are occupied by homes whose owners work either in Boston or in the factories of Watertown and Waltham."[30]

Many of the early twentieth-century subdivisions laid out in Arlington and Belmont were on farmland. Both these towns had numerous market gardens and greenhouses—in fact, hundreds of market gardens surrounded Boston—serving the booming metropolitan area between the Civil War and the 1920s. In the 1890s, Arlington had more acreage devoted to greenhouses than any other community in the country. Warren and Herbert Rawson alone owned twenty-three greenhouses. Yet, growing competition from the South and West eventually put the farms of Eastern Massachusetts out of business, making more land available for residential development.[31] The development of residential subdivisions became so rapid that the forty farms that existed in the town in 1910 were reduced to three by 1940.[32] Arlington developed along the Massachusetts Avenue spine, which was widened into a boulevard between 1914 and 1924. The widening encouraged automobile traffic along a route that had formerly been mainly used by streetcars. It spurred development of 1920s-style one-story "rent-payer" commercial blocks along the avenue as well as growth farther west in Lexington.

Since the 1820s, Belmont had grown fruits and vegetables to supply Boston's Quincy Market. By 1895, Belmont boasted sixty-three produce and dairy farms (today the town has one farm, Sergi Farms). The introduction of electric streetcar service in 1898 made Belmont's farmland more valuable for house lots than for market gardening. Passengers could travel from the Waverley section to downtown Boston in fifty minutes for five cents. Development pressures increased in 1912, when the Harvard Square subway station opened, and Belmontians could travel by streetcar and subway to Boston's Park Street in a half hour.[33]

Commercial real estate companies bought up Belmont farms and subdivided them into small lots for two- and three-family houses. Thirteen major subdivisions were laid out between 1898 and 1912. Developers tended to build dense, moderately priced housing, such as Wellington Park, which created eighty-eight two-family house lots of 1,500 square feet apiece.[34] Wealthier people decried this urban-scale density and the working class families it attracted, especially when the subway station opened in Harvard Square.

Controlling Growth

The process of growth generated significant class tensions, as suburbs became vehicles for social mobility. When middle-class families moved into communities with exclusive estates, such as Dedham, Medford, or Milton, those places lost their cache and stopped attracting wealthy families. Ultimately, most estates were subdivided for smaller house lots. When lower-middle-class families started moving into middle-class areas of Arlington, Belmont, and similar towns, the construction of two- and three-family houses caused concern. Towns could do nothing to control the development of multifamily housing. The outcry reached the State House, and the legislature passed the Tenement House Act (1912) to discourage the spread of lower-class houses in the suburbs. Tenements would be prohibited, but the real target was the three-decker, derisively named "Boston's weed." The Tenement House Act decreed that tenements could not exceed two-and-a-half floors nor could they house more than two families unless they were fireproofed, which would make them uneconomical to build. These three-decker houses could not occupy more than fifty percent of the lot or sixty-five percent of a corner lot. They were required to be set back at least ten feet from the lot line and twenty feet from other buildings.

The Tenement House Act was a prelude to broader zoning powers. Belmont became the first town to adopt the restrictive provisions, and Arlington, Watertown, and Winchester followed, guarding against the population influx predicted to be generated by the new Harvard Square subway. The *Boston Evening Transcript* explained how the Tenement House Act would protect the suburban quality of life and protect the standard of living for all: "A better distribution of the population in suburban territory will raise the standards of living, increase the thrift and savings of the people, and add immeasurably to the self respect of those hitherto forced to live under conditions subversive of all that makes for wholesome and clean living."[35] Adopting the Tenement House Act curtailed the construction of three-family homes and boosted single- and two-family houses.

Another step in land-use regulation was subdivision review. Boston obtained state approval for the Street Commissioners to control the layout of subdivisions along city streets in 1891. Before this, speculators had been responsible for laying out streets and house lots. The legislature extended subdivision control to other municipalities in 1907 and 1916. In 1913, the state legislature required communities with a population of more than 10,000 to establish planning boards, whose duties included planning to accommodate housing. Brookline and Cambridge immediately established planning boards. By 1922, twenty-three municipalities in the metropolitan area had planning boards.[36]

In 1918, Article LX of the Amendments to the Massachusetts Constitution gave the legislature the "power to limit buildings according to their use or construction to specified districts or cities and towns." Two years later, the Massachusetts Supreme Judicial Court upheld the constitutionality of zoning, and the state's first Zoning Enabling Act delegated zoning powers to municipalities. In 1924, the Massachusetts Supreme Judicial Court upheld zoning that restricted certain areas to single-family homes. Two years later, the US Supreme Court, in the famous *Euclid v. Ambler* decision, upheld the basic right of local government to zone land and exclude specific uses in various districts. Zoning became the primary tool for ensuring uniform development patterns and protecting property values. Because of zoning controls, suburbs were able to maintain a desired character and avoid the rapid changes that swept urban communities in the pre-zoning era.

By 1928, twenty-eight Greater Boston communities adopted zoning. One of the leading communities was Brookline, whose planning board was chaired by Frederick Law Olmsted, Jr. (chairman 1914–1926; member until 1938). Even before zoning was introduced, Olmsted, Jr., advocated restrictive property covenants to control uses, building setbacks, and tree belts. A 1915 planning board report published land-use recommendations illustrated with photos of development abuses, particularly stores built onto the front of houses and the encroachment of buildings onto sidewalks. The report led to the adoption of zoning in 1922.

Newton's 1922 zoning plan was crafted by landscape architect Arthur Shurcliff, who prepared zoning plans for twenty-six municipalities in Greater Boston. Newton's plan sought to restrict apartment buildings, like those in Brookline and Brighton. The new zoning restricted the commercial and multifamily housing to zones near the Boston-Worcester commuter rail route and the Highland Branch route. Most of the rest of the city was zoned for single-family houses, with two-family houses being extremely limited.

Communities like Newton found zoning to be an effective way to preserve the community's character. Arlington (1924), Winchester (1924), and Belmont (1925) each passed zoning codes that restricted two-family houses. Most new houses were for single families. With the rise of the automobile by the 1920s, people did not have to live close to transit stops, so housing density became less necessary. Lots could be larger and single-family homes could proliferate. Winchester, whose plan Shurcliff developed, prohibited apartment buildings and movie theaters. Wellesley (1926), with its restrictive zoning code, boasted as its motto: "We planned it that way."[37]

The zoning movement was motivated by a desire to secure the physical and social character of a community. As new suburbanites escaped the city, they wanted to insure that dirty industries, busy businesses, and families of a lower social class were not in their new neighborhood. Most suburban zoning required large lots and single-family homes and curtailed commercial uses, thus propping up housing values and excluding working and immigrant families. Zoning measures, thus, reinforced the social homogeneity of suburbs.

TABLE 5.2
Population growth in streetcar parkway–era suburbs

Municipality	1890	1910	1920	1930
Arlington	5,629	11,187	18,665	36,094
Belmont	2,098	3,999	10,749	21,748
Brookline	12,103	27,792	37,748	47,490
Milton	4,278	7,924	9,382	16,434
Newton	24,379	39,806	46,054	65,276

Note: Growth after 1920 reflected both increased transit use and the emergence of the automobile as a commuting vehicle. These communities were classic bedroom towns for Boston and Cambridge.
Source: US Census Bureau.

Exploring Streetcar Suburbs

Beacon Street, Park Drive to Cleveland Circle, Brookline

Frederick Law Olmsted laid out Beacon Street in Brookline for Henry Whitney, streetcar magnate and real-estate speculator. Sloping uphill toward Cleveland Circle, Beacon Street is an exhilarating urbanistic experience. Walk it, bike it (on new bike lanes), drive it, or ride the Green Line C Branch streetcar for the street's two-and-a-half-mile length. Coolidge Corner, Brookline's chief commercial district, is about midway. Today's appearance is not quite what Olmsted and Whitney had in mind—they saw Beacon Street lined by estates—but growth pressures became so great in the early twentieth century that apartment buildings replaced the mansions. During the 2000s, the Town of Brookline rebuilt Beacon Street, incorporating bike lanes, upgrading streetcar stations, and planting new trees. For another Olmsted-designed boulevard experience, travel by streetcar or automobile along Commonwealth Avenue from Kenmore Square to Boston College.

John Fitzgerald Kennedy National Historic Site, 83 Beals Street, Brookline

This National Park site is the birthplace of President Kennedy (1917). His family lived in this relatively modest middle-class house from 1914 to 1920. This Colonial Revival house, which was built in 1909, is typical of the streetcar suburb housing that was being built prior to World War I. It was refurnished in the period style by Rose Kennedy in the late 1960s.

Three-Decker Houses, Cambridge

Three-decker houses can be found by the thousands across Brighton, Dorchester, Jamaica Plain, South Boston, Cambridge, and Watertown. In Cambridge, there are streets made up of almost entirely three-deckers. They include Alberta Terrace, in North Cambridge; Marie Avenue, in Mid-Cambridge; Cambridge Terrace, near Porter Square. The three-deckers were a step up for working-class families from inner-city tenements. Three-deckers range from modest dwellings with no front porches to structures with ornate porches having Greek capitals. They are characteristic of the late nineteenth and early twentieth-century streetcar suburbs.

Metropolitan Parkway Suburbs (1895–1945)

Origins of the Metropolitan Park-and-Parkway System

A major shortcoming of the streetcar suburbs was the lack of green space. Frederick Law Olmsted designed the Emerald Necklace parks to compensate for the lack of open space in Boston's neighborhoods. He also advocated for a regional park system, which his protégé, Charles Eliot, planned. Boston's metropolitan parks carved out an unprecedented public realm for nature conservation and recreation, departing from the predominant mode of laissez-faire development, which conserved little green space. The parkways formed a network of landscaped greenways, which conveyed residents to parklands and paved the way for automobile commuting. The metropolitan park-and-parkway system produced a distinctive built landscape, with single- and two-family homes and ample green space. This suburban template represented the middle-class suburbia of the early twentieth century.

The metropolitan park movement began in response to the late nineteenth-century real-estate boom, when developers were building entire neighborhoods of dense, low-cost, working-class housing without regard to creating community amenities. Their goal was to maximize profit. Municipalities like Cambridge and Somerville were unable to regulate development or preserve open space as parks. Journalist Sylvester Baxter stated: "This naturally beautiful region is in danger of becoming a vast desert of house, factories, and stores, spreading over and overwhelming the natural features of the landscape . . . relieved by hardly an oasis."[1]

Reformers believed that new neighborhoods developing outside the inner city should be less crowded and should be interlaced with green space to provide residents with opportunities for recreation and experiencing nature. Landscape architect Charles Eliot argued: "For crowded populations to live in health and happiness, they must have space for air, for light, for exercise, for rest, and for the enjoyment of the peaceful harmony of nature which, because it is the opposite of the noisy ugliness of the town, is so refreshing to the tired souls of the townspeople."[2]

Sylvester Baxter and Charles Eliot believed that parks and suburban housing were necessary for relieving inner-city squalor, which was the most pressing social problem of the day. They advocated for preserving undeveloped open spaces on the perimeter of the cities to provide "green lungs" for city dwellers and to create a framework for more healthy and attractive neighborhoods. Eliot and Baxter's concerns dovetailed with the parks movement sweeping late nineteenth-century America. Ever since park pioneers Frederick Law Olmsted and Calvert Vaux had completed New York's Central Park in the 1860s, cities across the country developed parks as breathing spaces and civic ornaments.

Charles Eliot, who was a son of Harvard President Charles W. Eliot, set out to preserve scenic areas in Greater Boston that had not yet been over-run by urbanization. He sought to expand to a regional level the Emerald Necklace parks that Olmsted had created in Boston during the 1880s. Sylvester Baxter, a social reformer from Malden, promoted the visionary concept of regional planning and metropolitan government. He was the preeminent disciple of utopian novelist Edward Bellamy, author of *Looking Backward* (1888), and organized a Nationalist Club in Boston that advocated nationalization of railroads, telephones, and telegraphs. Eliot represented the environmentalist perspective, and Baxter exemplified the social reformer behind the metropolitan parks movement.

In 1891, Eliot and Baxter collaborated in establishing the Trustees of Reservations, the world's first private nonprofit trust designed to preserve scenic open spaces. Eliot explained that the mission of the Trustees of Reservations would be to hold "'small and well-distributed parcels of land . . . just as the Public Library holds books and the Art Museum pictures—for the use and enjoyment of the public.'"[3] The Trustees were able to obtain a handful of properties but could not move quickly enough to acquire the stretches of open space that Eliot had identified. Therefore, Eliot and Baxter organized a coalition of "gentleman reformers" to convince the Massachusetts state legislature to establish a Metropolitan Park Commission (MPC) to develop a plan for regional parks.

FIGURE 6.1
Charles Eliot. Charles Eliot's (1859–1897) 1893 plan for the Metropolitan Park System was the first regional planning effort in the United States. His goal was to create an open space network for the suburbs that surrounded Boston.
Source: Frederick Law Olmsted National Historic Site.

The Metropolitan Park Commission proposed establishing a regional agency, using the authority and fiscal resources of the state, to develop a park system and curb uncontrolled development. It was patterned on the Metropolitan Sewerage Commission (1889) and the Metropolitan Water Board (1895), which coordinated the sewerage and water supply systems for the metropolitan area's cities and towns. (The Sewerage and Water authorities merged in 1901, and they, in turn, were merged with the Park Commission to form the Metropolitan District Commission in 1919.) Sewerage and clean water were quintessential regional issues because polluted water did not respect municipal boundaries. When communities refused to be annexed by Boston after Brookline vetoed the merger in 1874, it became apparent that suburbs would not be able to build their own water and sewer systems and would require a metropolitan solution. These issues became more pressing as the germ theory of disease was accepted during the 1880s, and water filtration and sewerage treatment were deemed necessary for public health.

The Metropolitan Park Commission provided a broad-based approach to preserving open land and controlling development in an era before the adoption of land-use planning and zoning. The *Report of the Metropolitan Park Commissioners* (1893), which was authored by Eliot and Baxter, provided a brilliant blueprint for the Metropolitan Park System.[4] Eliot wanted metropolitan Boston to take advantage of its varied natural topography, situated between the sea and the rim of hills that surrounded the city, an area called the Boston Basin. A pioneer of environmental planning, Eliot proposed preserving and improving several types of natural spaces in the metropolitan area:

1. *Outer Rim Wild Forest* The large forest preserves were located on the edge of urbanized Boston along the ridge of the Boston Basin. They were as yet undeveloped because of the craggy terrain. The Middlesex Fells encompassed over 2,000 acres in Malden, Medford, Melrose, Stoneham, and Winchester. The Middlesex Fells, where local water supply reservoirs were located, truly were the wild, hilly country connoted by the English term "fells."

The Blue Hills, which encompassed 7,000 acres located primarily in Milton, were the highest point on the East Coast south of Maine. Charles Eliot remarked that the Blue Hills had "vastly finer scenery than any of the great public woods of Paris."[5] Eliot and Baxter's report also called for smaller wooded reservations at Stony Brook, in West Roxbury and Hyde Park, and at the Waverly Oaks in Beaver Brook Reservation, in Belmont and Waltham.

Outside the metropolitan park framework, Lynn and Waltham established their own forest preserves, at Lynn Woods (2,000 acres) and Prospect Hill (250 acres) respectively.

2. *Lakes* By the late nineteenth century, communities sought to curb development around water reservoirs to protect water quality and, secondarily, to create grounds for public enjoyment. Prior to the metropolitan parks plan, the Brookline and Chestnut Hill Reservoirs had become protected reservations. Under Eliot's plan Fresh Pond, in Cambridge, and the Mystic Lakes, at the head of the Mystic River in Arlington and Winchester, also became reservations.

3. *River Banks*   Three major rivers flow through Greater Boston into the harbor: the Charles River, Mystic River, and Neponset River. Most of the river banks were blighted and polluted by industry. Eliot argued that the watercourses should be kept clean and the banks beautified to provide recreational opportunities. The Metropolitan Park Commission developed three reservations along the Charles River—the Charles River Basin in Boston and Cambridge, the Upper Charles River at Newton and Weston, and Hemlock Gorge between Needham, Newton, and Wellesley. The Mystic River Reservation included the Mystic Lakes, which were the source of that river. One of its tributaries, Alewife Brook, also became an MPC reservation. During the twentieth century, a reservation was also created along the Neponset River.

4. *Oceanfront Beaches*   Boston was the first city to create public oceanfront reservations. Olmsted's Emerald Necklace plan of the 1880s had proposed the Strandway along the South Boston waterfront. Charles Eliot sought to expand on this example and create parkways and public beaches along the oceanfront of metropolitan Boston. Eliot proposed reservations at Revere Beach, north of Boston, and at Nantasket Beach, south of the city in Hull. The Metropolitan Park Commission also developed public beaches in Lynn, Nahant, Quincy, Swampscott, and Winthrop. Eliot even proposed preserving the Boston Harbor Islands for parkland, a concept that came to fruition in 1996, when Congress established the Boston Harbor Islands National Recreation Area

5. *Parkways*   To make the metropolitan reservations accessible, the Metropolitan Park Commission developed a network of parkways. Eliot designed the parkways as linear parks. He proposed four types of parkways. First, there were scenic drives through such reservations as the Middlesex Fells and the Blue Hills. These were pleasure drives and were not supposed to facilitate traffic movement. Second were the Blue Hills Parkway, the Fellsway, and Revere Beach Parkway, which connected the large reservations with urban neighborhoods. Third were the Charles River, Mystic Valley, and Neponset Valley Parkways, which turned the river banks into landscaped transportation corridors. Fourth, in a similar vein, the Lynnway, Quincy Shore Drive, and Winthrop Shore Drive provided attractive boulevards along the oceanfront.

The metropolitan parks plan attracted widespread support. The state authorized the Metropolitan Park Commission (MPC) to develop parks within the "Metropolitan District," which included Boston and thirty-five (it grew to a total of thirty-nine communities) other cities and towns within ten miles of the State House. As a state agency managed by three commissioners appointed by the governor, the commission

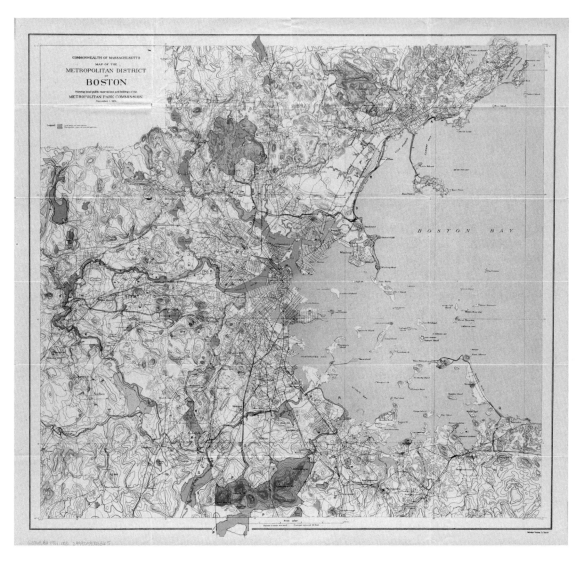

FIGURE 6.2
Metropolitan Park System map, 1901. This map depicts the extraordinary Metropolitan Park System
that was assembled in less than a decade. For $6.5 million, the park system acquired 9,177 acres of
reservations, thirteen miles of oceanfront, and fifty-six miles of riverbanks and built seven parkways.
Source: Map reproduction courtesy of the Norman B. Leventhal Map Center at the Boston Public Library.

avoided much city-suburban wrangling. Under the state's umbrella, the MPC utilized eminent domain powers to swiftly acquire vast tracts of endangered open spaces.

The Metropolitan Park System was an immediate success. The parks and parkways vision that Eliot and Baxter championed was realized within less than a decade, even though Eliot died suddenly at the age of thirty-seven in 1897. By 1900, the Metropolitan Park Commission had acquired 9,177 acres of reservations, thirteen miles of oceanfront, and fifty-six miles of riverbanks and built seven parkways. The $6.8 million price tag was a bargain.[6]

Boston's Metropolitan Park System became a national model, as it was the first regional park-and-parkway system in America and the first significant effort at regional land and open space planning. Boston's metropolitan park plan pre-dated by sixteen years Daniel Burnham's famous Chicago Plan, which featured a forest preserve encircling the city and preservation of the Lake Michigan shoreline. Frederick Law Olmsted regarded the metropolitan parks as the logical complement to his Emerald Necklace, arguing that "The two together will be the most important work of our profession now in hand anywhere in the world."[7] Sylvester Baxter claimed that Boston's metropolitan parks did "more to advertise Boston all over the world than any other modern factor." During the high tide of public parks, they influenced the development of metropolitan parks systems in New Jersey's Essex and Hudson Counties, Cleveland, Minneapolis, and Portland, Oregon.[8] Parks were as important to a city and region's self-image in 1900 as professional sports stadiums have become a century later.

British writer H. G. Wells reported favorably on the Metropolitan Park System when he visited Boston to research an article for *Harper's Weekly*—"The Future of America: A Search after Realities." Under the guidance of Sylvester Baxter, he toured the metropolitan parks and reported that, in comparison with New York, Greater Boston had been "planned out and prepared for growth." Wells found Boston "more impressive even than the crowded largeness of New York" and praised "the serene preparation Boston has made through this [Metropolitan Park] Commission to be widely and easily vast. New York's humanity has a curious air of being carried along upon a wave of irresistible prosperity, but Boston confesses design."[9]

The evidence of design is still apparent in the communities of the Metropolitan District, from Milton and Newton to Cambridge and Malden. In no other era was public space such an important element in defining the suburban landscape. The Progressive Era placed a premium on creating a sense of community cohesion, integrating city and suburbs, native-born and immigrants. Boston's metropolitan parks and parkways were a landmark material expression of those values.

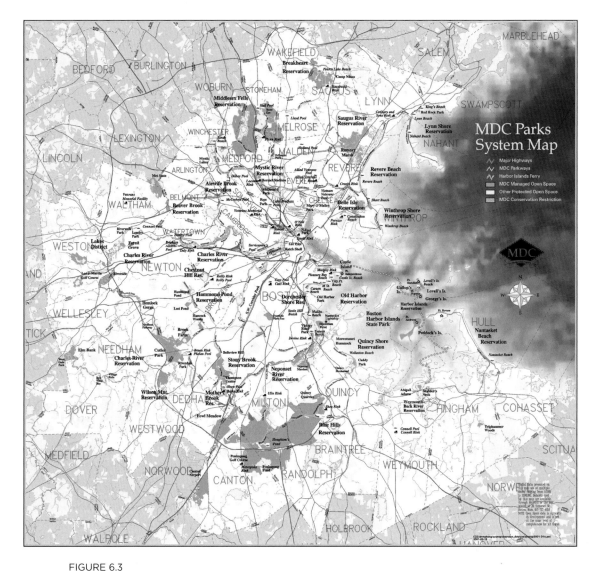

FIGURE 6.3
Metropolitan District Commission Parks map, ca. 1995-1996. This map depicts the Metropolitan Park System just before it was merged into the Massachusetts Department of Conservation and Recreation (DCR) in 2003.
Source: Courtesy of Massachusetts Department of Conservation and Recreation Archives.

Debate over Regionalization

The success of Boston's special-purpose metropolitan authorities instigated a debate about creating a comprehensive metropolitan government. In 1895–1896, Boston civic leaders persuaded the legislature to form a commission to study metropolitan government. The commission rejected a proposal for creating a "super-city" of Boston through annexation of suburbs and recommended a new County of Boston based on the Greater London County Council. The County of Boston, with forty communities, would have administered sewerage, water, parks, and possibly roads and public transportation. After reviewing the commission's proposal, the legislature let the matter die. Officials in the affected counties of Suffolk, Essex, Middlesex, and Norfolk and in suburban municipalities opposed metropolitan government because they did not want to give up any authority.

The high point of metropolitan sentiment was the "Boston—1915" campaign, initiated in 1909 by department store executive Edward A. Filene, lawyer Louis Brandeis, and financier James Jackson Storrow. (Storrow used this campaign as a launching pad for an unsuccessful 1910 mayoral run against John F. "Honey Fitz" Fitzgerald.)[10] These business-oriented leaders wanted Greater Boston to use metropolitan government and scientific management to create the best planned, most prosperous, and most socially stable city in the country. Though criticized as utopian by some, the "Boston—1915" plan recognized that social and economic problems threatened Boston's viability and required far-reaching solutions.

In 1911, the state created a special commission to make recommendations concerning the "Boston—1915" metropolitan government proposals. The commission members were Edward A. Filene, architect J. Randolph Coolidge, Jr., and nationally known planner John Nolen. The commission's final report proposed a metropolitan planning board for Boston and thirty-seven surrounding communities. Its purview would have included land-use zoning, transportation, beautification, and parks. The proposed body would have had power to approve municipal plans and evaluate them in the context of metropolitan goals. The primary incentive for surrounding communities to participate was funding from the metropolitan commission for a portion of local improvements. According to urban historian Mel Scott, Boston's metropolitan plan was the most ambitious and well-researched metropolitan planning effort in the country, at a time when Progressive planning efforts were at a peak.[11]

The Boston Chamber of Commerce supported a metropolitan planning board in its report *"Real Boston": The "Get Together" Spirit among Cities and Towns* (1911).

The Chamber of Commerce argued that "Real" Boston included 1.5 million inhabitants and forty municipalities stretching from Salem to Cohasset and including Canton, Framingham, Lexington, Lincoln, Sherborn, and Wayland. Boston Mayor John F. "Honey Fitz" Fitzgerald, seeking to strengthen the services and fiscal health of the central city, also supported the metropolitan scheme.

Within a few months of the commission's 1912 report, however, suburban legislators killed the metropolitan government plan. Once again, surrounding communities, led by the affluent suburbs of Brookline and Newton, refused to participate. The metropolitan plan was charged with being anti-democratic, and its purported benefits deemed doubtful. After this, the steam ran out of the metropolitan vision and the "Boston—1915" movement. Metropolitan government did not seem attractive to suburban communities because it appeared primarily to help the central city deal with its problems. Suburbs concerned with maintaining their socioeconomic status were wary of metropolitan planning.

In 1930, at the beginning of the Great Depression, Mayor James Michael Curley proposed a metropolitan scheme that would have federated Boston with forty-three surrounding communities and required them to pay their share of the region's public improvements. This proposal would have concentrated more power with the Boston Mayor than the "Boston—1915" plan. A hostile legislature rejected the proposal as a megalomaniacal power grab. During the 1930s, the state was at constant loggerheads with the City of Boston and Curley over construction and employment programs.

While Greater Boston was balking at regional planning, New York City assumed leadership in the field while avoiding creation of an integrated metropolitan government. The New York Regional Plan Association, a private nonprofit civic association with substantial business backing, published its first regional plan (strictly advisory but influential) in 1929. City builder Robert Moses, working through state-designated public authorities, implemented many of the transportation, recreational, and housing elements of the plan over a twenty-five-year period.

The idea of metropolitan government did not go away in Boston. In 1944, the Boston Society of Architects initiated the "Boston Contest of 1944" to obtain ideas for reviving the city's economy. The winning proposal came from Harvard political science professor Carl Friedrich, who argued that the metropolitan area had become "ill, decaying at the core, because its vitality has not been a common concern of all those having a stake in it."[12] Friedrich proposed that all communities within a twenty-five-mile radius of Boston should become part of the Boston Metropolitan Authority. The proposed Metropolitan Authority would use a city manager form of government with a legislative council that organized existing municipalities into districts.

Explaining support for Friedrich's proposal, Mel Scott stated: "The intellectual elite and many of the businessmen of the Boston area probably yearned more intensely for metropolitan planning and metropolitan government than community leaders anywhere else in the United States, partly from a sense of frustration."[13] Still, the suburbs remained unsupportive of regionalization, with about seventy percent responding that the "Boston Contest" proposal was only another approach to annexation. After Mayor James Michael Curley, under indictment for mail fraud, was reelected in 1945 voicing his support for a "Greater Boston" federation, there was no chance the legislature would approve regional government.

The public accepted professionally managed public authorities as appropriate entities for providing infrastructure services. When deemed necessary, the state created various regional public authorities—Metropolitan District Commission (MDC, 1919), Massachusetts Port Authority (Massport, 1956), Massachusetts Bay Transportation Authority (MBTA, 1964), Massachusetts Water Resources Authority (MWRA, 1984). But municipalities have not been prepared to cede responsibility to a state or regional body for land use planning and what would be located in one's backyard to a state or regional body.[14]

Parkways Shape the Suburban Landscape

Although metropolitan Boston failed to adopt regional land use planning, the parkways of the Metropolitan Park System made a transformative impact on the suburban landscape. The parkways that connected the Blue Hills and the Middlesex Fells Reservations with populated neighborhoods incorporated lanes for racing carriages, ordinary traffic, a right-of-way for streetcars, and sidewalks. This layout followed blueprints developed by Frederick Law Olmsted. In 1868, Olmsted designed America's first parkway—Brooklyn's Ocean Parkway, which connected Prospect Park to Coney Island. Starting in 1879, he incorporated into Boston's Emerald Necklace a network of parkways that included the Fenway, Riverway, Jamaicaway, and Arborway. As discussed previously, Olmsted developed a streetcar boulevard plan for Beacon Street in Brookline and the extension of Commonwealth Avenue. Olmsted parkways and boulevards served as models for the Metropolitan Park System parkways.

FIGURE 6.4
Mystic Valley Parkway, Medford, 1897. This view shows how Charles Eliot expected the metropolitan parkways would be used—by horsemen, pedestrians, bicyclists. Little did anyone anticipate that automobiles would soon dominate the parkways.
Source: Photograph by Nathaniel L. Stebbins. Courtesy of Massachusetts Department of Conservation and Recreation Archives.

Charles Eliot designed the metropolitan parkways originally for bicycles and horse-drawn vehicles. They provided a smooth, paved surface, a real improvement over rutted dirt roads. Ironically, the same year of Eliot's metropolitan parks plan, Charles and Frank Duryea drove America's first automobile through the streets of Springfield, Massachusetts. For about a dozen years, automobiles were leisure novelties that made occasional appearances on the parkways, but, after 1905, automobiles became so popular that the Metropolitan Park Commission had to repave the parkways with more durable asphalt. By the mid-1910s, the parkways evolved from being leafy pleasure drives to commuter corridors that improved access across the region and encouraged new real-estate development.

The Metropolitan Park Commission's work on parkways received unanticipated impetus from the Boulevard Act of 1894, which allocated $500,000 to build boulevards and parkways and provide work relief for those left unemployed by the Panic of 1893. Since there was no other agency remotely qualified to oversee the construction of parkways, the new Metropolitan Park Commission received the responsibility. The Boulevard Act funded not only the Blue Hills Parkway and the Fellsway but also the construction and widening of such major Boston arterials as Blue Hill Avenue, Columbus Avenue, Commonwealth Avenue in Brighton, Dorchester Avenue, Huntington Avenue, and Washington Street to Forest Hills.[15] Much of Boston's current arterial system dates from the 1890s efforts of the MPC.

Some of the most significant parkway planning took place north of the Charles River in communities that were poorly served by surface arterials. With a welter of small municipal geographical units, such as Cambridge, Everett, Malden, Medford, Melrose, and Somerville, there was no northern parkway counterpart to the Emerald Necklace parkways in Boston. Charles Eliot addressed this need with a circuit of parkway routes connecting Mount Auburn Street in Cambridge to Revere and Lynn.[16]

The parkway system, which took twenty years to construct, facilitated the flow of motor vehicles around Boston's perimeter, prefiguring the "ring roads" of Route 128 and I-495. The parkways formed the backbone of street systems, which provided the framework for developing new suburban neighborhoods in the first decades of the twentieth century.[17] In 1913, Sylvester Baxter wrote: "The connecting links of the park system—the parkways and the boulevards—have . . . filled a great need. Metropolitan Boston could hardly exist without these new elements in the general plan that originated in quite another purpose." Baxter forecast that, by 1950, the growth encouraged by the parkways in Greater Boston would reach out as far as Beverly, Canton, Framingham, and Wilmington—and he was correct.

Metropolitan Boston's boulevards and parkways reflected the City Beautiful planning paradigm of the late nineteenth and early twentieth centuries, which emphasized traffic mobility along broad roadways to accommodate the geographical expansion of the city.[18] They formed an elegant greenbelt that followed topographical contours, particularly river banks. The medians and borders of parkways were planted with shady oaks, elms, maples, and beeches. The authorities prohibited commercial and industrial uses from abutting the parkway. Buffalo, Chicago, Kansas City, Minneapolis, Washington, DC, and other cities developed urban parkway systems, but they did not extend them through the suburbs, as Greater Boston did.

The Metropolitan Park Commissioners observed, in 1911, that the timing of the metropolitan parks had been propitious for assembling open space and creating attractive suburban landscapes: "It was a fortunate beginning because the District was rapidly changing from one in which its population was gathered into detached cities and towns separated by intervening strips of land with sparse population, to one in which, by the pushing out of buildings to occupy these intervening and hitherto unoccupied lands, reasonable lines of intercommunication were becoming more necessary each year and increasingly more difficult to provide."[19]

The metropolitan park system promoted real estate development, attractive neighborhoods, and increased property values. The *Christian Science Monitor*, in 1915, noted how the MPC's "well kept public drives" evolved over a couple of decades from "the tough logging lanes and paths through undeveloped tracts." The improvements of metropolitan parks, particularly tree plantings along park borders and parkways "have been improved co-ordinately with the development of the surrounding territory."[20]

Public parks helped establish land uses. Prior to zoning, development could occur willy-nilly, with blighting, substandard development rapidly driving away other uses. Parks helped stabilize residential neighborhoods by creating open space buffers. Parkways maintained visual appeal by excluding commercial and industrial uses. According to the *Boston Globe*, the Fellsway promoted "artistic development and physical growth" in Medford and Malden, and "vast tracts of territory heretofore of no particular value" were brought into development.[21] By promoting automobile use, parkways enabled the construction of less dense housing.

The broad, tree-lined corridors seemed so attractive and up-to-date that they became appealing locations for affluent families in the first two decades of the twentieth century.[22] During this era, the splendid mansions along Boston's Jamaicaway included Mayor James Michael Curley's twenty-one-room mansion with the shamrock shutters situated overlooking Jamaica Pond. West of Boston, Commonwealth Avenue in Newton became a prestigious address, lined with Tudor, French Château, Colonial Revival, and Spanish Revival houses. Commonwealth Avenue spurred suburban development, as *A Handbook of New England* described:

This route [Commonwealth Avenue/Route 30 from Newton through Weston and Wayland] leads through some of the most delightful inland country in the vicinity of Boston, a region largely pre-empted for residential estates. The development of this region by Boston people in the last decade since the advent of the automobile has been rapid and continuous, promoted largely by the completion some twenty-five years ago of the Commonwealth Avenue Boulevard, which offers perhaps, the best entrance and exit to and from Boston.[23]

The suburban crescent north of Cambridge, which included Arlington, Winchester, and Melrose, used metropolitan parks and parkways to enhance its appeal. The preservation of the Mystic Lakes, between Arlington and Winchester, attracted prestigious residences. One real-estate ad praised the location: "'The Beauty Spot of Greater Boston—overlooking the Mystic Lakes on the Winchester car line—large lots—restricted to singles houses only.'"[24] Winchester beautified its townscape and secured its status as a prestigious suburb by extending the Mystic Valley Parkway from the lakes along the Aberjona River into the heart of town. Attractive single-family houses on spacious lots followed.

Traffic on the metropolitan parkways became heavy by the 1920s, with the explosion of automobile commuting. Massachusetts automobile registrations soared from 3,772 cars in 1904 to 102,633 in 1915 to 764,338 vehicles in 1925. By 1929, the state had 1,019,460 motor vehicles. Sylvester Baxter observed that automobiles were overwhelming the metropolitan parkways so that the Metropolitan District Commission (MDC) had to widen and resurface them.[25] Increasing traffic compromised the recreational and conservation functions of the parkways. The affluent families who had resided along parkways prior to 1920 abandoned the congested arteries and moved to country suburbs, prefiguring the middle-class suburban flight that occurred after World War II.

Country Clubs: Social Stratification in the Suburban Landscape

Not everyone flocked to the metropolitan parks. As suburbs filled out, affluent families felt the need to secure the "country" atmosphere that attracted them in the first place. The purpose was both topographical and social—to create private spaces where they could enjoy outdoor recreation and institutions that allowed them to congregate with their own sort. The solution was the "country club." It was quintessentially suburban, a place to enjoy recreational activities in a private setting outside the city.

The first club to focus on the country and recreation was the Myopia Club, founded by Boston Mayor Frederick O. Prince on his Winchester estate in 1879. The Myopia Club originally provided facilities for tennis, baseball, and boating, then shifted to fox hunting. Prince recruited members from gentlemen's clubs in the city, but since Winchester was a dozen miles north of Boston, it was an inconvenient location for many. In 1882, J. Murray Forbes, Augustus Hemenway, and thirty others, some of them Myopia Club members, leased 100 acres at an old racetrack and farm in South Brookline called Clyde Park. Park planner Frederick Law Olmsted was one of the first members. Clyde Park was closer to Boston and the estates of Brookline and Newton. The founders christened their association Country Club (the club later added "The" to the name), the first such named club in the nation. The new club was intended to be a destination for weekend coaching excursions and horse racing. The old farmhouse became the clubhouse, with a restaurant and tap room. Meanwhile, the Myopia Hunt Club moved to Hamilton, on the North Shore, where there was ample space for fox hunting, polo, and a golf course.

For a decade, The Country Club featured horse-related sports, as well as tennis, ice skating, and curling. Then, a new sport—golf—was introduced, which ended up making the "country club" virtually synonymous with the "golf club." The first golf course in America was St. Andrew's Golf Club, opened in New York in 1888. The first golf game played in Massachusetts took place four years later on seven holes laid out on the estates of Arthur Hunnewell and R. G. Shaw in Wellesley. Several who played the first rounds of golf in Wellesley became members of The Country Club. They advocated for laying out a course at their club in Brookline. Golf quickly became the primary recreational activity at The Country Club, as golf became the fashion among the upper classes.[26]

Around suburban Boston, golf spurred the development of many country clubs. By 1898, there were twenty-nine golf courses within a dozen miles of downtown. Newton quickly developed several courses on farmland: Newton Golf Club, Newton Centre Golf Club, Brae Burn Country Club, Chestnut Hill Golf Course/Newton Commonwealth Golf Course, Albemarle Golf Club, and Woodland Golf Course.[27] In some cases, country estates were turned into country clubs. For example, Watertown's Oakley Country Club placed a golf course on Harrison Gray Otis's Strawberry Hill estate and used his Charles Bulfinch–designed home for a clubhouse. The Oakley golf course is also famous for being the first American course planned by Scottish golf course designer Donald Ross.

2892—*Country Club, Brookline, Mass.*

FIGURE 6.5
The Country Club, Brookline, 1906. The Country Club was established as a private club in 1883 to provide grounds for horse-related recreation. Within a decade, the club added a golf course, becoming one of the first in the country.
Source: Author's collection.

By establishing country clubs in the 1890s, affluent society lost interest in gardening and took up more active recreational activities in leisure time. Golf became popular with women and mature men seeking a sport that was not dangerous or strenuous. The Country Club, in fact, hosted the National Women's Tournament beginning in 1902. Country clubs were open to the whole family, whereas city clubs were segregated by gender.

Country clubs provided social stability and a sense of community, first, to the Anglo-Saxon Protestant upper class and, later, to middle-class families. Tony neighborhoods grew up near many country clubs, forerunners of the "golf communities" of later years. Historian Richard Moss argues that the fear of immigrants, industrial life, and the tumult of the modern city drove the elite to suburban social institutions like country clubs. Moss asserts: "They founded country clubs to provide private spaces where the values and behaviors associated with gentility could be honored and maintained."[28] These behaviors were reinforced by US Golf Association rules (1894), which included the honor system as well as specified etiquette and clothing. At certain elite country clubs, golf pros were considered to be servants and were not allowed in the public rooms of the clubhouse.

To maintain social exclusiveness, private country clubs were segregated by class, ethnicity, and religion. Country clubs created a social pecking order, both within each club and among the clubs in a given region. Potential members, who were subject to the blackball, had to be sponsored by existing members. The most exclusive WASP country clubs excluded Catholics and Jews, not to mention Negroes. Along with The Country Club and Myopia, the Essex County Club (Manchester-by-the-Sea) and the Dedham Country and Polo Club were the elite WASP clubs. Predominantly Irish Catholic country clubs were Oakley (Watertown), Brae Burn (Newton), and Woodland (Newton), where Joseph P. Kennedy was a member—he was blackballed at the WASP Cohasset Country Club. Pine Brook Country Club (Weston) was one of first clubs to be predominantly Jewish. As late as 1962, a study by the Anti-Defamation League of B'nai B'rith found that a majority of American country clubs excluded Jews.[29]

The 1920s was the heyday of country clubs. Between 1916 and 1930, the number of the nation's golf courses jumped from 752 to 5,856; 4,613 of them were private.[30] Golf was particularly popular with the business and professional class, which regarded country clubs as an ideal place for social peers to mix in an informal setting and make connections valuable to their advancement.

Country clubs helped structure the metropolitan area's social hierarchy, creating suburban enclaves that expressed exclusiveness. The broad swaths of green lawn bordered by trees and plantings with clubhouses that resembled mansions expressed space that was privately controlled in the midst of teeming metropolitan growth. Richard Moss explained: "The thousands of country clubs built before 1930 were basically a private version of the public park movement. The general intention was essentially the same: both the park and the golf course were designed and manipulated natural settings offering people an easy route along a 'course' through nature."[31] But the parks created for country clubs were gated and guarded, the opposite of the democratic parks of Olmsted and Eliot. Just as public parks incorporated more recreational facilities between the 1920s and the 1960s, country clubs added tennis courts and, after World War II, swimming pools.

Country clubs never surpassed the status that they enjoyed in the 1920s. By the 1960s and the rising tide of egalitarianism, country clubs were pilloried for their snobbishness. Golf, often played at public and resort courses, grew in popularity, but the attachment to socially exclusive country clubs waned. Still, country clubs dot the region's landscape, remaining both a pleasant outdoor amenity and an emblem of the suburban ideal as it was conceived a century ago.

Suburbs in the 1920s and 1930s

Just as upper-crust suburbs clustered near country clubs, middle-class neighborhoods filled out around the metropolitan parks and parkways. Residents of both types of communities were drawn to the green space. The parkways, which promoted automobile commuting, transformed the residential landscape. The automobile allowed residents to forgo the dense transit-oriented neighborhoods and move further out to larger house lots. The average lots expanded from 3,000 to more than 6,000 square feet.[32] Homes incorporated garages, driveways, and larger yards, serving as a template for the post–World War II suburbs. Suburbs in the Metropolitan District, such as Arlington, Belmont, Melrose, and Milton, became built out, growing twice as fast as Boston.

The suburban boom reached many communities that had not experienced significant growth previously. It was not just a case of better transportation but new housing amenities and utilities that spurred the move to the suburbs. Developer Charles A. Gleason said that, with "twentieth century conveniences, there is nothing 'countrified' about country life today." Gleason praised emerging suburbs for their "country-club style." He argued that suburbs were no longer only for the wealthy: "The modest cottages which abound in most suburban towns, each with a convenient garage attached, bear witness that there is plenty of opportunity for all."[33]

As the metropolitan parkways provided an automobile network for Greater Boston, state highways were starting to open up the next band of rural communities as potential suburbs. In the 1910s, the state designated motor routes with color bands on utility poles and fence posts—blue for north–south routes, red for east–west roads, and yellow for secondary routes.[34] The state highway that became Route 20 west of Boston opened up development in Weston, Wayland, and Sudbury. *A Handbook of New England* reported in 1917: "Like the surrounding towns Sudbury is rapidly being transformed from an agricultural community into a region of gentleman's suburban estates."[35] For Wayland, the *Handbook* reported: "Once a rich agricultural town, most of the valuable farms have been taken up in the last decade for the homes of Boston professional and business men."[36]

Even Burlington, which was a farm community, experienced the first attempts to create suburbia. During the 1920s, that great decade of real estate speculation, developer John Hinston laid out the town's first subdivision. Hinston offered 5,000 square-foot lots for $9 to $29 and one-acre chicken farms for $59. Hinston's ad read: "Buy one or more acres of land in this fast growing Suburb, where you can make a good living on chickens and raise your own vegetables, keep a cow, where your family will be rosy and healthy, and you will be your own master and grow independent." The *Green Acres* sentiments were a stretch, as his only sales were to middle-class families desiring vacation camps.[37]

By the mid-1920s, the Massachusetts Department of Public Works (DPW) designated numbered federal (routes crossing state lines) and state routes. At first these highway routes were a patchwork of paved roads.[38] A noteworthy example is Route 128, the famous circumferential route through the suburbs of Boston. The original Route 128 followed a contorted route on city streets through Boston's inner suburbs, from Beverly on the north through the western communities of Lexington and Newton south to Hull and Hingham.[39] The traffic on suburban streets quickly became a mess. As an alternative, the Massachusetts Department of Public Works, under commissioner William F. Callahan and project engineer Frederick C. Pillsbury, planned a high-speed version of the highway, which would limit vehicular access. Between 1936 and 1941, they built the first stretch of the four-lane Route 128, between Wakefield and Danvers.

Pillsbury was also responsible for designing the Worcester Turnpike/Route 9, Providence Turnpike and Newburyport Turnpike/Route 1, and Concord Turnpike/Route 2 in the early 1930s.[40] These state highways were built along rights-of-way created for the turnpikes designed for horse-drawn transportation around 1800. The new state highways had four lanes. Commercial strips started to appear along Route 9 in Natick and Framingham and on Route 1 in Saugus, Dedham, and Norwood. Located on the edges of town, the strips became entertainment zones with restaurants and night clubs, providing the sizzle of highway culture and setting the stage for the post–World War II suburban commercial boom.

The immediate impact of Routes 1, 2, and 9 on suburbanization was small during the 1930s because the Great Depression dampened new housing construction. Two suburbs that grew substantially during the 1930s were Lexington—from 9,467 people to 13,187—and Wellesley—from 11,439 to 15,127. Although these communities were served by railroads, Lexington benefited from the construction of Route 2 and Wellesley benefited from Route 9. With the automobiles, development occurred along roadways, no longer in orientation to rail and streetcar lines.

By the late 1930s, the automobile was in widespread use. Rapid transit was still heavily used in the city, but the farther from Boston one got, the more likely the car would be the primary means of transportation. Suburbs were defining themselves as auto-oriented communities. *The WPA Guide to Massachusetts* (1937) called Newton "Commuter's Haven," reporting: "Its roads are excellent, its parkways beautiful, and its proximity to Boston, combined with its lavish natural beauty, places it in the front ranks of commuters' towns."[41]

TABLE 6.1
Population growth in early automobile suburbs

Municipality	1910	1920	1930	1940
Dedham	6,641	10,792	11,043	15,136
Lexington	4,918	6,350	9,467	13,187
Needham	5,026	7,012	10,845	12,455
Wellesley	5,413	6,224	11,439	15,127

These affluent and automobile-oriented suburbs enjoyed steady growth during the 1930s, when the population of most communities stagnated.
Source: US Census Bureau.

The Suburban House Becomes "Comfortable"

Emerging middle-class families sought to display their status by purchasing an attractive single-family home. The increase in such homes was evident. Between 1890 and 1920, about thirty-one percent of new Greater Boston housing was for single-families; between 1920 and 1940, fifty-four percent of new homes were single-family; and between 1940 and 1956, sixty percent were single-family houses.[42]

In the early twentieth century, the average American house slimmed down from Victorian excess, losing much of its size and gaining modern amenities. The prevailing style for the middle-class single-family house was the rectilinear center-hall Colonial Revival home, having two floors and six to eight rooms. The first floor had public rooms located off the axial hallway—a living room, dining room, and a kitchen toward the rear. The Victorian parlor was being replaced by the living room, which combined a public room and a family room. The private bedrooms and bathrooms were upstairs. Open rooms were designed to flow together, in contrast to the collection of small, box-like rooms that prevailed during the nineteenth century. The new emphasis was on "comfortable homes," as historian Alan Gowans called them. They eliminated formal parlors dedicated to displaying the family's prized possessions and single-purpose rooms like music rooms, sewing rooms, libraries, and conservatories.[43]

Suburban houses of the 1910s and 1920s featured modern appliance-filled kitchens, breakfast nooks, bathrooms, and recreation rooms. With labor-saving appliances and the rise of canned foods, kitchens were smaller. The kitchen was regarded as a home laboratory, the domain of efficient and hygienic food preparation technology. The use of electric appliances increased dramatically in American homes between 1916 and 1927, as the percentage of homes using electricity grew from sixteen percent to sixty-three percent.[44] The basement usually had a laundry room. Side sleeping porches, sun rooms, and dens replaced the sprawling front porch (by 1950s porches were at the back of the house facing a patio, partly to avoid car noise on the street).

Convenience, comfort, and cleaning efficiency became paramount considerations. Middle-class homes adapted to the disappearance of servants and a less formal lifestyle. The reduced role of servants led to the disappearance of service stairs, butler's pantries, and servant bedrooms. Entrance halls became smaller because it became less necessary to screen visitors in homogeneous suburbs. The size of homes was reduced to accommodate smaller, nuclear families and to compensate for increased expenses for plumbing, heating, and electrical service.[45]

Alan Gowans argues that "comfortable homes" reflected a change in the public mood from the latter nineteenth century, when unrestrained individualism called for ostentatious displays of wealth and status. In the early twentieth century, houses were supposed to promote convenience and coziness for the growing middle class. The houses employed architectural details of historical styles, whether Colonial, Dutch Colonial, Tudor, or Arts and Crafts, to convey an elevated status. The single-family "comfortable house" was a suburban creation. It was set back from street like a country house, but was situated on a relatively small lot. The new suburban home became the staple middle-class dwelling, a more private and comfortable home than those found in the city.[46] Such houses were popular in such inner suburbs as Belmont, Medford, Needham, Newton, and Winchester.

Neighborhoods with early twentieth-century homes have maintained their cachet, as communities close to Boston have increased in value because of a strong desire to

FIGURE 6.6
Dutch Colonial house, 64 Cedar Avenue, Arlington. The Dutch Colonial was a popular style for a middle-class single-family house in parkway suburbs during the 1910s to 1930s. Most have a side sunroom and sometimes a screened-in sleeping porch. More elaborate versions have gables and a center-hall entranceway. *Source:* Andrew McFarland.

live near the city. These are mature suburbs with sidewalks, full-grown trees, street lights, well-regarded schools, and a wealth of other institutions. The houses maintain their sense of comfort, spaciousness, and stylistic character. During the 1950s and 1960s, they were eclipsed by the "modern" ranches and split-levels but regained their allure with the rise of historic preservation during the 1970s. In fact, many homes built since then in outer suburbs have emulated the historic revival styles popular in the early twentieth century. It turns out that traditional architectural styles are the safest investments and, therefore, most resalable.

Exploring Metropolitan Parks and Parkways

Fenway-Riverway-Jamaicaway-Arborway-VFW Parkway, Emerald Necklace Parks,
Boston

The progenitors of the metropolitan parkways were the Emerald Necklace parkways
designed by Frederic Law Olmsted during the 1880s. These parkways, which link
the Charles River and Commonwealth Avenue with Jamaica Pond, the Arnold Arboretum, and Franklin Park, were intended to be park-like places themselves. The
parkways predate the automobile, so they are narrow and windy for the traffic they
now carry.

The attractiveness of the metropolitan parkways remains evident if one drives
along the Jamaicaway and the VFW Parkway to the Route 1 corridor. The parkways
are beautifully shaded by rows of trees. Parkway signs read: "Pleasure Vehicles Only."
The parkway ends at Dedham and Route 1 and becomes a treeless concrete stretch of
retail sprawl. Even where the banks of the Charles River appear, the highway obliter-
ates the scenic view. Because of utilitarian roadway design standards and strip commercial development, post–World War II suburban roadways failed to create an
appealing "sub-urban" setting, as the parkway system did.

Metropolitan Park System Parks and Parkways

The Metropolitan Park System (1893) provided the open space infrastructure for the
thirty-nine municipalities of Boston's Metropolitan District during the early twentieth century. The first expression of regional planning in the United States, the Metropolitan Park System helped shape the inner ring suburbs. The list of metropolitan
parks and parkways, some of which have been added more recently, is extensive, so
only a handful of the most important examples are listed here.

Beaver Brook Reservation/Waverly Oaks, Mill Street, Belmont and Waltham

This was the first reservation acquired for the Metropolitan Park System. The grove of
two dozen massive Waverly Oaks was one of the great natural landmarks of the Boston
area. Charles Eliot and Sylvester Baxter started The Trustees of Reservations and, then
the Metropolitan Parks Commission to protect these oak trees. Unfortunately, they
died off from disease within a couple decades. Today there are smaller oak trees at
Beaver Brook Reservation, descendants of the original Waverly Oaks. Also in the reservation is the home of Robert Morris Copeland, now used for park administration.

Copeland made a proposal to create a metropolitan park system in 1869 and was the author of the *Country Life: A Handbook of Agriculture, Horticulture, and Landscape Gardening* (1859), the voluminous guide for cultivating country estates.

Blue Hills Reservation and Blue Hills Parkway, Milton, Quincy, Randolph, Canton

Charles Eliot originally planned parkways as a means of transporting the public from built-up urban neighborhoods to the metropolitan park reservations on the periphery. The Blue Hills Parkway travels from Mattapan Square in Dorchester to the Blue Hills. With 7,000 acres, it is the largest reservation in the metropolitan park system. Fine views back toward the Boston skyline. The parkway no longer carries a streetcar line on the grassy median. The parkway is lined by early twentieth-century homes with a generous sprinkling of Dutch Colonials, the favored middle-class style of the 1920s.

Middlesex Fells Reservation and Fellsway, Malden, Medford, Melrose, Stoneham, Winchester

The northern wooded reservation counterpart to the Blue Hills, the Middlesex Fells have 2,000 acres of forests, reservoirs, wetlands, rocky hills, and great views. The Fellsway connects to the Middlesex Fells. Much of it is lined by early twentieth-century homes that developed near the now-defunct streetcar service.

Memorial Drive/Charles River Basin, Cambridge

In 1894, the City of Cambridge, under the guidance of Charles Eliot, purchased the banks of the Charles River to become a park. Gradually it was developed as a riverside embankment park and parkway. In 1923, the Metropolitan District Commission assumed management responsibilities and renamed the roadway Memorial Drive in memory of those who died in World War I. The stretch between the Boston University Bridge and the Longfellow Bridge affords one of the most striking urban park experiences in America.

Quincy Shore Reservation and Drive, Quincy

Quincy Shore Drive is an example of the waterfront parkways proposed by Charles Eliot, which include Revere Beach Parkway and Winthrop Shore Drive. Quincy Shore Drive, started in 1903, stretches for more than two miles, with Wollaston Beach/Quincy Shore Reservation on one side and residences on the other. It provides a pleasing view of Quincy Bay, Squantum Marsh, and the Boston skyline. Wollaston Park, a late nineteenth-century middle-class neighborhood, is situated on Quincy Shore Drive.

Commonwealth Avenue, Newton

Newton laid out its stretch of Commonwealth Avenue in 1893, extending Olmsted's Commonwealth Avenue from Boston College to Riverside Park and Norumbega Park on the Charles River. Streetcars traveled six miles along the grassy median to the popular parks until service was discontinued in 1930. Today, the lane on the north side of the median is used primarily by joggers and bicyclists. Commonwealth Avenue is noteworthy for its sinuous dips and curves. As the course for the Boston Marathon, it is the site, near Boston College, of the infamous "Heartbreak Hill." The early twentieth-century homes along Commonwealth Avenue feature a mixture of Colonial Revival, Spanish Mission, French Chateau, Tudor, and other eclectic styles that were popular in the period. The foremost landmark is Newton City Hall (1932), 1000 Commonwealth Avenue, an imposing red brick Georgian Revival structure surrounded by Olmsted Brothers–designed grounds.

Suburban Mill Towns (1820–2012)

Boston's Industrial Suburbs

Industrial cities and towns have long been components of metropolitan Boston. There have been two types. Some have been extensions of the city of Boston, dating back to the early nineteenth century. First, small-scale manufacturing sprang up in the abutting towns of Cambridge, Everett, Quincy, and Somerville, creating an urbanized continuation of Boston. The other, more typical industrial community was the self-contained mill town, which developed next to rivers to make use of waterpower. They ranged from the classic mill cities of Lowell and Brockton to the smaller factory villages of North Easton and Maynard. Investors built not only mills but also tenements and boardinghouses for the workers, a pattern that was copied in factory towns across New England. Although built with Boston capital and served by railroads, mill towns were places apart, where the lives of the workers were focused on the factory.

Although some industrial communities started as residential and light industrial suburbs, as in the cases of Malden, Quincy, and Somerville, they eventually became urbanized landscape, having lost the open green space that characterized most suburbs. Such industrial communities were inhabited primarily by workers who were often immigrants. This placed them at the bottom of the social ladder and created a long-standing dichotomy with residential suburbs, which were essentially middle-class.

The industrial towns surrounding Boston grew together as a continuous urban fabric around the waterfront, Mystic River, Middlesex Canal, and various railroad lines. During the post–Civil War industrial boom, the communities north of Boston filled up rapidly with smoking factories and congested worker tenements. One of the oldest industrial cities is Cambridge, which, in the popular mind, has been more associated with Harvard and the Massachusetts Institute of Technology (MIT) than industry. From the early nineteenth century well into the twentieth, East Cambridge and Cambridgeport teemed with the factories of Lever Soap, National Casket Company, the Riverside Press, Carter's Ink, NECCO (New England Confectionary Company), and plants manufacturing glass, rubber, wire cable, valves, boilers, and bricks. By World War II, Cambridge was New England's third most productive industrial city, trailing only Boston and Providence. After the war, the traditional industries in melted away, but Cambridge reinvented itself as a high-tech and biotech mecca feeding off research at MIT during the late twentieth century.

The diverse industrial districts of Cambridge spread north and east into Somerville, Medford, Malden, Everett, and Chelsea during the latter nineteenth century. This area was a mosaic of small geographic communities, which, if combined, could have been a large city. Combining these five municipalities with Arlington, Melrose, Revere, and Winthrop would have an area virtually the same size as the city of Boston—47.1 square miles versus 48.4 square miles (2010 population of 512,462 versus Boston's 617,594). Today, the population densities in the cities of Cambridge, Chelsea, and Somerville surpass Boston's. Most of the residences are in two-and three-family houses on small lots.

Somerville became a center of heavy industry after the Civil War. Between 1870 and 1900, its population boomed from 14,685 to 61,643. By World War I, Somerville's 4.2 square miles was virtually built out, being one of the most densely populated places in America. Slaughterhouses, brickyards, and iron and steel foundries were sited along Somerville Avenue and the railroad tracks. Into the 1930s, six Somerville plants were responsible for seventy-five percent of the state's meat-packing. The *Somerville Journal* lamented the unplanned growth: "Had it been possible to foresee how great the growth of the city would be and to make a general plan by which its growth might be regulated to the best advantage, Somerville today would be a much more attractive city than it is." While other communities created parks and attractive residential enclaves on hilltops, Somerville developers cut down hills to fill wetlands, where they built railroads and factories. In Somerville, only fifty-two of 2,400 acres were dedicated to parks and playgrounds. City fathers avoided building parks because they wanted to keep taxes low, and developers wanted the maximum amount of land to be available to the private market. By the time the *Somerville Journal* ran a story in 1896 headlined "Beauty or Business: Shall We Have Parks or Factories," the decision had been made in favor of industry.[1]

To serve the workers being drawn to Somerville, developers packed entire neighborhoods of densely built two- and three-family houses in such neighborhoods as Ten Hills and Mount Benedict in the northeast part of town. Subdivisions, with up to 500 house lots, had small yards and no public parks. Metropolitan parks advocate Sylvester Baxter wrote of Boston's northern industrial suburbs that "the suburban movement has already converted the outlying sections very extensively into tenement-house

FIGURE 7.1
Aerial of three-family houses, Somerville. Thickly settled industrial communities like Somerville had neighborhoods packed with two- and three-family houses.
Source: © 2012 Alex S. MacLean/Landslides, http://www.alexmaclean.com.

regions."[2] The living conditions in the park-less industrial cities north of Boston were cramped and unhealthy. According to the *Boston Evening Transcript*, in 1913, these industrialized "towns and cities are packed one against the other like sardines. A great part of this district is rather unattractive."[3] Since many factories paid low wages and much of their workforce was made up of unskilled immigrants, these communities ranked among the region's poorest.

Along the Mystic River, Everett became a center of heavy industry because of its riverfront location, where heavy barges could dock. Once again, streetcar magnate Henry Whitney played an important role, spearheading a scheme to import cheap coal from Nova Scotia, manufacture gas from the coal, and supply it by pipelines throughout metropolitan Boston. Everett became the site of these operations. The Mystic River waterfront was lined with coke and coal companies, the main gas plant of the Boston Consolidated Gas Company, and, later, oil storage tanks. Mystic Iron Works, the only blast furnace plant in New England, and DuPont, Monsanto, and Merrimac Chemical factories also were located in Everett. Near the plants grew up a dense web of two- and three-deckers to accommodate the workers and their families.

To the east along the Charles River, Watertown developed around the Watertown Arsenal (1816–1995). During peacetime, the arsenal was used for storing, researching, and testing military ordnance. During the Civil War, World War I, and World War II, the arsenal actively manufactured gun carriages and other heavy munitions. The area surrounding the Watertown Arsenal developed into an industrial area, spinning off businesses from the federal installation. The community's population quadrupled during the streetcar era between 1890 and 1920, from 5,426 to 21,457.

South of Boston, Quincy was originally famous for its granite quarries and later for shipbuilding. After Bethlehem Steel acquired the Fore River Shipyard in 1913, it became one of the world's largest shipyards. During World War I and World War II, the Fore River Shipyard built destroyers, battleship, cruisers, and aircraft carriers.[4] Quincy's shipbuilding industry disappeared with the closing of the Fore River Shipyard in 1986. Quincy had extensive working-class neighborhoods near the shipyard, quarries, and factories. Near Quincy Bay, there were streets of single-family homes where the middle-class enjoyed the salubrious environment. Because of their location near Boston and extensive streetcar and subway service, the industrial cities of Cambridge, Quincy, and Somerville, became integral parts of Boston. Workers could live in these places and commute to jobs in Boston.

TABLE 7.1
Population growth in inner industrial suburbs, 1840–1900

Municipality	1840	1860	1880	1900
Cambridge	8,409	26,060	52,699	91,886
Lynn	9,367	19,083	38,274	68,513
Somerville	Part of Charlestown	8,025	24,933	61,643
Waltham	2,504	6,397	11,712	23,481

Note: These communities started off as suburbs of Boston, but became cities with their own industrial base. The growth at the end of the nineteenth and beginning of the twentieth centuries reflects the heyday of dense industrial cities.
Source: US Census Bureau.

TABLE 7.2
Population growth in inner industrial suburbs, 1890–1930

Municipality	1890	1910	1920	1930
Everett	11,068	33,484	40,120	48,424
Malden	23,034	44,404	49,103	58,036
Medford	11,079	23,150	39,038	59,714
Quincy	16,723	32,642	47,870	71,983
Watertown	5,426	12,875	21,457	34,913

Note: The growth of these communities reflects the rapid urbanization that took place in the late nineteenth and early twentieth centuries, much of it driven by the growth of industry north of the Charles River.
Source: US Census Bureau.

Company Towns

Out of the immediate orbit of Boston were the classic single-industry mill towns. The first to arise were textile communities. Later, belts of shoe-making communities developed. These were all self-contained industrial towns with dense concentrations of factories and worker housing. Although they all were connected to Boston by the railroad, there was little inter-urban commuting.

In 1814, Francis Cabot Lowell built the first vertically integrated cotton mill, in Waltham at waterfalls along the Charles River, nine miles from Boston. Waltham's first red-brick cotton mill, which still stands on its granite foundation and features a wooden tower and full clerestory roof, became the model for other nineteenth-century New England textile factories. Around the factory, housing was built for workers and their families. After achieving success with his Waltham factory, Francis Lowell attracted Boston capital to build a larger textile plant along the Merrimack River at the thirty-foot drop of the Pawtucket Falls, but he died before the town, which his partners named for him, was established.

The city of Lowell (1822) is considered the first planned industrial community in America. It had an intricate system of locks and canals, eleven different factories, and rows of boardinghouses. Within a decade, the cotton mills had 7,000 employees. The "Lowell System" featured the mechanization of manufacturing functions, corporate finance and management, and a large, well-disciplined workforce made up of New England "farm girls."[5] Until the 1850s, the farm girls, with their churches, literary magazines, and sewing circles, helped form a sort of industrial utopia. Before the Civil War, Lowell was the largest industrial city in America and the second largest city in Massachusetts. The Boston Associates, the loose-knit group of capitalists who financed Lowell, introduced the "Lowell System" at mills in Chicopee (1825, 1838), Manchester, New Hampshire (1825), Nashua, New Hampshire (1836), Lawrence (1845), Holyoke (1849), and other locations.

After the Civil War, Fall River and New Bedford emerged as leading textile cities. They adopted steam power and more efficient technologies and used their ports for landing coal and cotton and shipping finished textiles. By the early twentieth century, they ranked as the top two US centers for cotton textile manufacturing. New Bedford, with sixty-five plants using over 50,000 looms, led the nation in manufacturing fine cotton goods and yarns.[6] These were dynamic communities that supplied industrial goods to the nation. Though workers were not well paid, they found opportunities in the mill towns that surpassed those in the countryside or the "old country."

FIGURE 7.2
Bird's eye view of Lowell, 1876. This view shows the density of mills, housing, and businesses of what was the largest textile city in America. Other Massachusetts mill towns had comparable density, though not the scale.
Source: Print by H. H. Bailey. Map reproduction courtesy of the Norman B. Leventhal Map Center at the Boston Public Library.

FIGURE 7.3
Boardinghouse, Lowell, ca. 1870. In Lowell's early years, company-owned boardinghouses provided housing for workers, particularly single young women.
Source: Photographer S. Towle. Lowell National Historical Park.

Mill towns tended to be self-contained communities. The workers were so busy in the factories that they had little time to do anything else. The Lowell farm girls originally worked eighty hours per week, but work weeks were reduced to sixty-six hours by the end of the nineteenth century. There were no paid vacations. As immigrants supplanted the farm girls by the 1850s, unskilled mill workers' pay ranked at the bottom of the economic scale. Low pay kept many mill families at a subsistence level. When recessions hit, mill towns were hit dramatically. In Lawrence, the "Bread and Roses Strike" of 1912 was precipitated by a drop in demand for products from the American Woolen Company's Wood Mill, the largest woolen mill in world. This brought about wage cuts that workers—60,000 of the city's 86,000 inhabitants relied on the mills for their living—could not sustain. The work options for mill families were drastically limited.[7]

Before the automobile era, workers tended to live within walking distance of their employment. If they could no longer find work in a specific community, workers would move to another. They did not tend to commute by transit because their wages were too low (Lawrence workers only made $8 to $10 per week in 1912) and the transit time was too long. By the 1920s and 1930s, when middle-class families could afford cars, most factory hands still could not.

Because of the density of the mill towns, there was little green space. The mill owners did not invest in park lands, since most did not live in the mill towns, which they considered places of production foremost. Workers had little leisure time and scant political clout to insist on public amenities.

The textile industry entered serious decline during the 1920s, even before the Depression. By 1930, 45 percent of New England's 280,000 textile workers had lost their jobs. In Lowell, the number of workers employed in cotton textile mills decreased by 85.8 percent between 1919 and 1938, from 12,479 to 1,769. In Manchester, the 6.8 million-square foot Amoskeag Mill, which at one time employed 17,000 workers, closed in 1935.[8] Textiles in New England were a mature industry that was at a competitive disadvantage to Southern textile plants, which had new machinery, lower wages, lower taxes, and proximity to cotton fields. Mill towns like Lowell and Lawrence suffered because they had not modernized their manufacturing systems nor diversified their products. When rayon fabrics were introduced, the textile mills did not convert their processes to supply the new products. The last great era of productivity for the remaining textile mills was World War II, when America's manufacturing capacities were utilized to their fullest. After the war, textile towns became partially abandoned landscapes of industrial decline, prefiguring the urban decay that would sweep single-industry communities in the Midwest Rustbelt in later years.

The leather and shoe industries, which were as economically important as textiles, endured a similar cycle of growth and decline. There were several major shoe-manufacturing subregions of Greater Boston. Lynn was a leading shoe city from the American Revolution on. In 1848, the invention of a shoe-sewing machine promoted mass production of shoes. The neighboring communities of Chelsea, Danvers, Peabody, Reading, Salem, Stoneham, Winchester, and Woburn also played roles in tanning and shoe making. Steam power enabled factories to be built virtually anywhere, not only by river banks. Beverly's United Shoe Machinery Corporation made the equipment that manufactured the shoes, leasing it to plants around the world. Haverhill specialized in high-quality shoes, surpassed in volume nationally only by Brockton. After a fire destroyed much of downtown Lynn in 1889, its status as a shoe manufacturer waned, but General Electric established a major presence there, making arc lights, electric motors, and, by World War II, aircraft electrical systems and engines. During World War II, the General Electric plant employed more than 10,000 people. General Electric has manufactured airplane engines into the twenty-first century, but federal budget cutbacks are terminating production.

By the twentieth century, Brockton, twenty miles south of Boston, emerged as the foremost "Shoe City." On the eve of the Great Depression, Brockton employed 30,000 shoe workers in sixty factories, some of which made tools and machines for shoe making. Communities surrounding Brockton also were active in this sector. They included Abington, Avon, Braintree, Randolph, Rockland, Stoughton, and Weymouth. Whitman specialized in manufacturing shoe nails. The Brockton shoe region received notoriety in the 1920s from the famous Sacco and Vanzetti case. Immigrant anarchists Nicola Sacco and Bartolomeo Vanzetti were accused of robbing a shoe factory and murdering two employees in South Braintree in 1920. Their controversial "Red Scare" trials, which ended in their execution seven years later, attracted international attention.

The western periphery of Boston also had a vibrant shoe industry. Natick was the third largest shoe producer in the country. Marlborough and Milford had shoe factories, while Framingham manufactured shoes and rubber. Framingham replaced its shoe industry after World War II with such companies as Dennison Paper and General Motors.

Woburn, a dozen miles northwest of Boston, had been a tanning center since the seventeenth century. The development of the Middlesex Canal and the railroad in the first half of the nineteenth century intensified industrial activity. By the Civil War, Woburn had twenty tanneries. Tanning supported a large shoe-making industry in town; in fact, the nickname of Woburn High School sports teams is the "Tanners." After World War II, the tanning and shoe-making industries started to decline and came under siege to foreign competition by the 1960s. The tanning industry spun off companies that produced chemicals used in the tanning process. Robert Eaton's factory, on the Aberjona River, became one of the country's largest chemical plants in 1900. Subsequently, Monsanto, W. R. Grace, and Beatrice Foods Company owned plants in Woburn. Woburn's chemical industries gained notoriety from *A Civil Action* (1995), Jonathan Harr's National Book Critics Circle Award for Nonfiction. Harr told the story of how the contaminants trichloroethylene (TCE) and tetrachloroethylene (PERC) got into the Woburn groundwater supply from chemical plants and caused fatal leukemia for at least six people.[9]

Although textiles and shoes were the leading industrial products of Eastern Massachusetts, the region manufactured a great variety of manufactures. Some communities had specialties—Attleboro and jewelry, Needham and knitwear, North Easton and shovels, Taunton and silverware, Walpole and roofing materials, and Waltham and clocks (the American Waltham Watch Company was the country's largest watchmaker). The arrival of high technology in the 1950s opened new chapters, while traditional manufacturing was eclipsed.

From Mill Towns to Suburbs

The automobile, by the 1920s, broke down barriers between Boston and outlying factory towns. State highways facilitated development on the outskirts of mill towns and commuting from greater distances. Communities that had been outside of Boston's commuting orbit became suburban. Prior to this period, the main areas of mill-town development existed around the factories and the train station.

Norwood, southwest of Boston, provides a good example. The town was home to two great printing companies, the Norwood Press and the Plimpton Press. Several tanning companies made bindings for the books. Industrial progress spurred modernization of the town. In 1915, tanning company executive George F. Willett became Norwood town manager, the first town manager in New England. Willett sought to introduce business efficiency and Progressive policies to town government. He built Norwood's Gothic Town Hall, Town Green, a new high school, and municipal athletic fields. With Willett's encouragement, Norwood built a community hospital, and developers constructed a string of commercial blocks on Washington Street. Willett even tried to build a 1,000-acre "garden village" on the English model, but it never came to fruition and the land was sold off for subdivisions during the 1950s.[10] Between 1910 and 1930, Norwood's population grew from 8,014 to 15,049.

The 1930s witnessed the decline of many local industries. Similar to situations in other industrial towns, the economic dislocations forced local residents to shift their work orientation away from Norwood, as they took jobs elsewhere in the region. The opening of Route 1 in the early 1930s spurred the development of a commercial strip on that roadway. The construction of Route 128 in the early 1950s hastened the process of Norwood's integration into the metropolitan area.

Neighboring Walpole went through a similar transition, guided by reforming local businessman Charles Sumner Bird, owner of the paper and asphalt roof shingle company Bird & Son. Bird, a pioneer in worker relations, was one of the first employers to adopt an eight-hour work day (as opposed to the traditional twelve-hour day), paid vacations, workmen's compensation, and an employee credit union.

As part of his campaign to improve working conditions, Bird became chairman of Walpole's Committee on Civic Improvement in 1912. The commission hired landscape architect John Nolen, a student of Frederick Law Olmsted, Jr., to develop a comprehensive plan for the town. Walpole's town plan called for grading roads to accommodate automobiles, widening streets, planting tree belts, and establishing building setbacks. The town adopted the Tenement House Act to prohibit three-family homes. In Walpole Center, Nolen designed a common around the Mill Pond to serve as a civic center with sites for a new town hall, railroad station, and fire station.

In the industrial village of East Walpole, Bird engaged Nolen to design the Neponset Garden Village to house workers in an English-style garden village, as advocated by Englishman Ebenezer Howard. When the village proved impracticable, Nolen turned the seventy-acre site into Francis William Bird Park, dedicated to Bird's son, who died in the 1918 influenza epidemic. The park combined meadows, wooded areas, and shaded pathways with athletic fields and a swimming area in a brook. Nolen set out to make Bird Park appear like "New England meadows and hillsides at their best." Today The Trustees of Reservations manages Bird Park, maintaining Nolen's design.[11]

John Nolen, who consulted with communities across the country on town plans, argued that he wanted to create "towns" and not "suburbs," since he believed that life in towns or small cities was preferable to that in large cities or their suburban append-ages. Of Walpole, he remarked that "No other small Massachusetts town has accom-plished so much towards its improvement based upon a definite plan and program."[12] The efforts of Charles Bird and John Nolen went some ways in transforming an unremarkable factory community into an attractive townscape that supported sub-stantial growth after World War II.

To the north of Boston in the Merrimack River Valley, similar experiments in improving workers' living conditions were taking place at Billerica Garden Suburb in North Billerica and Shawsheen Village in Andover. Billerica Garden Suburb, located south of Lowell, was one of the first American attempts to build a community like garden suburbs in England. Billerica Garden Suburb was intended for workers at the Boston & Maine Railroad repair shops. Reverend Charles Williams advocated a com-munity where workers could achieve home ownership by owning shares in the local housing corporation, and the Massachusetts Homestead Commission, a short-lived state agency, initiated the development.[13]

The garden suburb was designed by Arthur Comey, a city planning consultant from Cambridge, and Warren Manning, a renowned landscape architect and former Olmsted associate. Started in 1914, Billerica Garden Suburb was supposed to include about 300 worker cottages, curving streets, gardens, and playgrounds.[14] The Home-stead Commission, however, was abolished before the plans could be finished, and the remainder of the project was completed by private builders. The Billerica project was an attempt to deal with the problems of industrial squalor by building roomy and sanitary houses for workers in a suburban setting. It took until the post–World War II era and federal housing finance programs to enable large numbers of workers to purchase suburban housing.

Shawsheen Village was the product of William Madison Wood, President of the American Woolen Company, the world's largest woolen textile manufacturer. Wood wanted to move his administrative operations out of cramped, squalid Lawrence across the Merrimack River to the middle-class town of Andover. In the early 1920s, he built around the Shawsheen Mill a community with a post office, elementary school, stores, and approximately 230 residences. The village had two neighbor-hoods: Shawsheen Heights, or "Brick Shawsheen," having brick two-and-a-half-floor houses rented to executives; and Shawsheen Village, or "White Shawsheen," with smaller white clapboard houses intended for mid-level office workers. Wood also

MODEL SHAWSHEEN VILLAGE FROM THE AIR, LAWRENCE, MASS.

Compliments of Lawrence Daily Eagle and The Evening Tribune

FIGURE 7.4
Shawsheen Village, Andover, ca 1940. William Madison Wood, President of the American Woolen
Company, planned the industrial community of Shawsheen Village in 1921. The company buildings
are on the left. On the right are clapboard houses built for mid-level office workers. The company's
dormitory for single female employees is at the center bottom. Mill hands lived in Lawrence tenements.
Source: Andover Historical Society.

built a dormitory for single female employees, but he did not build housing for workers' families, who would still live in tenements. Wood provided a range of recreational facilities, including a golf course for executives, which later became the
Andover Country Club.[15] Designed primarily in the Colonial Revival style, Shawsheen Village was a decided effort to create well-ordered middle-class suburban alternative to the immigrant working-class city in Lawrence. Shawsheen Village and
Billerica Garden Suburb proved to be anomalies. Going forward in the twentieth
century, private employers would seldom build housing for employees.

Private individual builders, constructing single-family homes one at a time, created most suburban housing during the 1920s and 1930s. As workers increased their
income they moved out to the fringes of the mill towns and bought their own homes,

often financed by locally issued mortgages. Development occurred in an ad hoc fashion along local roadways. Little effort was made to plan a coherent suburban landscape. Such communities were reminiscent of the "self-built suburbs" of the early automobile age, which have been described by Dolores Hayden.[16]

This sort of development became widespread in industrial communities around Boston. North of the city, electric streetcars and parkways transformed the shoe-making towns of Reading and Stoneham from self-contained industrial communities into suburban residential areas. The Fellsway and the streetcar line that ran along it and through the Middlesex Fells spurred the population growth. Reading grew by forty percent between 1910 and 1930, and Stoneham grew by thirty percent.[17]

South of Boston, the US Census Bureau, in 1940, extended the metropolitan area to the shoe-manufacturing center of Brockton and the surrounding communities of Abington, Bridgewater, Hanson, Holbrook, Mansfield, Norwell, and Rockland. The suburbanization of these towns reflected the growing impact of the automobile on the region. Most of the communities were not bedroom towns for Boston but had their own places for work and shopping and maintained their small-town character. This was a portent of the suburban development that would ensue after World War II, when the automobile helped make mill towns into suburbs and created a multinucleated metropolitan area.

TABLE 7.3
Population growth of outer industrial towns

Municipality	1890	1910	1920	1930
Framingham	9,239	12,948	17,033	22,210
Natick	9,118	9,866	10,907	13,589
Norwood	3,733	8,014	12,629	15,049
Stoughton	4,852	6,316	6,865	8,204

Note: In 1890, these industrial towns were self-contained communities focused on the local factories. Thirty years later, automobiles began allowing residents of these towns to commute to other communities, including Boston.
Source: US Census Bureau.

New Uses for Old Factories

Mill towns underwent a cycle of establishment and growth, precipitous economic decline, and post-industrial redevelopment. The foremost example is Lowell, where workers were trapped in factory jobs during the decline that started in the 1920s. During World War II, workers started find new jobs out of town. Hundreds took positions at the Boston Navy Yard, the General Electric plant in Lynn, and the Watertown Arsenal because of better working conditions and superior pay. Through carpooling, buses, and railroads, they were able to commute to these workplaces. After the war, out-of-town commuting increased, as the textile industry declined and improved employment opportunities developed all around Eastern Massachusetts and Southern New Hampshire.[18] Meanwhile, the mill owners neglected to modernize the manufacturing operations. They invested in new plants with lower labor costs in the South. The number of Lowell's textile workers declined from 10,000 in 1940 to 4,000 in 1974 to none in 1980, the year Lowell's last textile mill—the Wannalancit Mill—closed.[19]

Just as Lowell was a case study for the development and decline of a mill city, it became a leading example of post-industrial redevelopment that started in the 1970s. Lowell had more than 1.5 million square feet of vacant industrial space. After years of agonizing over industrial decline, the city's leadership recognized that empty mills represented an asset that would benefit from historic preservation. They aggressively sought federal and state funding for redevelopment, and in 1978, Congress established the Lowell National Historical Park. This step initiated a movement to celebrate the history of industry, workers, and immigrants. Under the leadership of US Senator Paul Tsongas, Lowell brought in $250 million in grants from the federal government. The National Park Service turned part of the Boott Cotton Mills into an industrial history museum. *Historic Preservation* called Lowell "the relevant precedent emulated by gritty cities worldwide."[20]

The key to revitalizing Lowell and other New England factory towns was recognizing that vacant mill buildings could be profitably rehabilitated instead of being demolished. During the 1950s and 1960s, the solution to decaying nineteenth-century buildings was the bulldozer and the wrecking ball. Many of Lowell's mills and worker housing were torn down.

By the late 1960s, Americans began questioning this policy and rediscovered the appeal of historic buildings from the Victorian era. In 1966, Congress passed the National Historic Preservation Act and established the National Register of Historic

Places to encourage the preservation of important historic structures across the United States. The 1976 Bicentennial encouraged research on local history, listings on the National Register of Historic Places, and establishment of local historic districts to regulate the appearance of historic buildings. The preservation ethos transcended the instinct to preserve the homes of famous people and the works of noted architects. People recognized the craftsmanship, elegant simplicity, and future utility of factories and other vernacular buildings. This stemmed from the egalitarian spirit of the time and the desire to celebrate "history from the bottom up."[21]

One of the earliest efforts to rehabilitate an historic factory took place at the Prince Macaroni Company Building in Boston's North End. Built in 1917, the factory was superannuated by the 1960s. The architecture firm of Anderson Notter Finegold transformed it into apartments in 1969, astonishing the public that anyone would want to live in a former factory. The loft-style apartments caught on, however, as they would in the Soho warehouses of New York. Soon decrepit wharves on Boston's waterfront were rehabilitated and vacant warehouses were transformed into apartments, including Commercial Wharf (1969, 1971), Lewis Wharf (1971), and Mercantile Wharf (1976).

Lowell picked up on this trend and helped make the adaptive reuse of historic industrial buildings commonplace. Lowell and many other cities took advantage of a federal historic rehabilitation tax credit that was initiated in 1976 and peaked in use between 1984 and 1986. The federal tax credits made recycling historic buildings like mills financially competitive with new construction for the first time. In order to receive the tax credit, a developer had to follow the Secretary of the Interior Standards for Historic Preservation (1977), which detailed preferred methods and styles for achieving historic accuracy. Federal and state governments provided funding for subsidized housing, especially for the elderly, which was often used to rehabilitate historic buildings. For example, Waltham's Boston Manufacturing Mills, started by Francis Lowell in 1814, were converted to senior housing in 1979.

A further impetus to the redevelopment of industrial communities came from an emerging concern about leftover hazardous waste contamination, which has been termed "brownfields." The federal and state government established regulatory, tax, and grant policies to incentivize the transformation of former industrial sites into clean and functional features of the urban landscape.

As Lowell renovated mill buildings, the city also undertook streetscape improvements that recovered the historic setting and made the city more welcoming to shoppers, residents, and investors. The amenities included brick sidewalks, plantings, banners, benches, and period street lights. This reversed a tendency of modernist planning that had emphasized the automobile over the pedestrian. Introduced in Boston and Newburyport as well, period amenities became a stock feature of urban revitalization strategies.

Because of the newfound attraction and cheap cost of Lowell's nineteenth-century mill buildings and a lower-wage workforce, computer innovator An Wang moved his headquarters to Lowell in 1976. By 1984, 14,000 people were working for Wang Labs, and Lowell's unemployment rate was 3.8 percent (whereas the national average was 7.4 percent).[22] Lowell became "Exhibit A" for the "Massachusetts Miracle," which boosted Governor Michael Dukakis to the Democratic Presidential nomination in 1988. Unfortunately, Wang Labs went bankrupt in 1992, and thousands of jobs were lost. Yet Lowell benefited from being part of a much larger economic region. It continued the redevelopment process, expanding the campus of University of Massachusetts Lowell and attracting minor league hockey and baseball teams by building the Tsongas Center and LeLacheur Park.

Industrial cities have had mixed success at revitalization. Lowell and Waltham have been able to remake themselves because of their economic vitality. New Bedford Whaling National Historical Park has spurred revitalization in that city's historic downtown. Other mill cities with a dwindling industrial base and heavy concentrations of poverty, like Lawrence and Brockton, have been unable to match these achievements. The struggling downtowns have become symbols of not only industrial decline but also the social disintegration of communities that once melded the middle and working classes.

The issue of class continues to rear its head in the older industrial cities. In the contemporary metropolitan mosaic, these places are where the poorest and least employable live. The concentration of poverty feeds crime, disinvestment, and physical deterioration. Yet, there is a sense that aging mill towns, sometimes known as "gateway cities," can improve their situation. A "gateway cities" initiative has emerged from a 2007 study by the Brookings Institution and the Massachusetts Institute for a New Commonwealth, which set out a strategy for revitalizing eleven (later increased to twenty-four) old industrial cities that have below-average household income and education attainment.[23] Originally the Brookings Institution used the term "weak market cities" to describe poorer cities struggling with deindustrialization. This term seemed too pessimistic, so Massachusetts coined the euphemism "gateway cities" to express the sense that older industrial cities can offer opportunities for economic mobility to disadvantaged people, including immigrants. Important competitive advantages of these communities include the comparatively low cost of real estate, the existence of a comprehensive public works infrastructure, and the historic character.

The state has designated the Greater Boston cities of Brockton, Chelsea, Everett, Haverhill, Lawrence, Lowell, Lynn, Malden, Revere, and Salem as "gateway cities," to be targeted with special resources to support redevelopment. This strategic thrust differs from the initiatives of Governor Dukakis, who invested in physical improvements for aging cities. The "gateway cities" efforts focus more directly on job creation and training for disadvantaged workers. Aging industrial cities represent reservoirs of physical and human capital that must be tapped for the state's economy to be truly healthy. Smart growth advocates argue that, if Massachusetts is to both grow and control sprawl, it must reinvest in its cities. Turning earlier environmental assumptions on their head, planners now maintain that the "greenest" communities are cities, which reduce land consumption, automobile use, and the resource use entailed by new construction.

Exploring Industrial Sites

Boston Manufacturing Company Mills, 144–154 Moody Street, Waltham

This is where Francis Cabot Lowell opened the first mass-production textile mill in America, in 1814. This factory became the model for Lowell and countless other textile mills. The story of industrial development is told in the mill's Charles River Museum of Industry and Innovation. The majority of the mill has been recycled as apartments.

Lowell National Historical Park, 115 John Street, Lowell

The Boott Cotton Mills Museum, with an operating weave room of 88 power looms, tells the story of the textile industry in Lowell from its rise in the 1820s to its demise after World War II. At Boardinghouse Park, visit restored "mill girl" and immigrant housing. Lowell is not only significant as the premier textile city, it is also the place where America rediscovered industrial and immigrant history in the 1970s. Lowell has been influential in promoting the rehabilitation of historic factories across New England. The city's leading cultural event, the Lowell Folk Festival, takes place in Boardinghouse Park on the last weekend of July.

Lawrence Heritage State Park, 1 Jackson Street, Lawrence

In a restored boarding house, view exhibits on the industrial development of Lawrence, how workers lived, and the contributions of thirty different immigrant groups. A video presents the story of the Bread and Roses Strike.

Shawsheen Village and Shawsheen Heights, Andover

These neighborhoods were built by industrialist William Madison Wood around the Andover American Woolen Company mill during the 1920s. They are unmatched in metropolitan Boston for the quality of planning. The Balmoral apartment building housed single female workers. Shawsheen Village, on Argyll and Arundel Streets, had modest Colonial Revival houses for midlevel managers and office workers. Shawsheen Heights, on William and Kensington Streets, had solid brick Tudor homes for upper managers. The period street lighting and well-tended tree belts testify to the high quality of the planning. The Shawsheen neighborhood is particularly notable because it is across the Merrimack River from Lawrence, which had some of the most congested worker housing. The former woolen mill has been recycled as an office complex called Brickstone Square.

Prince Macaroni Building, 45–69 Atlantic Avenue, North End, Boston

This was one of the first industrial buildings (1917) to be adaptively reused anywhere. It was rehabbed between 1966 and 1969 by Anderson Notter Finegold.

8

Postwar Automobile Suburbs (1945–1970)

At the end of World War II, Boston and the rest of America's cities were poised for a suburban explosion. The Great Depression and the war had created a pent-up demand for people seeking new housing outside the central city. The result was suburban flight that drained Boston and other cities of people and businesses. Suburbs became the primary vehicle for improving the standard of living for middle-class and working-class Americans, just as they had previously served the privileged.

The postwar suburban template bore the imprint of government, more so than any period of suburbanization. The most consequential undertaking was highway construction, funded by both the state and federal government. Highways, particularly Route 128, dramatically expanded the amount of developable land outside Boston's inner suburban ring. An automobile-oriented landscape appeared that had mass-produced residential subdivisions, commercial strips, shopping centers, and industrial and office parks. The Federal Housing Administration (FHA) and the Veterans Administration (VA) financed mortgages for tracts of single-family ranch and split-level homes. Just as residents moved out to new suburbs by the tens of thousands, workplaces and retail stores migrated as well. The pattern of suburban commuting changed so that eventually there were more office and industrial employees working in suburbia than in the city.

As postwar suburbanization got underway, rural towns outside Boston seemed oblivious to the transformations ahead. These communities, which relied on agriculture and small manufacturing, were sleepy and self-contained. Few residents commuted to Boston. The novels of John P. Marquand and John Cheever help set the stage by describing midcentury Eastern Massachusetts towns. Marquand depicted Newburyport as the fictional North Shore town of Clyde in *Sincerely, Willis Wayde* (1955) and *Point of No Return* (1961). John Cheever wrote about the fictional South Shore town of St. Botolphs in *The Wapshot Chronicle* (1957). Cheever and Marquand both portrayed Yankee towns steeped in the past and WASP ethnicity. Characters in these novels seem trapped by family histories and class identities. In these novels, suburban out-migrants from the city were not evident. Cheever, in citing the names of deceased soldiers on the town's Civil War monument, remarked that "St. Botolphs would never muster as many soldiers again," implying that the days of the town's growth were behind it.[1]

During the 1950s, it became apparent that many small towns of Eastern Massachusetts were evolving into suburbs of Boston. They maintained a dense historic core, usually organized around a town common and/or a train station, while new residential subdivisions and commercial strips located on the outskirts. The traditional core provided a town identity that mitigated the sense of placelessness, which can exist in many suburbs around the country. There are dozens of these communities, with most located outside the Route 128 corridor. They include Braintree, Dedham, Natick, Reading, Wakefield, and Walpole.

Abetted by cheap land and cheap gasoline, Greater Boston grew most rapidly along the Route 128 beltway (later known as links in Interstate-95 or Interstate-93). Suburbs in that corridor grew by 36.4 percent in the 1950s and 25.7 percent in the 1960s.[2] The upscale suburbs of Concord, Dover, Lincoln, and Weston attracted professionals and technology executives with their countrified, carefully preserved landscapes. Subdivisions, with ranch houses, split-levels, neo-Colonials, and Cape Cod cottages, sprang up in Lynnfield, Needham, Norwood, and Reading. In Lexington, the population grew from 17,335 in 1950 to 27,691 in 1960, a 60 percent population jump. The number of its public school students leapt from 2,658 in 1949 to 6,280 in 1960 to a peak of 9,609 in 1969.[3] On the South Shore, rustic Duxbury's population grew from 2,359 in 1940 to 11,807 in 1980, spurred by the completion of Route 3 in 1963.

One of the suburban boomtowns was Framingham, whose population expanded from 23,214 in 1940 to 64,040 in 1970. Framingham had been an industrial town served by the railroad and State Route 9. As Framingham entered the auto age, it attracted a General Motors Plant that manufactured cars between 1947 and 1989. The factory employed 1,500 workers at its peak and attracted many new residents to town.

The Campanelli Brothers and Paul Livoli transformed Framingham into a classic subdivision suburb filled with thousands of ranch houses. The Campanelli Brothers built over 8,600 ranches in Greater Boston, mostly in the western suburbs of Framingham and Natick and the northern communities of Peabody and Beverly. In the 1950s, the Campanelli Brothers named their Framingham subdivisions with countrified appellations like Cherryfield, Fairfield, Ridgefield, and Woodfield. A decade later, the new neighborhoods were given posher names like Belknap Estates, Burgundy Estates, and Camelot Estates. In Framingham, master realtor Martin Cerel promoted this type of development by stressing the availability of Veterans Administration and Federal Housing Administration financing and used searchlights, fashion shows, and car shows to attract customers.[4]

Hilda Farrell recalled Framingham's suburban transformation: "When I married in the 50's, [Framingham] suddenly became suburbia, a town of unlimited space, clean air, and neat little affordable houses that extended the good life to new families with stay-at-home mothers, commuting fathers, and lots of children. Like thousands of my peers, I left the noisy crowded city behind and moved out to Framingham."[5]

Postwar middle-class and lower-middle class families were tired of living in five-story walk-up blocks in the North and West Ends, the decaying row houses of the South End, and the three-deckers and old fashioned single- and two-families on tiny lots in Cambridge, Dorchester, and Somerville. As a 1950s home-buyers survey put it, city dwellers "are reacting violently from the crowding of their environment." They were fleeing to the suburbs to make "new friends in new locations. But they want those neighbors to be as far away as possible."[6] They wanted a modern house with a yard. The single-family-house suburb was a "democratic utopia," the realization of the "American Dream."[7]

Young mobile families believed that suburbs were the best place to raise and educate children. The issue of school quality may have been the biggest factor in luring middle-class families to the suburbs. Suburbs readily built school after school to accommodate the flood of postwar "baby boom" children, increasing the tax rate when necessary. It is a great irony that, today, towns rezone property to make it difficult for families to move in and bring about the need for new school construction.[8]

The flight to suburbia reflected a profound rejection of the city. It seemed completely out of date. The neighborhoods built in the nineteenth and early twentieth centuries were deteriorating. Boston's industries suffered a deep depression, and vacant factories were everywhere. During this era, the growth of black neighborhoods spurred whites to leave the city, just as Irish immigrants a century earlier had induced Yankees to flee to the suburbs. The Great Black Migration from the South during the war years and after swelled Boston's black population. The number of blacks grew from 23,679 in 1940 to 104,707 in 1970, a leap from 3 to 16 percent of the city's population. Blacks were concentrated in Roxbury, the South End, and parts of Dorchester. Housing for poor blacks was provided in cramped, high-rise public housing projects, like Cathedral Public Housing in the South End or Columbia Point (currently Harbor Point) in Dorchester. Escaping urban "blight" and "crime" became code words for white flight.

Anthony Lukas's *Common Ground*, the Pulitzer Prize–winning account of Boston's busing crisis, explored the racial tensions that coursed through the city during the 1970s. One strand of his narrative was the story of ex-suburbanite reformers Colin and Joan Diver, who settled in the gentrifying South End out of a desire to live in a mixed-race, mixed-income neighborhood. At the end of the book, frustration with crime and weak municipal services drove the Divers to move to Newton, even though they were ashamed at abandoning their urban pioneer neighbors. Lukas summed up their motivations, which were similar to those of many other suburbanites:

> What was wrong with wanting to live in a community where he could walk the streets without fear, where he could leave his family at home without worrying about their safety, where he could send his children to public school with confidence they were getting a sound education? What was wrong with demanding effective police protection, efficient courts, clean streets, well-maintained parks, good lighting, adequate garbage collection?[9]

The high tide of anti-urbanism was bolstered by frisky American individualism. If urban social or physical conditions became unpleasant, those who could do so moved out to the suburbs. Sam Bass Warner, in *The Private City: Philadelphia in Three Periods of Its Growth*, termed this approach to metropolitan social policy as "privatism." This concept reflects strains of individualism, libertarianism, and the free market. In analyzing the roots of the wreckage of the central city and suburban flight, Warner identified privatism as a key factor.

The "private city" that Warner portrayed dealt with social issues through individual efforts, private enterprise, or nonprofit charities. Government efforts were underfunded because society wanted it that way. While suburban towns were able to

TABLE 8.1
Population growth of fast-growing postwar suburbs

Municipality	1950	1970	1980
Canton	4,739	17,100	18,182
Duxbury	3,167	7,636	11,807
Framingham	28,086	64,048	65,113
Lexington	17,335	27,691	29,479
Randolph	9,982	27,035	28,218
Sharon	4,847	12,367	13,601

Note: These suburbs were essentially built out by 1970.
Source: US Census Bureau.

provide schools, infrastructure, and safety to their residents, central cities became basket cases, unable to provide comparable services, even with federal and state aid. Warner observed, "What the private market could do well American cities have done well; what the private market did badly, or neglected, our cities have been unable to overcome."[10]

Gerald Gamm's case study *Urban Exodus: Why the Jews Left Boston and the Catholics Stayed* describes the forces that pushed much of Boston's Jewish population to the suburbs. The middle-class Jewish families that had settled in Upper Roxbury and Dorchester during the early twentieth century started to move to Allston/Brighton, Brookline, and Newton in the 1920s. By 1930, 8,000 Jews lived in Brookline, making up 17 percent of the population. By the 1940s and 1950s, Boston Jews were becoming alarmed at harassment directed at them by Irish Catholic toughs, and more families sought out the suburbs. Sharon, in particular, attracted many Jewish families. Half the town was Jewish by the end of the 1950s.[11]

The 1960s marked the last stage of the Jewish exodus from city, as blacks moved into traditional Jewish neighborhoods. The Jewish population of Dorchester and Upper Roxbury fell from 70,000 in 1950 to less than 16,000 by 1970. Along Blue Hill Avenue and Mattapan Square, which had long been a Jewish stronghold, the influx of blacks, declining housing prices, redlining, real-estate blockbusting, crime, and the reduction in municipal services drove Jewish families away. After fires were set at three Dorchester synagogues in 1970, the congregants moved out and the synagogues closed.[12] Gamm argued that Jewish suburban flight seemed precipitous because Jewish synagogues, schools, and other social institutions were not rooted in specific neighborhoods the way that Catholic parishes were. When Jewish families moved to the suburbs, their institutions moved as well, leaving a social and physical vacuum.

Living the American Dream

The postwar era marked the high tide of broad-based American affluence and economic egalitarianism. It was a period of rising expectations for the mass of society, which were expressed in the desire for a single-family suburban home. Metropolitan Boston's suburbs filled up with ranches, split-levels, Capes, and Colonials.

Personal taste and official policy discouraged the two- and three-family houses and apartment buildings found in cities. The Federal Housing Administration (FHA) and the Veterans Administration (VA), which insured mortgage financing for millions of homeowners in the postwar period, virtually required that their mortgages finance single-family homes. Federal mortgage regulations did away with the two- and three-family homes that had developed in cities and inner suburbs. Strict standards for lot size, house size, design, and cost produced cookie-cutter communities where the housing looked the same and the people were from the same social background.

Local zoning reinforced these standards. Federal mortgages led to redlining, namely the restriction of mortgages in areas whose housing failed to meet FHA or VA standards. Established urban neighborhoods were not provided housing financing or funding for renovations. The FHA and VA standards sought to prevent excess "lower-class occupancy" and "inharmonious racial and nationality groups" in neighborhoods where mortgages were provided. Racial segregation leaps out from these criteria. Such policies hastened the decline of the central cities with growing poor black populations and created a thriving housing industry in the suburbs. Dolores Hayden argues that "FHA programs were effectively a developer subsidy" that made "sprawl . . . the national housing policy."[13]

The Veterans Administration mortgages reflected how returning veterans spurred suburban development. There had been little new construction during the 1930s and the war years, so there was an acute housing shortage across the country. The tidal wave of returning veterans tended to marry quickly, starting a family and looking for an adequate place to live. In 1948, Newton used $1,250,000 of its own municipal bonds to build 418 small modern cottage-style homes for veterans' families in Oak Hill Park. The new development was located south of Route 9, on the site of the Highland Sand and Gravel Pit.

The Oak Hill Park houses resembled each other, like Levittown on Long Island. Although there were six designs to choose from, each house included a living room, dining area, bathroom, three bedrooms, and a utility room. The kitchens were small but could accommodate the latest appliances. The houses lacked basements, but they could add breezeways, porches, and garages. The base price was $8,000. During the mid-1950s, additional homes were built by private developers in the split-level style.[14] The house lots had ample backyards for the kids. Driveways were provided, as the automobile was the primary transportation mode in this neighborhood. The City of Newton even built a school and a shopping center for the new neighborhood, emulating "garden suburbs" like Radburn, New Jersey, and the "greenbelt" towns built by the New Deal outside of Washington, DC. In order to make the community less auto-oriented, interior walking paths linked homes.

Although the Oak Hill Park project contained only single-family houses, it is important to recognize that suburbs also built some multifamily housing. A prominent example is Hancock Village (1948), located on the Brookline-Boston line, off the VFW Parkway. Hancock Village has 759 garden apartments in fifty-seven buildings organized around green courtyards. The developer was the John Hancock Life Insurance Company, which, with other major insurance companies, became involved in developing (not just financing) residential communities across the country. This multifamily housing model was most often used in urban settings by public housing authorities, but it also was used by suburban housing authorities. The heyday for public housing was the 1950s and 1960s, when federal and state government provided funding to local housing authorities for multi-unit low-income family and elderly housing, even in the suburbs. Many middle-class suburbs from that era have public housing projects, either as attached townhouses or as mid-rise Modernist apartment buildings.

The craze for suburban living was promoted by movies, radio, and television. It was evident when a "dream house" in East Natick drew over 125,000 visitors over a month span in 1948. This was part of a promotion for the movie *Mr. Blandings Builds His Dream House* dreamed up by producer David O. Selznick. Seventy-three neo-Colonial houses were built across the country resembling the one that Cary Grant and Myrna Loy set out to build in the Connecticut suburbs. It was designed by General Electric and had the latest appliances, including air conditioning, food freezer, kitchen garbage disposal, dishwasher, washer-dryer, and television. Each "dream house" was supposed to be raffled off or sold at a nominal cost.[15]

Suburban subdivisions full of such Colonial and ranch-style houses sprang up across Greater Boston, from Hyde Park to Hopkinton. Since they were built with speed and economy, they tended to have a utilitarian aspect, lacking the sidewalks, tree belts, and park-like landscaping that ornamented earlier suburbs.

Some postwar homes were built one at a time on country roads, instead of en masse in planned subdivisions. These houses in the woods were built on the hundreds of small farms and woodlots that ringed metropolitan Boston. As farms became unprofitable, they were sold off for residential development. Because of their small size and hilly topography, it was often more feasible to build houses individually or in small groups, rather than in large standardized subdivisions. This sort of development occurred in communities outside Route 128, such as Carlisle, Medfield, Sharon, and Sudbury, where there was a lot of agricultural land available for development.

Postwar housing styles were strongly influenced by Modernism, which prioritized designing single-family "homes of the future." When Walter Gropius and Marcel Breuer, of Germany's Bauhaus school, started teaching at the Harvard Graduate School of Design in 1937, they both built Modern houses for themselves in Lincoln along Baker Bridge Road. With neighboring International Style houses designed by Breuer, they formed a nascent Modern community. The houses were white box-like structures with flat roofs and ample horizontal windows. Unpretentious industrial materials like wood siding, glass blocks, and chrome railings were featured. Streamlined and efficient was the style. These houses spurred an approach to residential architecture that was widely influential after World War II.

One of their architecture students, Carl Koch, designed Boston's first planned Modern neighborhood—Belmont's Snake Hill in 1940. The development had nine low-cost houses, and Koch lived in one of them. During the 1950s, Koch proceeded to design several more Modern neighborhoods, including Kendal Common and Spruce Hill, both in Weston. Koch's biggest project was Conantum, in Concord, which was inspired by MIT Professor W. Rupert McLaurin, who sought an affordable community for academics seeking to live in natural surroundings. Conantum advertised itself as being located "22 minutes from Harvard Square." Conantum had 100 houses on 190 acres with sixty acres of it preserved open space, an early gesture to nature conservation. The development featured one of first racial anti-discrimination covenants in the country.[16]

Carl Koch was named "The Grandfather of Prefab" by *Progressive Architecture* for his efforts to develop prefabricated houses in these neighborhoods. His best-known model was the Techbuilt house, which exemplified Koch's systems approach with prefabricated floors, walls, and roof panels. All the houses on Spruce Hill were Techbuilt, even though traditionalists in Weston wholeheartedly opposed them. Koch was decades ahead of his time, as builders long resisted the prefab approach.[17]

FIGURE 8.1
Gropius House, Lincoln. In 1938, Bauhaus architect Walter Gropius built this house for his wife and himself in Lincoln after being hired to teach at Harvard University. The house, which was one of the first Modernist houses in the country, influenced house design in Boston's postwar western suburbs. *Source:* Courtesy of Historic New England.

One of the best-known Modern subdivisions was the Six Moon Hill Road development, which had twenty-eight International Style houses on half-acre lots around common open space in East Lexington. Starting in 1948, members of the Architects' Collaborative, including Benjamin Thompson, designed and sometimes lived in these houses. Few of these houses exceeded 2,000 square feet and many were closer to 1,000 square feet, in dramatic contrast to the McMansions of the early twenty-first century. During the 1950s and 1960s, Lexington added eight comparable Modern neighborhoods, which are now being recognized by the National Register of Historic Places.

Architect David Fixler, in his article "Hipsters in the Woods," observed that Massachusetts in fact has "the richest and most diverse variety of Modern neighborhoods, some of which are the most architecturally influential and significant to be found anywhere in the world."[18] Modern architecture thrived in the affluent western suburbs stretching from Cambridge through Belmont, Lexington, Concord, Lincoln, and Weston. Scientists, engineers, architects, and academics, often of limited means, were seeking communities with up-to-date affordable houses, plenty of open space, and good schools.

The single-floor Modern houses as well as the more popular ranch houses were influenced by Frank Lloyd Wright's Usonian houses. The Usonian houses, introduced in 1936 in the depths of the Depression, were intended to be small, inexpensive, one-story homes that a family could assemble on its own using modular parts. They had no attics and no basements and were built on concrete slabs with piping in the floor to distribute radiant heat. The open living areas incorporated a hearth and flowed directly into the kitchen. In place of an enclosed garage, Wright provided a covered carport, a term that he coined. Although there is only one Wright-designed Usonian house in New England (it has Usonian design elements but is a more elaborate house than the basic prototype)—the Zimmerman House (1950), in Manchester, New Hampshire—Wright's influence can be seen in suburban housing tracts across the region. The Usonian houses were an expression of Wright's vision for suburbia, which he called "Broadacre City," in which each house would have one acre and grow its own food. Autos and highways would connect the low-density settlements.[19]

That vision became widely accepted during the 1950s and 1960s, when the ranch house became the leading house style. Built on one floor with a large picture window at the front of the house, it was often built on a slab to save money on digging a basement. Ranch houses originated in California and Southwest during the 1920s and 1930s and moved east after World War II. One of pioneers of the style was San Francisco architect William Wurster, whose buildings were intended to fit into the California landscape, but his skill and care did not carry over to the mass-produced subdivisions. A lot was lost in translation to the Northeast, but perhaps no more than was lost when Cape Cod houses were built by the Pacific Ocean.

Ranch houses, like those built by the Campanelli Brothers around Greater Boston, combined a low pitched roof, deep eaves, and strong horizontal lines with neo-traditional clapboards and shutters (not authentic because they did not match the width of the windows). The ranch lacked front porches. Inside, ranches had one floor with easy access between rooms, resembling bungalows of the early twentieth

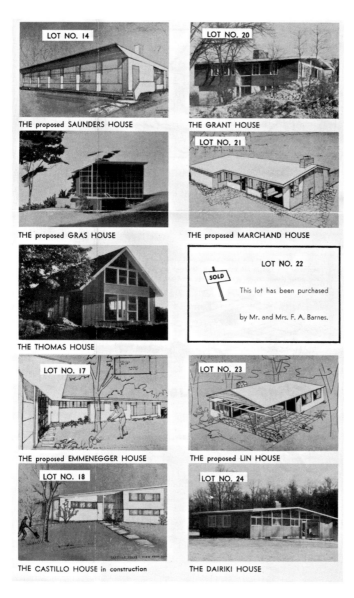

FIGURE 8.2
Kendal Common, Weston, ca. 1952. This advertisement for homes in
Kendal Common depicts the Modern, one-floor style that was popular
in the early 1950s in towns west of Boston. Carl Koch founded and
designed the early houses in the twenty-two home subdivision.
Source: Courtesy Weston Historical Society.

century. The most prominent interior features were appliances such as built-in ranges, dishwashers, refrigerators, garbage disposals, washers and dryers, and, of course, the television. These appliances provided the "pushbutton living" so coveted by mid-1950s suburbanites.[20] Ironically, despite all the labor-saving gadgets, the postwar suburban household relied on the unpaid labor of stay-at-home mothers to maintain the home and raise the children. Most suburban ranch houses had a front lawn, and many had patios in back. The garage, often attached, reflected the primacy of the automobile at the suburban home. A related housing style, the split-level house, had many of the same features as the ranch house. The main difference was the division between the main living area and the bedrooms, which were raised slightly and situated above a rec room and a built-in garage.

Despite the postwar interest in modern architectural styles, many traditional Cape Cod and Colonial houses were built in the Boston area. The foremost designer was Royal Barry Wills, who hailed from Melrose and designed hundreds of Capes, Colonials, garrisons, and saltboxes across the region. Through his books and published patterns, he popularized the Cape Cod house across the country. In a 1938

FIGURE 8.3
Colonial Revival house, VFW Parkway, Boston, 1951. During the early 1950s, the local Veterans of Foreign Wars (V.F.W.) raffled off a model home in a different architectural style each year. The houses, in West Roxbury, were fully furnished by Jordan Marsh.
Source: Courtesy of the Boston Public Library, Print Department.

FIGURE 8.4
Ranch house, VFW Parkway, Boston, 1952.
Source: Courtesy of the Boston Public Library, Print Department.

Life Magazine contest to design a house that an average family would choose to live in, Wills bested designs by Frank Lloyd Wright and six other architects. *Life* subsequently called Wills's Cape Cod prototype "the kind of house most Americans want."[21] The Cape Cod house provided the functionality and charm that was reassuring during the 1930s through 1950s. The Cape had an expandable form that easily accommodated extra rooms, dormers, and electric appliances.

The modest ranch and Cape Cod houses, which were smaller than the average 1920s home, were "dream houses" for many middle-class families. A 1955 survey taken in the Philadelphia area found that suburbanites viewed housing styles through strong class-tinted lens. Ranch houses appealed most to lower-middle-class and middle-class families and people who wanted to appear "sporty." The favorite housing type for middle-class families was the split-level. It represented "modernity, youthfulness and newness." Two-story Colonials housed upper-income professional people and executives, who were seeking to project the image of stability and success.[22]

Tastes and socioeconomic conditions evolved, however, and by the 1970s, Americans abandoned the ranches and split-levels for two-story homes. As suburbs became built out, land became scarcer and two-story homes could be built on smaller

FIGURE 8.5
Split-level house, VFW Parkway, Boston, 1953.
Source: Courtesy of the Boston Public Library, Print Department.

lots for less money.[23] By the twenty-first century, ranch and split-level houses became
so unfashionable, because of their small size and plainness, that they became prime
candidates for "tear-downs." They were replaced with McMansions, which came in a
variety of historical styles.

Route 128 and the Technology Boom

Of all the factors that contributed to the postwar suburban explosion, the most significant was the limited-access highway, which redefined the possibilities of life in suburbia. When World War II ended, metropolitan Boston was still oriented to the central
cities of Boston and Cambridge. Most suburbs were primarily residential, with little
in the way of work opportunities or shopping. The population of the Boston metropolitan area, according to the US Census, had reached 2,350,514 (eighty-three
municipalities) in 1940, up substantially from 1,623,149 (thirty-seven municipalities)
forty years earlier. In 1900, the metropolitan area was a compact urbanized area surrounding Boston. Forty years later, automobile highways had helped expand the

metropolitan area. Most of the population growth took place within the Metropolitan District, but the population was also spreading to the communities beyond.

Route 128 (parts of which were subsequently designated either I-93 or I-95) was the catalyst that oriented metropolitan Boston fully to the automobile. This legendary highway, America's first beltway, spurred the development of Boston's outer suburbs and encouraged the migration of industries, offices, and retail stores from the central city. It created a geographical corridor that demarcated the boundary between the metropolitan Boston of the early twentieth century and the suburbia that developed after World War II.

The first leg of the divided four-lane highway, between Wakefield and Danvers, was completed just before World War II interrupted construction. Between 1951 and 1958, the other segments of Route 128 were completed. Since most of Route 128 passed through farmland located a dozen miles from downtown Boston, it opened up extensive tracts of open land for suburban development.

The key figure in developing Route 128 was William F. Callahan, who served as the Commissioner of the Department of Public Works (DPW) from 1935 to 1939 and again from 1949 to 1952. During his first term at the DPW, Callahan initiated construction of the limited-access portions of Route 128. While many legislators derided Route 128 as "Callahan's Folly," Commissioner Callahan recognized that the circumferential highway would eventually create a significant economic spinoff. He even proposed building a public transit line down the middle of the highway, but skeptical legislators scuttled the idea.

Besides building Route 128, Commissioner Callahan embarked on an ambitious statewide highway construction program, implementing the 1948 *State Highway Master Plan*, which had been prepared by the Massachusetts DPW and incorporated federal highway guidelines. During his second term at the DPW, Callahan and Governor Paul Dever secured passage of a $100 million highway construction bond bill to implement the state highway plan. Among notable projects that Callahan undertook were the Central Artery through downtown Boston, Storrow Drive, the Southeast Expressway, and the Mid-Cape Highway/Route 6. By 1956, the Commonwealth had increased its limited-access highways from only 14.6 to 268 miles. Between 1952 and his death in 1964, Callahan served as Chairman of the Massachusetts Turnpike Authority, which built the Massachusetts Turnpike and the Turnpike Extension through downtown Boston. William Callahan has been compared to New York's Robert Moses for his comprehensive vision for highway development and the political ruthlessness with which he pursued his goals. By any account, he was the chief

FIGURE 8.6
Route 128, Lexington-Burlington, 1964. Before Route 128 west of Boston opened in 1951, the federal
government estimated that 15,000 vehicles would use the highway each day by 1970. On opening day,
18,000 vehicles used Route 128. The stretch in Lexington and Burlington was being widened in 1964.
Source: Massachusetts State Archives.

figure in creating a highway network in Massachusetts, with all the benefits and detri-
ments that were produced.[24]

When Callahan was building Route 128, some critics called it "the route to
nowhere." The Federal Bureau of Public Roads estimated that Route 128 would
carry 15,000 vehicles per day by 1970. The first day of operation in 1951 attracted
18,000 vehicles, 100,000 were driving the road by 1970, and there were 200,000
vehicles per day by the late 1990s.[25] The enormous influx of traffic spurred the state
to widen the highway in certain sections from four to eight lanes by 1958. So massive
were the road-widening efforts that fifty attractive bridges designed for the four-lane
highway had to be replaced.

The most dramatic result of Route 128 was attracting technology businesses. It became known as "America's Technology Highway" or the "Space Highway."[26] In 1948, Gerald Blakely, of the establishment commercial real estate firm of Cabot, Cabot, & Forbes, decided to start building industrial parks along the nascent Route 128 corridor.[27] During the 1930s and 1940s, almost no new industrial space was built in the developed central cities, so there was a pent-up demand after World War II. Blakely was particularly keen on luring scientists and engineers from the Massachusetts Institute of Technology (MIT) who might also be settling in new suburban communities. The first Cabot, Cabot, & Forbes project was the New England Industrial Center in Needham, which started with storage warehouses, then added manufacturing and offices. The development provided companies locating at the park with raw land, architects, contractors, financing, and an attractive park-like design. This is considered the nation's first master-planned business park. Cabot, Cabot, & Forbes went on to develop industrial parks in Peabody, Wakefield, and Waltham. By 1970s, the firm owned nineteen business parks in Greater Boston.

FIGURE 8.7
New England Industrial Center, Route 128, Needham, 1959. In 1948, Gerald Blakely, of Cabot, Cabot, & Forbes, started planning the region's first suburban business park. It was the New England Industrial Center, which started with storage warehouses and gradually added manufacturing and offices.
Source: Massachusetts State Archives.

The new business parks attracted widespread attention. Writer Elizabeth Hardwick observed: "For the engineer, the physicist, the industrial designer, for all the highly trained specialists of the electronic age, Boston and its area are of seemingly unlimited promise. Sleek, well-designed factories and research centers pop up everywhere."[28] Green space was an important factor in luring businesses out to the suburbs. Industrial parks were truly parks, with attractive garden landscapes surrounding Modernist boxes. R. John Griefen, of Cabot, Cabot, & Forbes, explained:

> The real selling point of 128 is the landscape there. The research-and-development industry depends almost wholly on scientists and engineers. A firm must be able to attract and hold them, perhaps lure them from other firms. It can't do this by money alone . . . , so it does so by offering nice surroundings. A scientist likes a quiet office with a blackboard, a window, and a tree outside, and it is better still if the tree has a squirrel in it. Route 128 supplies that kind of thing.[29]

In the office and industrial parks, most of the buildings had a single story because there was so much land and companies wanted to spread out more than they could in congested cities. Many of these buildings were generic, flexible structures that could be adapted for factory, warehouse, lab, or office uses. Such buildings could be leased to a single tenant or subdivided for several users.

Despite the popularity of industrial development, towns differed in their response. Burlington accepted every kind of commercial and industrial development, while neighboring Lexington allowed only research and development facilities. Towns liked locating industrial and office uses along the highway because it maximized tax revenues and employment while not disrupting town centers. George B. H. Macomber and the Nordblom Company attracted RCA electronics as lead tenant at Northwest Industrial Park in Burlington. Waltham industrial parks hosted Sylvania, Polaroid, the transistor company Clevite, and Canada Dry. Sylvania, Salada Tea, and General Aluminum opened plants in Woburn. Wilmington had AVCO, a defense firm with 3,500 employees. In Wakefield, developers razed the Pleasure Island amusement park (1959–1969) to create an industrial park.

The amount of investment along Route 128 was enormous. Between 1950 and 1957, $100 million was invested in commercial development and $400 million was spent to build housing. By 1955, there were fifty-three office and industrial companies located along Route 128; there were 223 by 1959 and 729 businesses with 66,000 employees by 1967. Between 1954 and 1967, 80 percent of Greater Boston's new industrial space was built in the suburban periphery.[30]

The driving force behind business expansion into the Route 128 corridor was MIT. After moving to its new Cambridge campus from Back Bay, MIT developed a Technology Plan (1918) to encourage large corporations such as General Electric, Eastman Kodak, and DuPont to provide financial support for university research. During the 1920s, MIT established the Division of Industrial Cooperation and Research to promote corporate research contracts. One of the first contracts was with Raytheon, which was manufacturing vacuum tubes for radios. (Raytheon's cofounder Vannevar Bush later served as MIT's dean of engineering and as President Roosevelt's science advisor in World War II.) During the war, Raytheon developed radar and, following the war, the company developed the transistor and the microwave oven. Raytheon became the region's premier electronics and defense contractor, producing sophisticated weapons systems, such as the Patriot Missile. To accommodate its dramatic growth during and after World War II, Raytheon established a major presence along Route 128, moving its headquarters from Cambridge to Lexington.

Another MIT-defense industry spinoff was the Lincoln Laboratory, which MIT established at the behest of the Air Force in 1951. Lincoln Lab was responsible for developing long-range radar, air-defense warning systems, and high-speed digital data processors. Lincoln Lab also opened a campus in Lexington. By 1958, Lincoln Lab spun off the MITRE Corporation, a nonprofit research and development firm specializing in air defense and missile warning systems. MITRE located in Bedford, near Hanscom Air Force Base, which was home for the Air Force's Electronic System Division. The Air Force Cambridge Research Laboratories also moved to Hanscom Air Force Base. MIT's Instrumentation Lab (now the independent Charles Stark Draper Lab) developed aircraft and missile guidance systems for the space race with the Soviet Union.

The formidable cluster of defense industry research entities, which employed thousands of scientists, attracted and spun off many for-profit companies. During the 1960s, Lincoln Lab spun off fifty new enterprises and Raytheon was the source of 150 start-ups.[31] MIT, together with the firms located near the junction of Route 128 and Route 2, formed the nation's leading electronics center. The region developed an innovative high-technology labor pool that would spur other industries.

One of the most famous Lincoln Lab alumni was Ken Olsen, who started the Digital Equipment Corporation (DEC) in 1957 to build electronic modules to design and test computers. This work led Olsen and his two partners, former Lincoln Lab researchers, to build the first minicomputer two years later. Looking for workspace convenient to his suburban home, Olsen rented 8,600 square feet in the hundred-year-old

Assabet Mill of American Woolen Company in Maynard, twenty miles from Boston. This move was an early step in opening up a second technology corridor along Interstate-495, which would be built about twenty-eight miles from Boston during the 1960s. Digital went on to become the second largest computer manufacturer by the late 1980s with over 100,000 employees. Unfortunately, it was not able to adapt to the emergence of the personal computer, and the minicomputer lost its market. In 1998, Digital was absorbed by Compaq, which was bought by Hewlett-Packard four years later. Hewlett-Packard maintains a presence in the I-495 corridor, though it is much diminished compared to Digital.

FIGURE 8.8
Digital Equipment Corporation, Maynard. Digital Equipment Corporation led high-tech development in the I-495 corridor. The minicomputer giant also pioneered the adaptive reuse of historic mills buildings when it made its headquarters in Maynard's former Assabet Mill.
Source: © 2012 Alex S. MacLean/Landslides, http://www.alexmaclean.com.

Another leading minicomputer company was Data General, which was established in 1968 when three Digital employees went off on their own. Led by Edson Castro, Data General became the nation's third largest minicomputer firm. Headquartered in Westborough, Data General was the subject of Tracy Kidder's Pulitzer Prize–winning book *The Soul of a New Machine* (1981). The book told the story of the Eagle Project, a group of Data General computer engineers who were in a race to develop a competitor to Digital's VAX computer. Like Digital, Data General bet its future on minicomputers and faded away during the 1990s, being bought out by EMC.

An Wang left Harvard's Computation Lab in 1951 to make electronic calculators. His firm Wang Labs started in Cambridge, then moved its headquarters to Tewksbury. Wang Labs ended up in Lowell, with the headquarters at the junction of I-495 and Route 3, before slipping into bankruptcy in 1992. At its peak, Wang Labs employed over 33,000 and earned revenues of $3 billion. Its product line included word processors, minicomputers, and data processors.

The minicomputer industry took off during the 1970s, grabbing the high-tech baton from the defense and space industries, which shed 30,000 jobs between 1970 and 1972. During the 1970s and early 1980s, minicomputer companies Digital, Data General, Wang Labs, Honeywell, Prime Computer, and Computervision created 100,000 new technology jobs and controlled more than two-thirds of the minicomputer market. These jobs were mainly in manufacturing hardware, not in developing software. The Massachusetts unemployment rate, which was the highest in the country in 1975, at 11.2 percent, dropped to the lowest in 1987, with 3.2 percent. This was the era of the "Massachusetts Miracle," which propelled Governor Michael Dukakis to the Democratic Presidential nomination in 1988. The 1980s boom fueled speculation in housing and commercial real estate across the Commonwealth, particularly in the Route 128–I-495 region.

Just as the Dukakis presidential campaign ultimately withered, so did the Massachusetts high-tech economy. In the late 1980s, the minicomputer industry lost 50,000 jobs, and only Digital remained profitable. During the early 1990s, each of the minicomputer giants either was acquired by other companies or went out of business. The Massachusetts minicomputer industry lost much of their market to emerging personal computers. They had not regarded desktop computers as a threat. Considering it a toy, Ken Olsen predicted that "the personal computer will fall flat on its face in business" and prohibited even the use of the term "personal computer" at DEC.[32]

Technology analyst Annalee Saxenian, in *Regional Advantage: Culture and Competition in Silicon Valley and Route 128*, observed that, not only had the Massachusetts technology sector lost market share, it was losing its edge in innovation to Silicon Valley. Saxenian wrote: "By the end of the 1980s Route 128 had ceded its position as the locus of computer innovation to the West Coast."[33] Saxenian blamed the decline of the Greater Boston computer industry on the self-contained, vertically integrated business model of companies like Digital and Data General that made it difficult to adapt to changing markets. Silicon Valley was more adaptable and flexible because its companies were less hierarchical and much more open to cross-pollination between companies. Silicon Valley encouraged an open exchange of information and job hopping, which did not occur around Boston. In socially conservative Boston, tech workers tended to stay with the same company. They went directly home after work and socialized at golf courses and dinner parties, not at tech bars and hangouts. Even during the Massachusetts Miracle years of 1975–1990, Silicon Valley created three times as many jobs as Route 128.[34]

Despite the fact that the minicomputer industry went belly up and the lead in technology shifted west to Microsoft, Intel, Apple, Hewlett-Packard, and Google, Greater Boston maintained a technology base, with branch facilities of these tech giants and many other firms. Greater Boston gradually became more like Silicon Valley in encouraging the exchange of talent and ideas between companies and universities. Although office construction continues along Route 128, there are perceptions that the locus of innovation has shifted to Cambridge, which is the nation's leading biotechnology center. In 2009, Microsoft CEO Steve Ballmer said of the Greater Boston tech sector: "Cambridge is a great brand. Route 128, I don't think is a tech brand any more. The mentality is more around MIT, Harvard, and other universities than it is in the 128 corridor."[35] The cutting edge of innovation has moved back to the city, where the "creative class," to use urban theorist Richard Florida's term, is concentrated.[36]

Birth of the Shopping Center

The image of post–World War II Boston posed a dichotomy between the city and the suburbs. The central city was deemed to be fading. Yet, the suburbs were national leaders in automobile-oriented development. Besides having the nation's first suburban beltway, Greater Boston claimed the first regional shopping center on the East

Coast (it opened only days after Seattle's Northgate, considered the country's first regional mall)—Shoppers' World in Framingham.

Before World War II, regional retail activity was heavily concentrated in downtown Boston. The suburbs were primarily residential and had little more than local convenience shopping. Even services like cobblers, florists, watch repairmen, and candy shops tended to be located at downtown train stations, where commuters could pick up goods on their way back to the suburbs. The streetcar lines were laid out to funnel shoppers into downtown. Wagons and, later, trucks delivered packages from department stores and other retailers to suburban homes, facilitating the experience of downtown shopping. In the 1920s, with the popularization of the automobile, suburban shopping districts started to appear in town centers. For example, E. P. Slattery, an upscale downtown women's store, opened in Wellesley in 1923 and in Brookline in 1927. Filene's and Jordan Marsh department stores also opened branches in suburban town centers.[37]

In 1951, Shoppers' World opened on Route 9 in Framingham, twenty-one miles from downtown Boston. Changing the region's shopping patterns, the shopping center collected together forty-four stores arrayed along covered walkways. Prefiguring the enclosed regional mall, Shoppers' World had two levels connected by second-floor pedestrian bridges. The "Futurama-style" shopping center had a flying-saucer-shaped Jordan Marsh department store, as well as a courtyard designed by landscape architect Sidney Shurcliff to resemble a New England town common. The courtyard had a water fountain with synchronized music and colored lights patterned on fountains at the 1939 New York World's Fair.

Architect Morris Ketchum, Jr., had been partner of the "Father of the Mall" Victor Gruen, who designed prototypical shopping centers at Northland Mall outside Detroit (1954) and Southdale Mall near Minneapolis (1956). Ketchum set out to design a trendsetting shopping center, and he succeeded. Surrounded by over 6,000 free parking spaces, Shoppers' World drew hordes of shoppers away from the downtowns of Boston and Framingham, where it was difficult to park all those Fords, Chevys, and Ramblers. The exceedingly popular shopping center influenced the development of shopping centers around Boston and across the country.

The key to Shoppers' World's success was Jordan Marsh, which made a major commitment to the suburban market by building an anchor store with 250,000 square feet. Building in Framingham was a leap of faith that was quickly rewarded. The areas of Framingham and Natick around Shoppers' World on Route 9 became a busy commercial strip, the second most profitable retail location in the state after

FIGURE 8.9
Shoppers' World, Route 9, Framingham. The first East Coast shopping mall was Shoppers' World,
opened in 1951. This shopping center revolutionized Greater Boston's shopping patterns by drawing
away shoppers from downtown with acres of free parking spaces. The Jordan Marsh department store
made a splash with its flying-saucer architecture.
Source: Courtesy of the Framingham Historical Center.

downtown Boston. Originally called the "Golden Mile," the retail district became the
"Golden Triangle" as the shopping district expanded to include five shopping cen-
ters. The Natick Mall, which opened in 1965, was the second enclosed mall in
Greater Boston.[38]

During these years, a more modest commercial node appeared on Route 9 closer
to Boston to tap the upscale suburbs of Brookline and Newton. In 1948, the Metropolitan District Commission sold a dozen acres of the Hammond Pond Reservation to
the Chestnut Hill Shopping Center, which originally accommodated an R. H. Stearns
department store and ten other stores. Next door, the upscale Chestnut Hill Mall

opened in 1974, also on former Hammond Pond Reservation land. Five hundred yards west on Route 9, another upscale mall, the Atrium Mall, opened in 1986.

In 1963, Brockton's Westgate Mall, off Route 24, became the first enclosed mall on the East Coast. Along the arc of Route 128, three major regional malls appeared: North Shore Mall in Peabody (1958), South Shore Plaza in Braintree (1961), and Burlington Mall in Burlington (1968). Cabot, Cabot, & Forbes was responsible for developing both the South Shore Plaza and the North Shore Mall. In the case of the North Shore and Burlington malls, the Jordan Marsh and Filene's department stores were original anchor tenants, while Filene's was the main anchor at the South Shore Plaza. Department stores, whether local companies like Jordan Marsh or Filene's or national retailers like Sears Roebuck and J. C. Penney, were the key to a shopping center's feasibility. Suburbs were becoming more than bedroom communities for Boston: they were economic centers that undermined the retail primacy of downtown Boston.

FIGURE 8.10
South Shore Plaza, Braintree. The South Shore Plaza, along with the Burlington Mall and the North Shore Mall, developed along Route 128. The South Shore Plaza, which opened in 1961, is the largest shopping mall in New England.
Source: Andrew McFarland.

From "Stringtowns" to "Strips"

As shopping moved to the suburbs, major roadways became commercial strips. From the 1920s on, country roads evolved into busy roadways lined by homes and businesses. Some stretches sprouted eateries, motor courts, gas stations, car dealers, and supermarkets. Businesses put up idiosyncratic signage and architecture to attract motorists. Quincy-based Howard Johnson's pioneered the standard orange roof and colonial-revival cupolas on their restaurants. Springfield-based Friendly's built red brick, peak-roofed restaurants with trademark colonial-style cupolas and weather-vanes. By the high tide of automobile obsession in the 1950s, drive-in restaurants, drive-in banks, drive-in cleaners, and drive-in theaters were appearing on strips all around Boston. The highway strip was the domain of private enterprise.

Route 9, which connected Boston with Worcester (formerly known as the Worcester Turnpike), became a prominent strip. It was home to restaurants, night-clubs, and local shopping. Some of the most popular spots in Framingham were the Abner Wheeler House, a historic New England inn; Ken's Steakhouse; the Maridor Restaurant; and big band leader Vaughn Monroe's nightclub and restaurant, the Meadows. The Red Coach Grill was located on Route 9 near the Framingham exit of the Massachusetts Turnpike. Over the years, it has been site of six other restaurants.

The mutating strips were cute, eccentric, and convenient, but they alarmed Shirley-based conservationist Benton MacKaye (1879–1976), who criticized them as "stringtowns," "roadtowns," and "auto slums." In the mid-1920s, MacKaye recognized that the sprawling commercial roadway landscape threatened to drain vitality out of the centers of established communities and deface the countryside. In one of the first critiques of urban sprawl, MacKaye advised the Cape Cod Chamber of Commerce, in 1927, to implement planning measures that constrained the development of "stringtowns."[39]

Despite MacKaye's warnings, commercial strips proliferated after World War II. By the 1960s, national franchises came to dominate the suburban strip with standardized signs and facades and vast parking lots. Eric Schlosser, author of *Fast Food Nation*, argued that the fast-food industry was the key force in developing the commercial strip. According to Schlosser, "The fast-food chains were the first companies to demonstrate that you could create identical retail environments and sell the same products in thousands of locations. The huge success of McDonald's spurred countless imitators. The founders of the Gap later said they were inspired by McDonald's and Kentucky Fried Chicken." Between 1970 and 2001, American purchases of fast food increased from $6 billion to $110 billion, and commercial strips expanded commensurately.[40] The ubiquity of a chain like McDonald's is demonstrated by the fact that there are thirty-five McDonald's restaurants within twenty miles of both Natick and Peabody.

As the chain business model depends on capital from Wall Street, it relies on a predictable, standardized product to attract investment. This requires creating an easily identified corporate brand, which is expressed on the landscape by recognizable signs, buildings, and colors. Many corporate products—hamburgers, gasoline, motels, and so on—are virtually indistinguishable, so they rely on marketing to differentiate them. According to landscape historian Edward Relph, the strip became a "television road" where corporate outlets compete with their repetitive signs and buildings. The strip makes visual sense at 30–50 mph, but at a pedestrian pace, Relph believes it is a "hideous confusion of ill-formed spaces, dirty surfaces, rusty poles, vehicles, and competing signs."[41] American highway strips tend to look the same, regardless of the climate, the terrain, and the culture. They are built to facilitate auto access and commerce, and their design leaves little room for social interaction, pedestrians, or public transit.

It seems ironic that many towns seeking to preserve their rural character end up zoning roadways for intensive commercial use. They have done so because strip businesses contribute substantial property taxes, reducing the tax burden on homeowners. Some regard homes as a drain on municipal coffers because of the students that must be educated by public schools, so they seek commercial development as an alternative. Since Massachusetts municipalities rely on local property taxes for 52.9 percent (2004 data) of their total budgets, municipal officials are eager to approve new commercial development.[42] This is referred to as "fiscal zoning."

According to former Director of Urban Design for the Boston Redevelopment Authority Brenda Case Scheer, America veered toward sprawl when the highway strip replaced the speculator grid as the primary land-use form. The grid produced the traditional urban landscapes of New York, Philadelphia, Chicago, and countless smaller communities, except for Boston, which has a hodgepodge of irregular blocks and small, unconnected grids. The grid made it simple for developers to construct buildings on tightly arranged blocks. This land-use form encouraged pedestrians and mass transit.

The highway strip facilitates a different real-estate development pattern. The community provides the highway (usually with federal or state funding) and the commercial-use zoning, and investors do the rest. There are two types of commercial strips: (1) the state roads with four lanes or more, like Routes 1 or 9, which attract shopping centers, big box stores, and chain stores and restaurants; (2) the secondary two-lane state highways, like Routes 18, 20, and 28, which are lined by some franchises, but many local restaurants, auto-repair stations, and tradesmen's shops. On the strip, most buildings sit behind their parking lots and face the main roadway. The few side streets channel their traffic onto that main road, creating traffic congestion. Scheer calls the roadway "an elastic tissue that allows adaptation to rapid change." Because buildings are often cheaply built and are intended for a single use, they can be easily demolished when a new use is proposed.[43]

The most obvious visual aspect of the strip is the parking lot. Strip shopping centers have long provided ample free parking situated in front of the shopping outlets. According to the Metropolitan Area Planning Council, seventy-four of 101 Greater Boston communities currently require retail establishments to provide a minimum of four parking spaces per 1,000 square feet of retail space. This means that pavement for parking takes up more land than the floor area of a typical one-story building.[44] Communities have recognized problems associated with excessive parking requirements and have reduced the required amount of parking spaces. This encourages public transit use and walking, improves the strip's appearance, and diminishes impervious surfaces that concentrate rainwater runoff. Some communities are forcing parking lots to be located behind the stores, so that buildings can be moved closer to the street line.

Greater Boston has many strips, most notably Route 1 north of Boston (formerly known as Newburyport Turnpike), which has elements left over from pre-corporate chain days. *Buildings of Massachusetts: Metropolitan Boston* calls the array of commercial architecture and signs along Route 1 in Saugus "among the finest displays of strip development on the East Coast dating from the suburban migration after World War II."[45] Some of the standout landmarks include Weylu's Chinese restaurant, Kowloon Polynesian restaurant, Hilltop Steak House and its plastic giant cactus, the leaning tower of Prince Pizzeria, and the two-masted frigate that is Ship's Wharf (formerly the Ship Restaurant). Of course, Route 1 has the Square One Mall and a selection of Target, Kohl's, and Dunkin' Donuts. All along the route, the full range of national and regional chains can be found.

Route 1 and other strips pose a paradox. The public flocks to strips, eager for the stores, eating places, and services. The more popular it is, the more congested the traffic becomes. The strip, however, undercuts the suburban claim to be quieter, more scenic, and more community-oriented than the city. The placelessness of the

FIGURE 8.11
Hilltop Steak House, Route 1, Saugus. In 1961, Frank Giuffrida opened the Hilltop Steak House on
Route 1. Its giant neon cactus is a classic of 1960s' roadside signage.
Source: Andrew McFarland.

strip has become a target of reproach. When critics assail "sprawl," they are usually
reacting against commercial strips like Route 1 in Saugus, Route 1 south of Boston in
Dedham and Norwood ("The Auto Mile"), and Route 9 in Natick and Framingham.
The strip has become a major planning challenge, but, if it is sensitively redeveloped,
it could provide a springboard for suburban revitalization.

Shaping the Postwar Suburban Landscape

During the postwar era, suburbs focused on shaping communities that safeguarded the enormous psychological and economic investments being made. As suburbs filled out, it became apparent that each suburb was developing a distinct social character. Historian Lizabeth Cohen has observed that people moving to the suburbs increasingly "selected among homogeneous suburbs occupying distinctive rungs in a clear status hierarchy of communities."[46] Just as *US News & World Report* ranks colleges, *Boston Magazine* ranks communities based on the "best places to live," the prestige of certain streets, the price of homes, and the quality of the schools. Even without consulting *Boston Magazine*, most Greater Boston residents carry a mental picture of the class gradation of communities around in their heads and can provide an opinion about the relative prestige of specific cities or towns similar to those reflected in *Boston Magazine's* annual rankings of "the best places to live."

To maintain their investments and class distinctions, suburbanites fought to protect the historic character of their communities and celebrated home rule, town meeting, and local schools as graspable havens in a vast metropolis. Strategies for maintaining social exclusivity and high real-estate values included restrictive property covenants, large-lot zoning, the exclusion of industrial and commercial uses, and land conservation.

Many urban politicians, intellectuals, and city planners criticized the localism of the suburbs as a threat to the viability of the metropolitan region. They advocated metropolitan planning, an extension of the Metropolitan District Commission (MDC), or even broadened powers for Boston, but they could gain little traction in the suburbs, where citizens favored the status quo and locally managed town services and finance.

Whenever there was discussion about expanding the MDC to include additional suburbs, there was resistance. In 1940, the Trustees of Reservations proposed enlarging the metropolitan park system to include eighty-six new communities located within a twenty-five-mile radius of downtown Boston (approximately as far as today's I-495 beltway). The MDC, City of Boston, and State Planning Board approved the idea, as did a special committee established by Governor Leverett Saltonstall. They believed that an enlarged park system could protect more open space and make available a wide array of recreational opportunities. But representatives of more than forty of the potential new communities came out strongly against the proposal. They wanted no new tax assessments and no interference from the MDC or Boston

interests.[47] In these years, towns were fiscally autonomous, almost completely reliant
on the property tax for revenues. It was only by the 1970s that the state started offering substantial local aid for education, highways, and general expenditures, appor-
tioned from state tax and lottery revenues.

There were other efforts at regionalization. When Governor John Volpe's 1961
commission on MDC reorganization called for adding new communities stretching
out to Bedford and Avon, the resistance again was strong. Boston Mayor Kevin
White, in order to stabilize the central city, proposed in 1970 to transform the MDC
into a "regional federation" comprising ninety-nine communities, but his proposal
also received a negative response from the outer suburbs and went nowhere.[48] During
the urban crisis of the 1960s, some reformers advocated sharing suburban tax
resources with the city and distributing low income housing and schoolchildren
throughout the metropolitan area, but the suburbs wanted nothing to do with urban
social problems.

Greater Boston established a regional planning entity in 1963 with the creation
of the Metropolitan Area Planning Council (MAPC) to coordinate transportation
planning for 101 cities and towns. The legislature, with the approval of the municipalities, made sure that MAPC would have no regulatory powers and would be
strictly advisory. To this day, MAPC has no power to implement its plans, and
municipal zoning remains the arbiter of local land uses.

Towns were in control over land use and open-space protection, and they tried
to maintain a rural landscape as much as possible. The outer suburbs developing in
the postwar era considered their landscapes to be different from the Metropolitan
District suburbs, which were more urban and likely to value programmed parks.[49]
The country town ideal influenced communities to seek open space, without the
MDC-style refinements of public parkways, picnic groves, and recreational fields. A
popular model for open-space conservation was the state park or forest, which usually
had woods and ponds and was situated remote from population centers. A drawback
of state parks and forests was that they were not linked together in a planned geographical network as metropolitan parks were. The state park model was promoted
by a 1957 Massachusetts Department of Natural Resources plan for new state parks,
mainly in rural areas.[50]

The country suburb ideal had deep roots in the nineteenth century, when
wealthy families established rural retreats. Country estates provided their own open
space, so wealthy families did not feel the need for the common spaces that public
parks provided. They did, however, defend the country town look. In the face of

postwar growth pressures, affluent rural suburbs such as Dover, Lincoln, and Weston maintained their countryside qualities by rigorous efforts at single-family, large-lot residential zoning and the conservation of forest and underused agricultural lands. These communities set a tone for suburbs to be distinctive from the city, not integrated with it, as Metropolitan District suburbs had been. To maintain a country atmosphere, suburbs even avoided building sidewalks and street lights. Today, 58 percent of streets and roads in Greater Boston have no sidewalks, as outer suburbs seek to maintain a rural and auto-oriented character.[51]

In middle-class suburbs, many homeowners had lots of one-quarter acre or more by the 1960s. With ample private space, suburbanites felt they did not need the public parks provided in older, denser suburbs. In any case, unless parks were within reasonable walking distance of homes, families were unlikely to use them.

In the face of declining suburban interest in parks, the MDC still tried to use its 1956 Parks Plan to promote open space conservation. The MDC plan had a section on "Metropolitan Sprawl" that discussed the problem of unplanned development, arguing that suburbs outside the Metropolitan District were incapable of preserving adequate open space in the face of residential, commercial, and industrial development.[52] The MDC proposed creating new reservations in Braintree (at Great Pond, which abutted the Blue Hills Reservation) and Weymouth, but developers built housing on the targeted open space before it could be purchased. In an era marked by privatism, suburban communities showed little interest in creating significant public spaces.

Within its inner suburban communities, the MDC turned its attention to recreational facilities, building twenty-seven skating rinks and nineteen swimming pools between 1950 and 1975. The MDC built these facilities to accommodate baby-boom children.[53] Outside the MDC jurisdiction, growing suburbs built school athletic fields and playgrounds. Focusing on athletic facilities, Bostonians neglected the scenic beauty and natural attractions of parks. This was in line with park developments elsewhere in the country, as large urban parks almost everywhere, including Boston's Franklin Park, deteriorated. Parks suffered a precipitous decline from the late nineteenth and early twentieth centuries, when parks were the pride of their cities and park expenditures were generous. Many people came to believe that parks were a drain on taxes and that using parkland for development would expand the tax base. The MDC Commissioners, in their 1956 Plan, recognized that "The changing patterns of land use, and in particular the almost fantastic increases in land values in some localities, have created enormous pressures for the release of parklands to private ownership or their diversion to highways, to military use or for other public purposes."[54] After a decade-and-a-half of Depression and wartime stagnation, public opinion "favored development over open space."[55]

The biggest threat to parkland was highway construction. The increasing speed of automobiles created a demand for functional highway design that consumed wide swaths of land for rights-of-way that ranged from 200 to 300 feet. Highway construction chewed up city neighborhoods, open country, and even existing parks. The landscaped parkway designs, which predominated before World War II, were discarded in favor of highways that optimized traffic flow.[56] Harvard landscape architecture professor Norman T. Newton, in *Design on the Land: The Development of Landscape Architecture*, lamented: "All too often the reservations have been gouged out for the sake of highways, but this is only one manifestation of a still larger fault: utter obeisance to the automobile in administration of what was born as a park system. The focus is no longer on the parks themselves, but primarily on a series of highways—to call them parkways is in most cases fallacious."[57]

The most controversial loss of MDC parkland occurred in 1951 when Storrow Drive was carved out of the Charles River Reservation. A decade later, the state DPW plowed I-93 through the middle of the Middlesex Fells and the Mystic River Reservation. I-93 cut the Middlesex Fells in two, removing 100 acres of open space and increasing noise, air, water pollution, and visual blight.

The state missed a major opportunity to preserve open space in Boston's outer suburbs when the Bay Circuit was proposed. The Trustees of Reservations and regionalist Benton MacKaye proposed to the Governor's Committee on Needs and Uses of Open Spaces, in 1929, creating a greenbelt encircling Boston about twenty miles from the State House. MacKaye, a Shirley resident who was creating the Appalachian Trail at the time, proposed that the Bay Circuit should start on the north at Plum Island, in Newbury, and circle through preserved open spaces to the west of Boston and around to Duxbury on the south. It would provide an outer belt counterpart of open space to the Emerald Necklace and the metropolitan parks. The greenbelt would include state forests, water reservoirs, and privately managed nature preserves. The missing links would be filled in with strategic land acquisitions, usually undeveloped forests, farmland, or wetlands. A Bay Circuit Parkway would provide a greenbelt that would combine recreational and transportation functions while providing a "panorama of the countryside."[58]

Benton MacKaye believed that a well-designed Bay Circuit could help to conserve the countryside from being "metropolitan-ized" and "motor-slummed."[59] The Bay Circuit proposal anticipated the development pressures of the 1950s and provided a strategy for containing sprawl and creating a planned green landscape for Boston's outer suburbs, comparable to the Metropolitan District, but more rural in character.

The closest the Bay Circuit came to fruition before World War II occurred when it was part of the unsuccessful proposal to expand the metropolitan park system to eighty-six new communities in 1940.[60] In 1955, Charles W. Eliot II (nephew of Charles Eliot), a landscape architecture professor at Harvard, played an instrumental role in finally convincing the legislature to designate the Bay Circuit Trail. Lack of enabling legislation and funding, however, stymied the project. The state was reluctant to proceed with the Bay Circuit Parkway because it feared that, with the lack of appropriate zoning in local communities, "the Bay Circuit route could easily become lined with hot-dog stands and gasoline stations, thus destroying its whole purpose."[61]

The legislature, at the urging of Governor Michael Dukakis, finally allocated land acquisition funds for the Bay Circuit Trail in 1983. By this time, much of the prime open space that was originally targeted had been developed. The Bay Circuit became a hiking trail through preserved open space, some of it publicly owned and some private. There was not enough land to create a parkway or enough political will to provide coordinated management. The trail received a valuable impetus in 1990, when the Bay Circuit Alliance was formed to coordinate land purchases and conservation easements. Fortunately, a patchwork of open spaces existed in a circumference about twenty miles from Boston. They included state parks and forests, Massachusetts Audubon nature sanctuaries, properties of the Trustees of Reservations, Boy and Girl Scouts reservations, and town and local land trust conservation areas. It became apparent that almost three-quarters of the Bay Circuit Trail could be created by routing it through these conservation lands and the remainder could be pieced together by new acquisitions and land easements.

Today, almost the entire 200 miles of the Bay Circuit Trail have been preserved, with the largest remaining gaps being located in Southeastern Massachusetts. Because of the geographic dispersal (thirty-eight communities) and number of separately owned properties (eighty-five), the Bay Circuit is not the cohesively planned entity proposed before World War II, but, remarkably, it does provide a de facto Greater Boston greenbelt. The big drawback has been the lack of coordinated management and publicity. That is changing, however, as the Trustees of Reservations and the Appalachian Mountain Club are assuming responsibilities for management, public outreach, and trail maintenance. Because of these efforts, the Bay Circuit Trail preserves "the illusion of wilderness" for Boston's outer suburbs, as the *Boston Globe's* Sam Nejame has observed.[62]

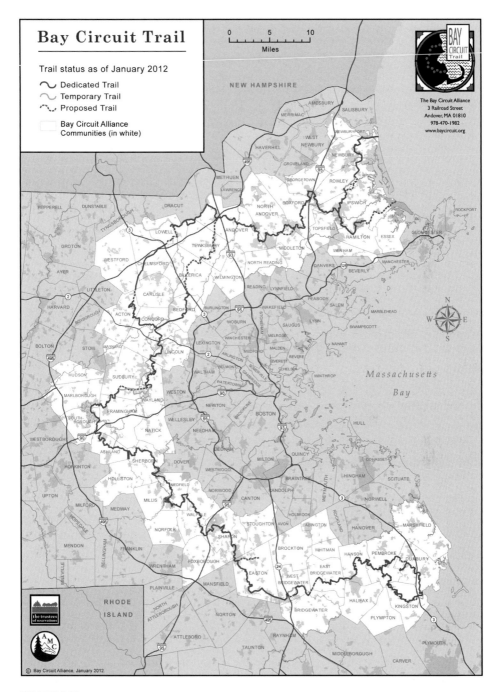

FIGURE 8.12

Bay Circuit Trail map. Benton MacKaye proposed a greenway encircling Boston's suburbs in 1929, but it did not begin to come together until the 1980s. Today, the 200-mile Bay Circuit Trail passes through thirty-eight communities, from Newbury in the north to Southborough in the west to Duxbury in the south. *Source:* Bay Circuit Alliance, Inc.

The Role of Zoning and Land Conservation

In the mid-1960s, historian Walter Muir Whitehill observed that the postwar rush to the suburbs was destroying much of the countryside:

> "Ranches," "Capes," and "splits" mushroomed speculatively where there had been market gardens, pastures, and pleasant woods, thus almost instantly eliminating the country that the migrants sought. . . . The automobile, with its attendant acolytes of traffic engineers and real estate speculators, in the single decade of the nineteen fifties all but accomplished the ruination of both city and country in Eastern Massachusetts.[63]

The spoliation of the countryside spurred suburban communities to adopt zoning to protect their historic character. In the 1920s, the suburban communities that adopted the first zoning regulations sought to separate residences from shopping, offices, and industry and limit two- and three-family houses and apartment buildings. Lot size requirements for single-family houses were fairly modest in Arlington, Milton, and Winchester. Postwar suburbs outside the MDC required increasingly larger house lots in an effort to preserve rural character. In many subdivisions, zoning did not produce a country atmosphere because there were few areas of protected open space. Wealthier suburban communities were more successful in preserving the rural character. Mandating large lot sizes forced homes to be a certain size and cost, thus reinforcing the community's class orientation.

This has been especially true in the cluster of affluent communities west of Boston. In 1951, the year Route 128 was opened, Lexington doubled the size of house lots in outlying areas from 15,500 square feet to 30,000 square feet. Feelings ran high against development spun off by Route 128. A 1953 ad in *Lexington Minuteman* called for reducing development opportunities further:

> DANGER! <u>LEXINGTON</u> IS BEING <u>EXPLOITED</u>! DO YOU WANT TO RETAIN AS LONG AS POSSIBLE THE RURAL ATMOSPHERE OF LEXINGTON? VOTE YES ON THE ZONING AMENDMENT . . . DO YOU WANT TO AVOID THE CITY ATMOSPHERE WITH ACCOMPANYING HEAVY STREET CONGESTION? VOTE YES ON THE ZONING AMENDMENT![64]

In a similar vein, Weston's Board of Selectmen expressed alarm, in 1952, about the avalanche of development they feared was coming: "Of the many problems that have confronted the town in the past year, the most important can be described in one word, 'GROWTH'—more houses, more families—more children, more roads, more school facilities, more public services and—more and heavier taxes."[65] These sentiments reflected Weston's longtime concerns about limiting growth.

The town's first zoning bylaw (1928) had created single-residence, general-residence, business, and industrial districts but placed almost the entire town in the single-residence district. This district had a minimum lot size of 10,000 square feet (almost a quarter acre). Within six years, town meeting increased the minimum lot size to 15,000 square feet. Two years later, Weston, divided the single-residence zone into three classes, with minimum lot sizes of 20,000, 30,000, and 40,000 square feet. To little surprise, the great majority of the town's landscape was zoned for 40,000-square foot lots. With the postwar boom along Route 128, Weston undertook its last increase in lot sizes, in 1954. The town created classes of 30,000-, 40,000-, and 60,000-square foot lots, with the largest amount of remaining open space being required to have 60,000-square-foot lots. Similar zoning methods for protecting the community's character were adopted by other affluent towns.[66]

In contrast with restrictive zoning initiatives in Weston and Lexington and other upscale communities, Framingham resisted restrictive zone changes that might exclude the middle class. When neighbors advocated zone changes to limit development on the Pinewood Golf Club in 1954, the planning board resisted, stating: "'Framingham does not want to exclude the working man, and the young couples who want a home. . . . All of the Planning Board members are fathers and we are reluctant to recommend a zoning program that makes it too expensive for their own children to build their home in Framingham.'"[67] As a result of its welcoming approach to development, Framingham built middle-class and lower-middle-class subdivisions.

As a complementary strategy to zoning, many suburbs initiated efforts to conserve open space so it could not be built upon. Once again, the affluent suburbs west of Boston led the way. Wayland sought to control land uses by conserving open land. The Wayland Planning Board determined, in 1945, that: "The town of Wayland is facing an era of unprecedented development. . . . What the townspeople can do is to try to guide this growth, so as to retain the village atmosphere and the charm of the ponds, rivers, woods, farms, and natural features, while fitting into the environment the new neighbors who hope to join us." In 1953, several Wayland citizens helped establish the Sudbury Valley Trustees to preserve open space and protect wildlife in the Sudbury, Assabet, and Concord River Basin. In its first decade, the Sudbury

Valley Trustees bought thirty-two parcels with 525 acres, much of it old farmland. Such land conservation was a significant innovation because, at this time, virtually no private organizations existed for conserving land.[68]

Elsewhere in the region communities acquired conservations lands. The Commonwealth of Massachusetts chipped in to help municipalities preserve open space for natural resource and passive recreation purposes with the Self-Help Land Acquisition Program. Between 1961 and 1975, the state provided funding for acquiring 17,405 acres in 121 projects. Some of the leading beneficiaries were Carlisle, Concord, Lexington, and Lincoln. Since this program required a local match, the communities that took advantage of it were fairly well off. Less wealthy and urban communities tended not to use the Self-Help program.[69]

Communities along the Concord and Sudbury Rivers strategically engaged the federal government to establish the Great Meadows National Wildlife Refuge along those waterways. In 1944, Samuel Hoar, of Concord's politically eminent Hoar family, donated a 250-acre stretch of Concord River wetlands to the US Fish and Wildlife Service. A significant bird sanctuary, the Great Meadows Wildlife Refuge, has grown to over 3,800 acres.

Besides protecting their natural environment, suburban towns sought to preserve their historic character. In 1913, a *Boston Evening Transcript* feature on suburban development noted of Lexington and Concord: "Proud of their wealth of history and jealous of their well-earned reputations as model and righteous communities, they have been cautious as to their residential development." Even where new residential development did take place, Lexington encouraged historical revival styles.[70] In 1925, landscape architect Arthur Shurcliff observed that the landscape along the historic Battle Road, which stretched five miles through Lexington, Lincoln, and Concord, was "'part of a quiet countryside, not unlike that of the early days.'"[71] In order to preserve that landscape, Shurcliff recommended measures which resulted in the creation of a national park.

In 1958, a federal report found that growth was rapidly transforming the rural appearance of the Battle Road and that a National Park should be established to preserve the historic route. A year later Congress designated Minute Man National Historical Park to preserve the Battle Road. The area around the Old North Bridge in Concord and historic homes of authors Nathaniel Hawthorne and Louisa May Alcott were also included in the park. The Town of Lexington initiated its own preservation efforts in 1956, when it established its first historic districts to control demolition and the exterior appearance of buildings, one of the earliest preservation programs in the state.

One of the foremost communities in taking a comprehensive approach to protecting its landscape was Lincoln. The town became one of the first to adopt zoning. During the late 1920s, when developers proposed subdivisions that would create relatively dense housing, the town adopted a zoning code that required that single-family homes be built on minimum 10,000-square-foot lots. Lincoln's Zoning Committee explained its action: "That purpose [of the zoning bylaw] is to keep Lincoln the same type of community which it now is. Normal growth is both desirable and welcome, but it should be of such a character that it will not harm one single home of Lincoln."[72]

During the early 1930s, when the Massachusetts Department of Public Works was planning Route 2, it intended to route the highway through Lincoln and Concord Centers, but the town officials successfully resisted. Route 2 was built across the northern edge of Lincoln and the southern end of Concord. After the four-lane highway was completed, development pressures increased and Lincoln raised its zoning in 1936 to almost an acre (40,000 square feet) per single-family house.[73] Postwar growth spurred by Route 128 pushed Lincoln to become the first Massachusetts community to require 80,000-square-foot lots, in 1955.

Despite zoning controls, Lincoln residents felt that to preserve their rural community they needed to permanently preserve open space. The Lincoln Land Conservation Trust (1957) accumulated hundreds of acres of natural areas and created sixty miles of hiking trails. The municipal Conservation Commission (1959) made comparable land acquisitions and protected wetlands. As a result of various land donations, conservation restrictions, deed covenants, and agricultural preservation restrictions, Lincoln has been able to preserve 40 percent of its land as open space, making the homeowners on the remaining land truly feel as if they are living in the country, not in a suburb directly abutting Route 128.

The effectiveness of Lincoln's strategic planning is particularly evident in the work of the Rural Land Foundation (1965), which, in the 1970s, acquired seventy-two acres of farmland near the town center. The foundation preserved fifty-five acres as open space and developed the remainder for low- and moderate-income housing and the modest Mall at Lincoln Square (which is only one of three small commercially zoned areas in Lincoln). The Rural Land Foundation has used the revenue from the mall to conserve additional open space.

Lincoln's strategic planning approach has also led to affordable housing, to comply with state regulations intended to curb the practice of using zoning to exclude lower classes. By the late 1960s, it was apparent that many suburbs were using zoning to exclude lower-income, usually black, families. To address this problem, the Massachusetts legislature, in 1969, passed an "anti-snob zoning" law referred to as either the Comprehensive Permit Act or Chapter 40B. Chapter 40B requires that at least 10 percent of the housing stock of each community should be "affordable." Under this policy, a housing unit, whose "affordability" is subsidized for the long term, can be bought or rented by a household earning up to 80 percent of the local median income. If less than 10 percent of a community's housing stock fails to meet these guidelines, the state allows developers of affordable housing to circumvent local zoning. As the *Boston Globe* has stated, "the anti-development urge in many towns cannot be overcome without some mechanism for reconsideration of rejected proposals—a mechanism that 40B provides."[74]

Approximately fifty Massachusetts communities—and Lincoln is one of them—have 10 percent of their housing considered "affordable." Lincoln citizens have made the calculation that it makes more sense for the town to decide where affordable housing should be located than leaving it up to private developers. A notable Lincoln multiple-unit housing project is Battle Road Farm, which has 120 mixed-income units in a village-like landscape. Noted architect William Rawn designed the housing, and landscape architect Michael van Valkenburgh designed the grounds.

Statewide, Chapter 40B has led to the production of approximately 58,000 housing units for working and middle-class families and senior citizens over a forty-year period.[75] Because it subverts local zoning and promotes social diversity, Chapter 40B has angered some communities that feel they have had dense affordable housing forced upon them. Yet, in 2010, the electorate voted in a statewide referendum to maintain the Chapter 40B out of a concern for maintaining "affordable" housing.

Greater Boston's affordable housing predicament spotlights the locally-based planning paradigm that prevails in the region. Home rule drives land-use planning. Although the state sets goals for housing, economic development, and natural resource conservation, local communities can undercut them. There are no regional land use controls, with the Metropolitan Area Planning Council (MAPC) having only an advisory planning role. Compared with the nation's leading metropolitan areas, many of which have strong county government, Greater Boston's regional capacity is scant and local interests predominate.

Exploring Post–World War II Suburbs

Gropius House, 68 Baker Bridge Road, Lincoln

People do not always think of Boston as being on the cutting edge of Modern architecture in America, but it was. The foremost leader was Walter Gropius, of Germany's Bauhaus school, who came here to teach at Harvard's Graduate School of Design. The Gropius House (1938), in Lincoln, was one of the region's first Modernist houses. The flat-roofed, white clapboard box was designed for maximum efficiency, yet it emanates simple beauty. Americans dabbled in Bauhaus design but gradually retreated to the safety of the Colonial Revival house and the Cape Cod cottage. The house is owned by Historic New England and is open to the public year-round. It is furnished with Bauhaus-style furniture designed by Marcel Breuer, who built his own Modernist house nearby. Despite the house's machine-like quality, it harmonizes with the rolling landscape surrounding it.

Snake Hill Road, Belmont

In 1945, *Progressive Architecture* called the Snake Hill Modernist houses "one of the best known and most significant groups of contemporary houses in the world." Carl Koch, who had trained with Walter Gropius and Marcel Breuer, built these nine houses between 1940 and 1946. The single-story, wood-frame houses blend into the trees and the rocky hillside. Koch's own home was at 77 Snake Hill Road.

Six Moon Hill, Moon Hill Road, Lexington

Between 1945 and the 1960s, nine Modernist neighborhoods were developed in Lexington. The first was Six Moon Hill (1948), which architect David Fixler has called "the gold standard for the Modern suburban neighborhood in terms of planning and architectural quality."[76] All but two of the thirty homes were designed by members of The Architects Collaborative (TAC). The flat-roofed houses have vertical redwood or cypress siding and ample glass. They are nestled between trees and shrubbery. An important feature of this development is the community room and open space designed to foster a strong community spirit.

Isadore and Lucille Zimmerman House, 223 Heather Street, Manchester, New Hampshire

The Zimmerman House (1950) is Frank Lloyd Wright's only Usonian-style house in New England. It can be visited only by reservation, which can be made through Manchester's Currier Museum of Art. It is more high-end than the typical postwar single-floor home, since Wright also designed the interiors, furniture, gardens, and even the mailbox.

Oak Hill Park, Wiswall and Spiers Roads, off Baker Road, Newton

Oak Hill Park (1949) originally had 412 single-family homes built by the City of Newton for returning war veterans. Although many homeowners have made modifications to the houses, Oak Hill Park still provides a sense of what postwar housing subdivisions looked like. The houses south of Saw Mill Brook Parkway have maintained their orientation toward a network of footpaths.

Hancock Village, Gerry Road, Independence Drive, Sherman Road, Thornton Road, Brookline and Boston

Hancock Village (1948), which is listed on the National Register of Historic Places, is an example of garden village housing. The model was adopted for public housing in some cities and postwar suburbs. John Hancock Mutual Life Insurance Company developed the 789-unit garden village on the Weld Golf Course. Two-story townhouses built in a stripped-down postwar traditional style are arrayed in fifty-seven buildings situated around grassy courtyards. An adjacent strip shopping center is located on the VFW Parkway in Boston. Two architectural firms worked on the plans—Boston's Perry, Shaw, and Hepburn and the Washington, D.C. firm of Louis Justement and Francis Koenig. The Olmsted Brothers firm, of Brookline, prepared the landscape design.

Cape Cod and Colonial Revival Houses, Wellington Estates, Constitution Road, Revolutionary Road, Paul Revere Road, Lexington

Lexington, which is notable for its collection of Modern houses, also has many neo-traditional Cape Cod and Colonial houses. The Wellington Estates district, developed in the late 1940s, is full such houses, designed by Royal Barry Wills, perhaps the leading designer of these styles nationally during the postwar era. Comparable Capes and Colonials can be found in many postwar neighborhoods across the region.

Campanelli Brothers Ranch Houses, Streets off Elm Street, Framingham

There are thousands of streets throughout Greater Boston that are lined with ranch and split-level houses from the 1950s and 1960s. A majority of them are located in communities along Route 128 and the Massachusetts Turnpike, towns like Bedford, Braintree, Burlington, Canton, Dedham, Lynnfield, Needham, Norwood, Wakefield, and Wilmington. The Campanelli Brothers built some of the most extensive subdivisions around Saxonville, on the north side of Framingham. Off Pinewood Drive, Griffin Road, and adjacent side streets there are scores of one-story ranch houses. Several basic styles are repeated from street to street. The houses are over fifty years old now and have lost their original feeling of being modern. Many of the houses have been updated with family rooms, dormers, and Palladian windows. Where one spies a two-story house in this neighborhood, it is usually a "tear down" of an aging ranch. There is an adage that architecture is least appreciated fifty to seventy-five years after its construction. That is the period when it is most prone to alteration or demolition. Historic styles are rediscovered once they are being lost. This is an important phenomenon to contemplate while exploring 1950s and 1960s subdivisions.

Battle Road Farm, Old Bedford Road, Lincoln

In carefully planning its buildout, Lincoln has made sure that 10 percent of its housing stock is "affordable," thus meeting the state's mandated threshold. Battle Road Farm (1991) was planned specifically to help the town achieve its affordable housing goal. The development has 120 mixed-income units in a village-like landscape nestled between Minute Man National Historical Park and Hanscom Air Force Base. The semi-attached houses, which resemble either New England farmhouses or turn-of-the-century carriage houses, were designed by architect William Rawn. The landscape was designed by Michael van Valkenburgh. This is an early work of two nationally distinguished designers.

Route 128 (I-95), from Exit 12, Canton, to I-93 at Exit 36, Reading

This is the most developed stretch of Route 128, where "America's Technology Highway" got its name. You can take almost any exit and find an office park. Try driving on a Sunday morning when the traffic is light and you can rubberneck a bit.

New England Business Center, Highland Street at Exit 19A, Route 128, Needham

Gerald Blakely of Cabot, Cabot, & Forbes started the first suburban industrial park in Greater Boston off Route 128 in 1948 just as the highway was being built. The utilitarian industrial park was originally called New England Industrial Center, but the name has been changed to reflect the evolution of many industrial and warehouse parks to office parks. Unlike later business parks that included a lot of green space, this business park was built on a grid of shoulder-to-shoulder buildings. Visitors can obtain a sense of the original park layout on First Avenue, which parallels the highway. Keeping up with the mixed-use development approach of the present day, the business park has a new apartment building at the rear called Charles River Landing.

Waltham Business Parks, Winter Street, Exit 27, Route 128, Waltham

This area hosts some leading Route 128 corporations in a setting designed during the 1990s to be more park-like than earlier "industrial parks." Waltham Woods Corporate Center, 840–870 Winter Street, is a landscaped campus overlooking the Cambridge Reservoir. With 70 percent tree cover, it includes Raytheon Global Headquarters; Health Point, where the Boston Celtics practice; and Massachusetts Medical Society, which publishes the *New England Journal of Medicine*. One reason these corporate offices exist here is the proximity to Weston and Lincoln, where many executives live. Bay Colony Corporate Center, at 950–1100 Winter Street, boasts of award-winning landscaping by Sasaki Associates.

Digital Equipment Corporation, Intersection of Main Street (Route 62) and Great Road (Route 117), Maynard

The Mill in Maynard is a perfect example of the economic transition from textiles to high tech. From 1847 until 1950, the Mill manufactured woolen textiles and employed 2,000 workers during World War II. It closed in 1950, and the building was leased out to small businessmen. In 1957, Ken Olsen and partners started Digital here. Eventually, the corporation used the entire mill complex as its headquarters. During the 1990s, Digital struggled to compete and was bought out by Compaq in 1998. Now, the Mill is called Clock Tower Place and houses such enterprises as the job search firm Monster.com.

Shoppers' World Site, Shoppers' World Drive and Route 9, Framingham

Just over the border from Natick there is a sign for "Shoppers' World." You enter and find a rectangular shopping center of category killers that include Toys"R"Us, Office Depot, and Sports Authority. There is a huge parking lot in the middle. Gone is the streamlined 1950s Shoppers' World, which was demolished in 1994. The eight lanes of Route 9 provide one of the region's most intense traffic experiences. West of the strip on steroids is a lower-intensity strip of smaller buildings, including houses converted for commercial use.

Natick Mall, Route 9 at Speen Street, Natick

Just east of Shoppers' World is the Natick Mall, which replaced the original Shoppers' World as the premier shopping destination on this stretch of Route 9. A 2006–2009 redesign gives the mall some flash. In seeking to rebrand the shopping mall, owner General Growth Properties sought to rename it simply "Natick." This was too much for town meeting, and its members voted a resolution in opposition, saying that the regional mall could not just name itself "Natick." The real-estate company withdrew its proposal and renamed the mall "Natick Collection." This name was too precious and never stuck, so the mall returned to its original appellation in 2011. The most unusual aspect of the redevelopment is the 215-unit condominium building that flanks the mall. It is an effort to mix uses and create greater density.

Like the Natick Collection, the South Shore Plaza in Braintree, Burlington Mall, and the North Shore Mall in Peabody, have undergone major renovation and expansion since the construction, so it is difficult to still experience what enclosed shopping malls were like in the 1960s.

Route 1, between Malden and Lynnfield, Saugus

This four-mile commercial strip retains some of the roadside funkiness from the 1960s. The most celebrated landmark is the Hilltop Steak House, distinguished by its plastic cactus and cows. Weylu's Restaurant, the Kowloon, Prince Pizzeria, Ship's Wharf (formerly The Ship Restaurant), and the Christmas Tree Shops add to the high kitsch. Other strips in the region have been homogenized by national chains and have lost most of their local quirkiness.

Bay Circuit Trail

The Bay Circuit Trail can be considered an outer greenbelt counterpart to the Metropolitan Park System that was established in 1893. The Bay Circuit was first proposed in 1929, but the state did not start implementing the proposal until 1983. Only during the past two decades has the trail come together. It is a postmodern pastiche (in comparison with the comprehensively planned Metropolitan Parks) of state parks, town conservation lands, Massachusetts Audubon Society nature sanctuaries, properties owned by the Trustees of Reservations, and other private land trusts. The eighty-five-plus parcels that make up the Bay Circuit Trail offer a fascinating variety of hills, forest, grasslands, wetlands, and other open spaces. The best way to learn about the Bay Circuit Trail is through the website http://www.baycircuit.org.

Rewarding Bay Circuit Trail experiences await at:

Ward Reservation, off Prospect Street, Andover

Holt Hill, at 420-feet, is the highest point on the Bay Circuit Trail. You can see the Boston skyline over twenty miles to the south. The intervening landscape looks like a forest, which conceals the region's buildings. This view provides a sense of the extensive geographic reach of metropolitan Boston. Managed by the Trustees of Reservations.

Tippling Rock, in Nobscot Boy Scout Reservation, top of Brimstone Lane, off Route 20, Sudbury

Pleasant woodsy walk and a view of metropolitan Boston from the west.

Moose Hill Farm, Massachusetts Audubon Sanctuary, 396 Moose Hill Street, Sharon

The view from the top of Moose Hill takes in downtown Boston and nearby Gillette Stadium in Foxborough.

Cranberry Watershed Preserve, behind Silver Lake Regional High School, Kingston

Along the Jones River, this preserve, owned by the Town of Kingston, includes 270 acres of upland and twenty-two acres of cranberry bogs. Abutting along the Jones River is the Hathaway Preserve. A great place to experience the wetlands of Southeastern Massachusetts.

9

Boston Redefines the Center City (1945–2012)

Urban Decline

During the post–World War II era, the city of Boston reached a low ebb vis-àa-vis the suburbs. The suburban tide seemed inexorable and urban decay endemic. Boston was forced to take stock of its weakened condition and decided to launch a series of revitalization initiatives. The issue remained in doubt for many years, but Boston ultimately reinvigorated its role as metropolitan hub. The city pioneered several planning paradigms—urban renewal, Modernist architecture, historic preservation, waterfront reclamation, greenways, curbing highway construction, and supporting public transit. The city and state undertook major planning and infrastructure initiatives, while tens of thousands of individuals and businesses made investments in Boston. They rehabilitated historic structures and opened a host of businesses. By the 1990s, American cities became fashionable again, and Boston was in the forefront. Its decline and rebirth has been a classic urban story.

During the late nineteenth and early twentieth centuries, Boston was a city with a complicated reputation. On one hand, Boston was at the cutting edge of what it meant to be a city in America. Boston pioneered the public school, the commercial bank, the Visiting Nurse Association, countless medical advances, Alexander Graham Bell's telephone, the subway, professional baseball, and mutual funds, as well as suburbia. Boston was prosperous, and, as late as 1929, it had the highest per capita retail sales in the nation, the highest blue-collar wages, the third most wholesale trade, and the fourth most banking assets.[1]

Yet, Boston could seem more antiquated than other American cities. By the early twentieth century, its economy was stagnating. Jane Jacobs, in *Cities and the Wealth of Nations* (1984), explained Boston's economic decline: "The old textile, shoe and railroad fortunes were tied up in routinely invested trusts, the city as a whole had become an exporter of capital, not a place in which capital was being put to work to compensate for the losses nor replacing wide ranges of its current imports."[2] Boston's conservative attachment to its past carried over from economic activity to the local culture. Brahmins under siege by the influx of immigrants made a cult of the city's historical heyday, a nostalgic perspective that handicapped its economic and cultural development in the face of the future-oriented dynamism of New York and other cities.

Boston's backward-looking quality did not help as it tried to modernize and compete with the suburbs. Like other central cities, Boston struggled to maintain a viable economy in the face of dramatic change. Suburban flight, which started in the 1850s, picked up momentum in the late nineteenth century, as immigrants streamed into the city. Because there was no zoning, any kind of industry or noxious use could pop up near a residential neighborhood. The city's aged and densely built housing stock was inadequate to provide the desired standard of living for the rising middle class. The South End, which started as a prestigious neighborhood similar to Back Bay, saw its townhouses turn into boardinghouses during the 1870s. By 1890, the neighborhood housed immigrants and African-Americans. Back Bay was the preeminent residential district until the 1920s, when wealthy families lost interest in living in the city and sought out spacious homes in garden suburbs. The last Back Bay townhouse was built in 1917. The growth of shops and offices on Newbury and Boylston Streets and the transformation of townhouses into boardinghouses led Back Bay to be dubbed a "potential slum" by 1935.[3]

The Depression brought on a slump in real-estate values that persisted for decades. Between 1930 and 1939, the assessed valuation of taxable property in Boston declined from $2 billion to $1.52 billion. By 1951, the assessed valuation was still only $1.57 billion (partly because of faulty assessment practices). Between 1937 and 1951, municipal expenditures rose from $80 million to $132 million. The city's tax rate became the highest and its bond rating became the lowest of the country's large cities.[4] Between 1930 and 1960, there was scant investment in Boston. Boston lacked skyscrapers because of little business growth. The insurance industry was an exception. The New England Life Building (1942) and the first John Hancock Building (1947), in the Back Bay, were only major buildings erected during these decades. In the meantime, New York's skyline was astonishing the world.

Some of the reluctance to invest stemmed from the conflict between the Yankee-dominated business community and the Irish-oriented City Hall, which was especially contentious when James Michael Curley was mayor. Curley's City Hall was charged with waste, corruption, and destructively high commercial property assessments. There was also deep mistrust between City Hall and the Republican-dominated state government, and Boston found it difficult to obtain state assistance in tackling its problems.

FIGURE 9.1
Scollay Square, Boston, 1954-1959. This scene is typical of much of central Boston during the fifties, from the West End and Scollay Square to the South End and Roxbury. Boston's deteriorated cityscape drove thousands to the beckoning suburbs and instigated slum clearance and urban renewal.
Source: © Massachusetts Institute of Technology, Courtesy of MIT Libraries, Rotch Visual Collections; Photograph by Nishan Bichajian.

The physical decay and poverty of the central city frightened investors. Uncompetitive industries closed down, and new technology industries located in the suburbs. Boston's port was half abandoned. Planners labeled neighborhoods such as the West End, North End, South End, Charlestown, and Roxbury slums. The blighted buildings seemed beyond redemption, so banks redlined investment in many neighborhoods, reinforcing a downward spiral. Scollay Square, just around the corner from the State House, offered burlesque shows at the Old Howard Theater, tattoo parlors, flophouses, and dive bars. The Washington Street shopping district, which had been Boston's great magnet of attraction, gradually lost customers to suburban shopping centers, while the great movie palaces went dark or were converted into porno theaters. Aging Northeast cities never looked so undesirable compared to the glamour of Sunbelt destinations like California.

Meanwhile, the urban landscape was being torn apart to make it easier to drive through town. Entire neighborhoods were cleared for highways, and downtown buildings were demolished to create parking lots. The highway routes cleared for the Central Artery, Massachusetts Turnpike, Southeast Expressway, and the Inner Belt route that was never built destroyed neighborhoods and the city's walkability. The highway-oriented landscape reinforced the primacy of mobility and undermined the viability of urban life.

Boston's very soul seemed sick. Writers sketched Boston as a decaying city. Edwin O'Connor's *The Last Hurrah* (1956) portrayed the "red brick city" whose machine-style politics—patterned on James Michael Curley—was entertaining but parochial and anachronistic. John P. Marquand's *The Late George Apley* (1937) satirized insular Brahmins stuck in the past.

Elizabeth Hardwick's essay "Boston" (1959), published in *Harper's Magazine*, was particularly harsh. Hardwick pilloried Boston for its "lowly image, a sort of farce of conservative exclusiveness and snobbish humor." She excoriated "the dying downtown shopping section" and "feckless, ugly, municipal neglect." Hardwick summed up the sentiment of many critics: "The weight of the Boston legend, the tedium of its largely fraudulent posture of traditionalism, the disillusionment of the Boston present as a cultural force make quick minds hesitate to embrace a region too deeply compromised."[5]

After peaking in 1950 at 801,444, Boston's population dropped from 801,444 to 562,994 in 1980. The loss of downtown's prestige, physical decay, racial strife, and increasing crime drove people by the tens of thousands to the suburbs. The flight of the middle class sapped Boston's socioeconomic health and its civic cohesiveness.

Urban Renewal

From the abyss, Boston launched a recovery that makes the dark days of the 1950s seem impossible to comprehend. Thomas H. O'Connor's *Building a New Boston: Politics and Urban Renewal, 1950–1970* argues that the turnaround started with the 1949 mayoral victory of John B. Hynes (1950–1960) over James Michael Curley. Although the city suffered demographic and economic decline during Hynes's term, he began to restore fiscal probity and cooperation with the business community. The Hynes administration demonstrated energy by initiating the Boston Redevelopment Authority, Central Artery, Columbia Point public housing, and the Prudential Center. The administration also made its share of strategic mistakes.

The Planning Board's *General Plan for Boston* (1950) called for demolishing and redeveloping 20 percent, or 2,700 acres, of the city's land area. This plan spurred the West End urban renewal project, which displaced over 7,000 residents in the neighborhood around the Massachusetts General Hospital and the Boston Garden between 1958 and 1960. Sociologist Herbert Gans, who chronicled the demise of the West End in *The Urban Villagers*, claimed that Boston pursued wholesale urban demolition because it was considered a "poor city" desperately in need of gleaming new buildings. Gans argued, however, that, despite its aging buildings, residents still considered the West End "a good place to live."[6] The dislocated residents and the general public considered the destruction of the West End to be a catastrophe.

Race also was a factor in urban renewal. Most of Boston's African American population lived in the South End and Roxbury. These older neighborhoods had much substandard housing and were considered slums. The city was aggressive in clearing these areas. Many African American families were relocated to public housing projects in those neighborhoods as well as to Columbia Point on the Dorchester waterfront. Critics who protested the injustice of these actions said urban renewal was really "Negro removal."[7]

Urban renewal projects were driven by the availability of federal funding during the 1950s and 1960s. Starting with Title One of the Housing Act of 1949, the federal government paid two-thirds and local government paid one-third of the cost of acquiring properties that were considered "slums and blight."[8] After clearance, these sites were made available to private developers to build residential or commercial structures. About one-third of Boston's historic core was demolished for urban renewal or highway projects during this period.

Contemporary Bostonians excoriate the destruction of urban renewal, but Boston had to take some measures to ease automobile movement through the windy warren of streets. The problem was that the city used the bulldozer rather than a surgical scalpel to modernize the urban landscape—but that happened everywhere during the 1950s and 1960s. The conventional thinking was that cars had to be accommodated, regardless of the harm done to the urban fabric, local businesses, pedestrians, or public transit.

Under Hynes's successor John F. Collins (1960–1968) and his Boston Redevelopment Authority (BRA) Development Administrator Edward J. Logue, Boston embarked on the urban renewal project at Government Center (replacing tawdry Scollay Square), planned the revitalization of the waterfront, and spurred the development of office skyscrapers. Collins and Logue brought competence and dynamism to city planning and captured a disproportionate share of federal dollars. The Brutalist concrete architecture of Kallman, McKinnell and Knowles's City Hall (1968) became a vivid symbol of Boston's ambition to move to the forefront of modernism. The urban renewal projects of the 1960s, which are criticized today for their sterility and disruption of the pedestrian urban scale, nevertheless generated civic pride in Boston.

Demonstrating optimism about Boston's direction, historian Walter Muir Whitehill wrote a volume in the "Centers of Civilization Series" titled *Boston in the Age of John Fitzgerald Kennedy*. Whitehill observed: "Thanks to changes in the political climate, national and local, Boston began in the nineteen sixties to seem a better and more hopeful place to live in than it had for some decades."[9] The buzz grew when the "Impossible Dream" Red Sox of 1967 injected an enthusiasm for experiencing Boston that had been missing for decades. The darkest days for Boston and for baseball had occurred when the Boston Braves moved to Milwaukee in 1953 and the Red Sox fell into irrelevancy. The resurgence of baseball at Fenway Park paralleled the revival of the city. The highways that had been drawing residents out to suburbia carried enthusiastic thousands back for sporting events.

Mayor Kevin White (1968–1984) brought the work of Collins and Logue to fruition with a flurry of development. The most effective project was Quincy Market, the 1826 wholesale food market that morphed into the nation's first festival marketplace under the guiding hands of Mayor White, architect Benjamin Thompson, and developer James Rouse. Quincy Market, opened for the Bicentennial in 1976, was a revolutionary combination of historic preservation, food court, boutiques, vendor carts, and buskers. Quincy Market became so popular that it attracted more annual visitors than Disney World.

FIGURE 9.2
City Hall, Boston, ca. 1968. Designed by Kallmann, McKinnell and Knowles, City Hall was a Modernist symbol of Boston's resurgence. It was part of the Government Center urban renewal project that replaced tawdry Scollay Square.
Source: Courtesy of the Boston Public Library, Print Department.

The Quincy Market project played a major role in spurring the historic preservation movement. During the 1950s and 1960s, scores of historic landmarks were lost to urban renewal. Yet the basic idea of preservation was taking hold with the introduction of the "Freedom Trail," which was proposed by *Boston Evening Traveler* columnist Bill Schofield in 1951. Connecting Boston Common with the North End and Charlestown, the Freedom Trail is considered the world's first heritage trail.[10] During the 1970s and the Bicentennial, the enthusiasm for preservation led to the rediscovery of historic architecture and urban landscape of Beacon Hill, Back Bay, the South End, and other neighborhoods. From these efforts emerged a residential revival in historic neighborhoods and a dramatic rise in real-estate values.

As part of his Bicentennial public works, White inaugurated the Christopher Columbus Park, the first public park on the harbor front in both Boston and the nation. This initiative followed up on the opening of the New England Aquarium on the harbor in 1968 and the rehabilitation of historic warehouses on Commercial, Lewis, and Mercantile Wharves. These efforts transformed the way cities thought about their waterfronts.

A major boost for Boston's image came from the July Fourth Bicentennial Boston Pops concert on the Charles River Esplanade. (The first July Fourth Pops Esplanade concert had been held two years earlier.) This concert attracted 600,000 for fireworks and Tchaikovsky's "1812 Overture." The annual Esplanade Independence Day celebration opened the eyes of suburbanites to the pleasures of Boston's parks and public events. The event has even achieved national attention and continues to be broadcast on network television.

Even though Boston's revitalization efforts turned the corner during the 1970s, it was not totally apparent at the time. Boston remained gritty, and increasing crime scared many away. The city suffered rising tensions between whites and blacks, epitomized by the busing crisis of the mid-1970s, when whites in South Boston, Charleston, and Dorchester resisted efforts to bus blacks from Roxbury to their neighborhood schools. These events exacerbated suburban flight. The 1970s were also a period of comparatively high unemployment and decline in both traditional industries and the defense industry that flourished along Route 128. Boston still had a down-at-the-heels side, which was portrayed in the George V. Higgins novel and film *The Friends of Eddie Coyle* (1972). A Brookings Institution study ranked Boston one of the country's most decayed cities because of high unemployment, declining per capita income, and substandard housing. On an urban distress scale from -5 to +5, Boston earned a -5 score.[11] During the 1970s, Boston's population declined from 641,071 to 562,994, its biggest decadal percentage decrease. Even the metropolitan area lost population.

FIGURE 9.3
Quincy Market, Boston. The rehabilitation of Quincy Market for the 1976 Bicentennial not only marked a new trend in tourism and downtown retail but also helped spur the historic preservation movement. The complex is currently referred to as the Faneuil Hall Marketplace.
Source: © 1977 Steve Rosenthal.

FIGURE 9.4
Row houses, South End. Most of the row houses of the South End were built between the 1850s and the 1870s. They were intended to be middle-class housing, but they turned into houses for the working class. In the 1970s, historic preservation promoted gentrification of the neighborhood.
Source: Andrew McFarland.

But major policy decisions were being made that would support Boston's long-term turnaround. Boston's urban core was strengthened by transportation policy decisions that other cities did not make. After decades of highway building and gutting urban neighborhoods to accommodate the automobile, Governor Francis Sargent (1969–1975) reversed the trend when he decided to stop construction of the Inner Belt Expressway in 1970. Governor Sargent said: "Four years ago, I was commissioner of the Department of Public Works—our road building agency. Then, nearly everyone was sure highways were the only answer to transportation problems for years to come. But we were wrong."[12] Following his freeze on highway construction, Sargent successfully applied to the federal government to use transportation funds for upgrading the transit system, in particular the Red and Orange Lines. By shifting back toward a balanced transportation strategy that included mass transit, Sargent strengthened the urban core.

Less heralded but also important in promoting transit use was the parking cap that the US Environmental Protection Agency (EPA) imposed in 1975 to curb air pollution in downtown Boston. The EPA froze the number of parking spaces in commercial parking facilities and at curbsides at a maximum of 35,556 commercial spaces. These spaces had to serve well over 100,000 downtown workers and tens of thousands of shoppers and visitors. Restricting the number of parking spaces has made Boston's parking rates the highest in the country after New York City. Besides making it more difficult to drive downtown, the parking freeze made it nearly impossible for developers to tear down a building and put up a parking lot, as was done in many cities around the country.[13]

The 1970s marked the high watermark of federal intervention in cities. The Federal Clean Water Act of 1972 also had a major effect, precipitating the cleanup of the Charles River, Mystic River, Neponset River, and, most significantly, Boston Harbor. Under a $4 billion court-mandated cleanup, the state, in 1991, started treating raw sewage that had been pouring into Boston Harbor. The harbor cleanup spurred the 1996 establishment of the Boston Harbor Islands National Recreation Area, under the National Park Service. The cleanup efforts allowed beaches along Boston Harbor to be reopened and trails and other park amenities to be developed along riverbanks and Boston's waterfront.

"World-Class City"

Despite planning missteps, industrial decline, and social tensions of the 1970s, Boston was on the upswing. Mayor Kevin White was immensely proud of Boston's turnaround and contended it was a "world-class city." As detractors scoffed, Mayor White organized an international conference in 1980, the 350th anniversary of Boston's founding, to substantiate his claim. He invited mayors from thirty-six large world cities, including Bombay, Dublin, Hangchow, Hong Kong, Istanbul, Jerusalem, Leningrad, London, and Rome, for a week-long conclave held at Faneuil Hall, MIT, and Harvard's Kennedy School of Government. White's keynote address, reflecting his perception of Boston's redevelopment successes, called the conference "a celebration of cities in an age when our potential to be great finally outweighs the crises of day-to-day survival."[14]

Though driven by boosterism, Mayor White sensed the changes that were happening to his city and region. Yet even he probably could not have foreseen the transformation that would occur during the 1980s. This was the decisive decade of the "Massachusetts Miracle," when Greater Boston's struggling economic base transmuted into a leadership role in the postindustrial economy. Just as Boston had been one of the first American cities to industrialize and then lose its industries, it became one of the first to adapt to the high-tech and services economies. During that decade, Boston was the fastest growing city in terms of median family income, and its suburban family income growth ranked second nationally.[15] After the recession of the early 1990s, Greater Boston's employment growth surged again during the so-called "dot. com Revolution."

Barry Bluestone and Mary Huff Stevenson's *The Boston Renaissance: Race, Space, and Economic Change in an American Metropolis* explained that a "triple revolution" swept Boston's economy, demographics, and spatial development after 1980. Bluestone and Stevenson explained how the knowledge-based industries have transformed the regional economy. On the social front, Latin, Asian, and African immigrants have made the region multi-ethnic. Although a majority of immigrants have settled in Boston and smaller surrounding cities, they have also spread to many suburbs. The region's spatial revolution has entailed the revitalization of Boston and other urban communities.[16]

During the 1990s, some observers thought that the rise of the Internet would encourage decentralization and the ultimate demise of cities. If the Internet allowed people to live and do business anywhere, the primary reason for urban proximity would disappear and people would move to more remote locales. Why put up with the hassle of Boston, when you could live in Vermont or the Ozarks and work electronically.

The Information Age, however, has saved Boston and other cities. The telecommunications infrastructure has magnified the power of certain cities in the globalization of economic, cultural, and political life. The great financial capitals—New York, London, Tokyo, Frankfurt—have been strengthened as nodes of international networks of economic and information exchange. Columbia University's Saskia Sassen observed this phenomenon in *The Global City: New York, London, Tokyo*, calling "global cities" "command posts for the world economy." Information technology is essential to the economic salience of global cities, but sophisticated economic, educational, and governance institutions and up-to-date transportation facilities are also necessary. The face-to-face exchanges that are facilitated by these urban institutions are essential for facilitating the flow of information that generates economic and cultural innovation.[17]

Besides the major economic capitals, there are global cities that play specialized roles in the Information Age urban hierarchy. This is where Greater Boston finds a niche. Its specialization is in knowledge-based industries—universities, hospitals, life sciences, technology R&D firms, design firms, and mutual fund and pension management. According to the "Global Cities Index," compiled by *Foreign Policy* in 2010, Boston ranked as the nineteenth city in the world for economic development, earning ninth place for human capital. The Institute for Urban Strategies at the Mori Memorial Foundation in Tokyo (2010) ranked Boston twentieth on its "Global Power Index" and rated it sixth for research and development. The Melbourne-based "2thinknow Innovation Cities Global 256 Index" ranked Boston first in the world in relation to 162 "innovation indicators."[18]

Buttressing these evaluations of Boston's global economic significance is a 2005 study by PricewaterhouseCoopers of the gross domestic product (GDP) of the world's 150 leading metropolitan areas. Greater Boston ranked eleventh in the world with a metropolitan GDP of $290 billion (Tokyo ranked first with $1,191 billion GDP and New York City was second with $1,133 billion GDP).[19]

Boston's economic rise has been remarkable. In the 1950s, Boston was an economic basket case. Economic historian Peter Temin argued that the extensive Interstate Highway System that served the mid-twentieth-century American industrial economy "diminished the importance of urban clusters in producing and distributing goods." Central cities suffered as business relocated to the suburbs. Explaining Boston's turnaround, Temin stated: "With the emergence of the knowledge-based economy in the final quarter of the century, the ability of cities to speed the flow of people and ideas grew more important."[20]

The key element of the dynamic regional economy has become the clustering of skilled people. Economic development theorist Richard Florida has written that globalization, by increasing the financial return on innovation, has made the pull of innovative places only stronger. According to Florida, "Talent-rich ecosystems are not easy to replicate. To realize their full economic value, talented and ambitious people increasingly need to live within them."[21]

Richard Florida's influential book *The Rise of the Creative Class: And How It's Transforming Work, Leisure, Community, and Everyday Life* argues that the most successful cities attract the "creative class"—essentially educated workers creating value-added innovative goods and services. He estimates that the American "creative class" numbers forty million (30 percent of the United States workforce). The key to economic development is attracting highly skilled workers, who are mobile and can live where they want. Key ingredients for city-regions to attract the "creative class" (places called "IQ magnets" by Bill Gates) are three "Ts": talent (a highly educated population), tolerance (a diverse community, which has a relatively large gay population), and technology (infrastructure that supports economic innovation).[22]

Some of the leading "creative" cities are San Francisco, Minneapolis, and Seattle as well as the university cities of Austin and Raleigh-Durham-Chapel Hill. Greater Boston, with its strength in the three "Ts" and an array of educational and cultural opportunities, is very attractive. Richard Florida ranks Boston third in the country behind San Francisco and Austin in the percentage of its workers involved in the "creative" sectors, second in high-tech jobs, and sixth in innovation (patents per capita).[23] Boston's universities have spun off significant local concentrations of business consultants, architects, landscape architects, medical researchers, web designers, and artists of every stripe. Boston's specialization in money management originated with nineteenth-century conservative family trusts and evolved into the mutual fund, pension fund, and insurance industries and the rise of Fidelity, Putnam Investments, State Street Corporation, Liberty Mutual, and John Hancock Life Insurance.

In order to attract "creative" workers, a stimulating quality of life is essential. Boston has demonstrated that higher education, attractive architecture, abundant green space, walkability, public transit, theaters, museums, and sports are keys to urban revitalization. With myriad restaurants, pubs, coffeehouses, sidewalk cafés, street furniture, festivals, and public cultural events, Boston offers stimulating pleasures. Its walkable historic cityscape attracts students, young professionals, and empty-nesters who are drawn to cities.

The city has redeveloped the Charlestown Navy Yard and the South Boston Seaport District and created the Rose Kennedy Greenway along the route of the Central Artery. The HarborWalk provides pedestrian and bicycle access to forty-seven miles of Boston's waterfront. The "Big Dig's" burial of downtown highways has eased traffic congestion and vastly improved access to Logan Airport. The office sector in the financial district and Back Bay is healthier than most American central cities. In Cambridge, MIT spinoffs and other tech businesses are thriving in R&D space around Kendall Square, which is a dynamic hub of the global biotech industry. Cambridge companies include Akamai Technologies, Amgen, Biogen Idec, Genzyme, Google, Microsoft, Nokia, Novartis, Schlumberger, and the World Wide Web Consortium. Historian Stephen V. Ward has written: "If it is valid to speak of a formula for the postindustrial city, Boston stumbled across it first."[24]

FIGURE 9.5

Aerial view of the Rose Fitzgerald Kennedy Greenway, Boston. Perhaps Boston's most striking (and controversial) public improvement of recent years has been the replacement of the elevated Central Artery by a highway tunnel with a 1.5-mile linear park on the surface. The Rose Kennedy Greenway (2008) is the latest example of Boston's knack for creating networks of high-quality open spaces.
Source: Photograph © Alex MacLean. Courtesy Rose Fitzgerald Kennedy Greenway Conservancy.

FIGURE 9.6
Aerial view of Kendall Square, Cambridge. Kendall Square has become the region's center for technological innovation, especially for biotechnology. MIT (dome of MIT's Rogers Building in the lower right-hand corner) is the progenitor of much innovation. The high-rise office buildings contain such companies as Amgen, Biogen Idec, Genzyme, and Microsoft, which draw on talent largely produced by MIT.
Source: © 2012 Alex S. MacLean/Landslides, http://www.alexmaclean.com.

The relative popularity of Boston is indicated by the high cost of residential real estate. Between the 2005–2006 peak and 2010, Greater Boston's housing prices held their value better than most other places. Boston's high-price-tier houses were down 10.7 percent from the peak, while the high-price houses in Las Vegas were down 54 percent, Phoenix was down 49.4 percent, and San Francisco was down 24 percent. Boston's low-price-tier homes declined 26.8 percent from the peak, while Las Vegas declined 66.5 percent, Phoenix declined 69.8 percent, and San Francisco declined 58.4 percent. Denver was the only metropolitan market whose high-end houses declined less than Boston's. Housing prices did not decline substantially because Boston did not experience the over-building of other metropolitan areas. Real estate has even appreciated in Cambridge, Back Bay, and the South End since 2006.[25]

Yet Boston has its weaknesses. The region has experienced slower growth than other parts of the country, and its cost of living is high. And there is a social under-side to the "creative" or "knowledge" economy. Less skilled workers—and there will always be less skilled workers and a need for their services—are being left behind. Massachusetts, which is at the head of the nation's "knowledge" economy, also leads the country (tied with Arizona) in income inequality. According to the Center for Labor Market Studies at Northeastern University, Massachusetts has "the largest gap between the haves and have-nots of any state." The top 10 percent of households earned as much income in 2009 as the bottom 70 percent combined.[26] This reflects the wealth that can be created by a highly skilled creative class and the powerlessness and inequality that can accompany it. Although Greater Boston has strong compara-tive advantages, there are serious problems that could hinder its economic advance.

As experience has taught, the economic vitality of one generation can be super-seded by a period of decline, particularly with fast-moving global competition. Yet, Boston has strong potential to cling to its niche as an educational-research center in the global city hierarchy. The key for Boston is keeping an eye on the global economy and undertaking the strategic moves necessary to remain competitive.

The metropolitan area of the "knowledge economy" has become a mosaic of development stretching from downtown to established suburbs to the exurban fringe. Though downtown Boston remains the leading business center, it is one among many places of economic activity in the metropolitan area. The stark dichotomy between city and suburbs no longer exists as it did in the 1950s and 1960s. Just as the "modern" industrial age model of suburban development located workers, industry, and business in the city and the middle and upper classes living in bedroom commu-nities on the periphery, the postmodern era of sprawl has each type of land use scattered through the metropolitan area. The stereotype of poorer minorities living in the city and upper middle- and middle-class whites living exclusively in the suburbs no longer applies. There has been substantial urban gentrification and movement of African Americans, Latinos, and immigrants to suburban communities, even though the largest concentrations of minorities and poverty remain in urban centers.[27]

Barry Bluestone and Mary Huff Stevenson's *The Boston Renaissance* observed that suburban sprawl has not "hollowed out" the urban core as it has done to other cities. The city's population has been on the rise since 1980, reaching 617,594 in 2010. Greater Boston has both a strong central city and a network of smaller urban and suburban nodes. According to Bluestone and Stevenson, "eastern Massachusetts can now be conceived of as an economically interrelated unit—not just a patchwork of urban villages, towns, and cities."[28]

Exploring Redevelopment in Boston and Cambridge

Prudential Center, 800 Boylston Street

An example of private-sector mid-1960s urban renewal. The Prudential Center (1965) was designed to have several smaller buildings surrounding the fifty-two-story tower, the city's second tallest. Its separation from the street level originally isolated the Prudential Center. The shopping arcades (1990) have enlivened the complex, and the Top of the Hub Restaurant provides the city's highest public viewing place.

Boston City Hall, City Hall Plaza, Boston

Boston City Hall (1968), designed by Kallmann, McKinnell, and Knowles, is a Modernist landmark. It is loved by architects and hated by much of the public. When it was opened, City Hall was a concrete statement that Boston was heading into an innovative and dynamic direction. The sprawling brick plaza designed by I. M. Pei is the epitome of 1960s urban renewal Modernist design and a problematic space to this day.

Faneuil Hall Marketplace/Quincy Market, Faneuil Hall Square, Boston

The historic rehabilitation of Quincy Market for the 1976 Bicentennial is the mid-1970s redevelopment counterpart to City Hall, which is across the street. Quincy Market bolstered a trend for recycling historic warehouse and industrial buildings for postindustrial consumer use. The food court inspired copycats across the nation. For thirty-five years, it has been the leading attraction in Boston, a gathering place for visitors of all kinds.

Rose Fitzgerald Kennedy Greenway, above I-93, between South Station and North Station, Boston

The Big Dig replaced the overhead Central Artery/Fitzgerald Expressway with a multilane Interstate highway below ground and a one-and-one-half-mile surface greenway. The Kennedy Greenway (2007) is a work in progress as an urban open space. The cultural institutions that had been originally planned to sit on the Greenway are not being built, so the Kennedy Greenway Conservancy is developing a range of less capital-intensive, yet engaging activities. Part of the Greenway's appeal is that it is only a block from the harbor front. The Boston Harbor Islands Pavilion, at the corner of State Street and Atlantic Avenue, provides information about visiting the Boston Harbor Islands National Recreational Area.

HarborWalk, Boston

In 1984, Boston set out to create a pedestrian walkway along its harbor front from the Neponset River at Quincy to Chelsea Creek. The forty-seven-mile walkway is about 80 percent complete. It has been a success because harbor front abutters are required to allow the public access. The HarborWalk is most noticeable near downtown, the Charlestown Navy Yard, and the South Boston Seaport District. Christopher Columbus Park (1976), which is between Quincy Market and the North End, is considered the first harbor-front park to be built in America. It provides an excellent opportunity to experience the harbor that produced a great city. The HarborWalk is another example of Greater Boston's facility at creating first-rate walking trails and linear connections.

Massachusetts Institute of Technology/Kendall Square, East Cambridge

Urban revitalization is built on wealth. Arguably, the leading source of Greater Boston's wealth in recent years has been the Massachusetts Institute of Technology and the tech businesses it has spun off. MIT offers a cornucopia of architectural landmarks, including the Great Court (William Welles Bosworth, 1916), Baker House (Alvar Aalto, 1949), MIT Chapel and Kresge Auditorium (Eero Saarinen, 1955), Simmons Hall (Steven Holl, 2002), and Stata Center (Frank Gehry, 2004).

The center for tech business migrated to Route 128 in the 1950s, but over the past couple of decades, the presence of technology companies has intensified near Kendall Square. This area is the world's greatest concentration of biotechnology business. Designed by Stefan Behnisch, the Genzyme Center (2003), 500 Kendall Street, has been acclaimed as one of the "greenest" office buildings in the country. Tours of the buildings are offered to the public.

South Boston Waterfront, Seaport Boulevard and Summer Street

The South Boston Waterfront, also called the Seaport District and the Boston Innovation District, is the city's development frontier. It plays off the brick warehouses of the Fort Point Channel District, which were developed a century ago. The decline of shipping and railroads opened up the area next to Fort Point Channel for development. In recent years, various projects have started to fill out the area: Moakley Federal Courthouse (1999), Boston Convention and Exhibition Center (2004), Institute of Contemporary Art (2006), and the restaurant complex at Liberty Wharf (2011). The MBTA's Silver Line (2004) underground transit service has connected the South Boston Waterfront to South Station and Logan Airport.

A combination of offices, apartments, hotels, and restaurants are popping up, now that the 2008 financial meltdown has receded. Mayor Menino's Innovation District concept is drawing dozens of emerging tech companies. The South Boston Waterfront provides an example of urbanism in the making. The HarborWalk and waterfront amenities provide allure, while many of the buildings are of the contemporary global glass-and-steel brand.

10

Interstates, Exurbs, and Sprawl (1970–2012)

Edge Cities

The signal event of the early 1970s for metropolitan development was the completion of the Interstate Highway System. Interstate-495 was the most consequential route for Greater Boston, circling on a radius almost thirty miles from downtown and spreading development into Central Massachusetts, Southeastern Massachusetts, and Southern New Hampshire. The region's spiderweb of highways, which also included the Massachusetts Turnpike (Interstate-90), Route 128, Route 3, Interstate-93, spurred land-use patterns that were even less dense than those of the 1950s and 1960s. Businesses, developers, and public officials wanted low-density, auto-oriented development because it was easy to build and was most likely to promote economic growth.

Interstate highways and cheap gasoline allowed farming communities, which had been too distant from the city to allow commuting, to attract suburban development. Extensive amounts of open land were carved up into large house lots. Two types of residential templates were prevalent—the tract subdivision, where a developer would build an entire neighborhood, and the individually built houses located in the woods or fields. The former form of development was relatively dense suburbia, while the latter became known as "exurbia."[1]

Nodes of commercial development appeared near highway exits to accommodate motorists. Greater Boston became a multinucleated region with many centers for work, habitation, shopping, and recreation. The city of Boston was no longer the preeminent focus of the region's economy, and suburbs were no longer simply bedroom communities. Gillette Stadium and Patriot Place and the Comcast Center (formerly Tweeter Center) established major regional entertainment venues near the interstates and far from downtown. Many suburbs became a blend of residential neighborhoods, business parks, and commercial strips. The traditional dichotomy between city and suburbs no longer described reality. The spread of low-density, highway-driven development created a backlash. The ravenous consumption of open land, proliferation of corporate big box stores and fast food franchises, and increased traffic congestion was referred to pejoratively as "sprawl."[2]

When the federal government established the Interstate Highway System, transportation engineers did not expect that highways would facilitate commuting and the wholesale movement of housing and business to areas far from the central city. They anticipated that interstates would carry long-distance traffic. It was surprising when the new highways enlarged the potential commuting area exponentially. Traffic experts explained that, with an average national commute of 24.3 minutes (Greater Boston's average is 27 minutes), a driver traveling at thirty miles per hour has a twelve-mile commuting radius. This computes to a commuting zone of 463 square miles. Driving farther or faster would enlarge the potential commuting zone even more. As commuters figured out how to navigate the highway system, they moved farther from their places of work.[3]

The highway system gave birth to "edge cities," as the new mix of malls, office buildings, cinemas, fast food restaurants, and warehouses were christened by journalist Joel Garreau in his eponymous book *Edge City: Life on the New Frontier*. According to Garreau, edge cities were significant suburban concentrations located ten or twenty miles from downtown. Edge cities developed because the commuting distance into the central city had become too long. Office parks were developed near the suburban residences of workers, especially the executives who wanted to work near home. For example, business parks on Route 128 spurred an influx of executives into Lincoln and Weston. According to Garreau, a full-fledged edge city had at least 600,000 square feet of retail space, much of it located in a regional mall (the typical regional mall has 400,000 to 800,000 square feet with at least two anchor stores), and five million square feet of leasable office space. With such a concentration of business activity, edge cities became the locus for job growth in most metropolitan areas.[4]

In Greater Boston, the first edge cities developed along the Route 128 and Route 9/Massachusetts Turnpike corridors. They were located around the Burlington Mall, Shoppers' World/Natick Mall, and the South Shore Plaza. By 1980, the shopping centers and office parks at Natick and Framingham produced almost 100,000 jobs.[5] Burlington took off as an office center when the Lahey Clinic moved there from Boston in 1974. Between 1950 and 1980, Framingham's population grew from 28,086 to 66,113 and Burlington's grew from 3,250 to 23,486. By the 1980s, edge cities started emerging around the North Shore Mall and Liberty Tree Mall at Peabody/Danvers and the intersection of the Mass. Pike and I-495 in Marlborough. In Southern New Hampshire, a major edge city arose between Nashua and Manchester.

Garreau argued that Boston was not only one of the first metropolitan areas to spawn edge cities but was also the first to have its edge cities "built out." By this he meant that new suburban edge cities could not keep developing farther out from the city, as was happening on unincorporated rural land around the Sunbelt cities of Atlanta, Houston, or Phoenix. Because of the Atlantic Ocean, Boston could not

TABLE 10.1
Commuters working in the City of Boston, 2000

Residence	% of Commuters Working in Boston
Boston	66.42%
Brookline	46.98%
Newton	29.21%
Cambridge	26.71%
Arlington	21.48%
Foxborough	14.19%
Wilmington	13.68%
Beverly	10.92%
Framingham	10.83%
Burlington	9.95%
Bedford	8.22%
Wrentham	7.32%
Maynard	6.63%

This table showing selected communities within the I-495 beltway indicates which communities are most oriented to Boston for jobs. Not surprisingly, communities closer to Boston are more likely to have residents who commute to the central city. Many outer suburbs are more oriented to edge cities than Boston for work. *Source:* Metropolitan Area Planning Council, Transportation Program, "Journey to Work Data, 2000" (US Census Bureau, American Community Survey).

expand to the east; in other directions, metropolitan Boston bumped into Worcester, Providence, Lowell, and other established communities. Since Boston could not easily spread out further into undeveloped territory, growth intensified in existing centers and housing and commercial leasing costs rose, creating the high real-estate-cost structure that the area is noted for.[6]

The growth of Boston's metropolitan area due to the automobile has been traced by the federal government—the US Office of Management and Budget (OMB) designated an ever-larger metropolitan boundary and the US Census Bureau tracked the population growth. In 1910, Boston's Metropolitan District had thirty-seven cities and towns. By 1950, the Boston Standard Metropolitan Area included 2,369,986 people living in sixty-five municipalities. In 1980, OMB created a new metropolitan area category—the Consolidated Metropolitan Statistical Area (CMSA), which combines two or more contiguous metropolitan areas. The CMSA reflected a new geographic reality defined by sprawl, lengthy commuting patterns, and the blending together of metropolitan areas. In Boston's case, the smaller metropolitan areas of Lawrence-Haverhill, Lowell, Salem, and Nashua, NH, were added to Boston to form the Boston-Lawrence-Salem, MA-NH CMSA, which had 169 municipalities. By 2010, the Boston-Worcester-Manchester-MA-RI-NH Combined Statistical Area (a new name for the CMSA) had grown to a population of 7,559,060 living in 385 communities, which makes it the country's fifth largest CSA.[7]

Economists created new categories to describe metropolitan regions, such as the regional "labor market area" or "retail trade area."[8] Another variation was the regional "television market," which measures the television sets and watching habits. In this case, Nielsen rates Boston as the seventh largest television market in the country, behind New York, Los Angeles, Chicago, Philadelphia, Dallas–Fort Worth, and San Francisco–Oakland–San Jose. If you added the Providence–New Bedford television market to Boston's, you would have the fourth largest television market.

Metropolitan areas have grown so large that they blend into others, forming a larger entity called the megaregion. The first megaregion to be recognized was the Northeast Boston–New York–Philadelphia–Baltimore–Washington conurbation, described in geographer Jean Gottmann's study *Megalopolis*. Regional planners now argue that the true building blocks of economic development are not cities, states, or nation-states, but megaregions that can span state and even national boundaries. The Northeast "Bos-Wash" "megalopolis" is the world's most potent economic megaregion, with fifty million inhabitants and a gross domestic product (GDP) of $2 trillion, more than that of the United Kingdom or France.[9]

Yet, American megaregions like the Northeast Corridor do not operate as entities capable of coordinated development strategies. Cities and states are the primary political units. States are the most effective players in addressing megaregional infrastructure issues—witness high-speed rail projects and the Northeast Regional Greenhouse Gas Initiative to promote carbon trading—but they lack the resources and the political capacity to undertake megaregional transportation and urban infrastructure projects comparable to Europe or East Asia. Under President Obama, the federal government has funded high-speed rail, but Republicans have tried to undo these efforts. Without a positive role for government at each level and a structure for megaregional coordination, America's megaregions will have difficulty planning effectively for global competitiveness in the twenty-first century.[10]

TABLE 10.2
Geographical expansion of Boston's metropolitan area

Year	Number of Municipalities	Federal Metropolitan Designation
1910	37	Boston Metropolitan District
1950	65	Boston Standard Metropolitan Area
1960	78	Boston Standard Metropolitan Statistical Area
1970	92	Boston Standard Metropolitan Statistical Area
1980	106	Boston Standard Metropolitan Statistical Area
	282	Boston-Lawrence-Salem, MA-NH Consolidated Metropolitan Statistical Area
1990	129	Boston Primary Metropolitan Statistical Area
	282	Boston-Worcester-Lawrence, MA-NH-ME-CT Consolidated Metropolitan Statistical Area
2000	234	Boston-Cambridge-Quincy, MA-NH Metropolitan Statistical Area
	385	Boston-Worcester-Manchester, MA-NH Combined Statistical Area

Note: The Office of Management and Budget (OMB) has made many changes to the terms and definitions related to metropolitan areas over the years. The terms "Standard Metropolitan Statistical Area," "Primary Metropolitan Statistical Area," and "Consolidated Metropolitan Statistical Area" have been used and discarded.
Source: US Census Bureau.

The Interstate-495 Landscape

Interstate-495 (first section completed in 1966) encouraged low-density sprawl thirty miles from downtown Boston. As land along Route 128 was developed, companies looked to I-495 as a second technology corridor. During the minicomputer boom that fueled the "Massachusetts Miracle" of the late 1970s and 1980s, Data General, Digital Equipment Corporation, Honeywell, Prime Computer, and Wang all located near I-495. More recently, such companies as Boston Scientific Bristol-Myers Squibb, Cisco Systems, Compaq, EMC Corporation, Fidelity, Genzyme, Hewlett-Packard, and Intel opened facilities in office parks along I-495. A leading reason corporations located near I-495 was that they could draw workers from a wide area reaching from New Hampshire and Rhode Island to west of Worcester, where housing cost less than it would closer to Boston.

I-495 also has clusters of warehouses that serve as regional distribution centers for a wide variety of products. During the nineteenth and early twentieth century, warehouses were located near downtown Boston to take advantage of the railroad lines. By the late twentieth century, the Interstate Highway System became the lifeline of wholesale distribution. The warehouse and distribution function became so prevalent along the I-495 corridor that business areas like Taunton's Myles Standish Industrial Park are now filled with warehouses, not factories that manufacture products.

Most highway exits have seemingly interchangeable clusters of mainly retail development. These business nodes have the same mix of gas stations, convenience shopping and eating, and offices. The investment in site and building design is minimal. Dolores Hayden, in *Building Suburbia*, writes: "For the most part, edge nodes are uncomfortable and ugly places. Building is cheap; depreciation is accelerated; obsolescence is rapid. Money might be spent on a corporate headquarters when a corporation intends to stay, but developers of speculative office parks design for rapid turnover. There is little site design beyond inexpensive buildings with big signs and parking lots."[11]

Perhaps the most powerful evidence of I-495's capacity to spur development can be found in entertainment and shopping sites that have grown up along the beltway. The Boston Patriots were pioneers in moving out from Boston to a newly created highway interchange, when it opened Schaefer Stadium (subsequently called Sullivan Stadium and Foxboro Stadium) in 1971. Located thirty miles from downtown Boston and twenty miles from Providence, the new stadium inspired Patriots owner

William Sullivan to rename his team grandiosely the "New England Patriots." The stadium's location at the interchange of I-95 and I-495 certainly helped the Patriots evolve from a Boston-oriented team to a team that is not more than a two-and-a-half-hour drive from any New England state. The Kraft family replaced the original stadium with Gillette Stadium in 2002 and built the popular Patriot Place shopping-entertainment center in the parking lot five years later.

The next exit over on I-495, in Mansfield, an amphitheater-style concert venue Great Woods opened in 1986. Currently called the Comcast Center (it was also called the Tweeter Center), the music venue accommodates up to 20,000 for popular music acts. In the other direction on I-495, there is a mammoth off-price shopping center called Wrentham Village Premium Outlets (1997). The Wrentham Outlets draw on an enormous market area created by the highway system. Characteristic of late twentieth-century edge nodes, these projects are stand-alone pods oriented to the highway system. They do not connect physically to each other or fit into the surrounding townscapes (although both Patriot Place and the Wrentham Outlets attempt to create their own versions of car-less pedestrian streets with traditional New England architectural ornamentation). They create a pastiche suburban form in the outer ring of Boston's metropolis.

One project that could have made a major impact on the I-495 landscape was a proposed commercial airport at the surplus Army base at Fort Devens in Ayer, near the interchange of I-495 and Route 2. One of the more consequential examples of NIMBYism was the local opposition to the proposed airport. In 1990–1991, the state studied potential sites for a counterpart to Logan Airport on the perimeter of metropolitan Boston. Even though Fort Devens had plenty of land, neighbors adamantly opposed it out of concern for traffic and noise. The state backed down on the second airport and decided to upgrade Logan.

Twenty years later, some are having regrets. John D. Kasarda and Greg Lindsay, in *Aerotropolis: The Way We'll Live Next*, describe how airports with vast amounts of surrounding developable land have become major engines for economic growth, comparable to port or railroad cities of earlier eras. With global corporations placing a premium on easy access to air transportation both for passenger and high-value freight service, office parks, warehouses, and attendant retail and housing have grown up around such airports as Atlanta, Chicago's O'Hare, Dallas–Fort Worth. Because East Boston is built out, Logan lacks land to accommodate growing enterprises and misses out on airport-induced development. Peter Canellos, editor of the *Boston Globe's* editorial page, has called Massachusetts's failure to create an aerotropolis west of I-495 "a big mistake, the kind that separates the truly global metropolises from the boutique cities."[12] Because local residents wanted to maintain the status quo in their communities, they opposed significant new growth and the establishment of the aerotropolis planning paradigm.

Much of the land near the I-495 corridor has been dedicated to residential development. Families seeking a lower-cost, rural setting bought houses amid the woodlots and abandoned farms of Central and Southeastern Massachusetts. Residential growth was rapid after I-495 opened. By the 1980s, there were as many people in Greater Boston living outside the Route 128 beltway as inside it. Between 1970 and 2010, the population of the I-495 community of Franklin expanded from 17,830 to 31,635. Westford doubled from 10,368 to 21,951, and Hopkinton grew from 5,981 to 14,925. When Hopkinton became the starting point of the Boston Marathon in 1924, the town was in the countryside, far beyond Boston's suburban belt. Only in 1980, did the Office of Management and Budget recognize Hopkinton and other I-495 communities had become part of the Boston Standard Metropolitan Statistical Area (SMSA).

The prevailing land-use pattern along Boston's I-495 corridor has been low-density residential zoning. More than half of the municipalities (95 of 187) in Eastern Massachusetts and most of the I-495 communities zone over half of their land area for lot sizes of one acre or more per home.[13] In Hopkinton, approximately 76 percent of developable land is zoned for housing lots of 60,000 square feet. Large-lot zoning has become the norm during the past two decades, as the size of the average house lot has virtually doubled since 1990.

Ironically, Greater Boston is less dense than other regions, especially in the West. Los Angeles is almost twice as dense as Greater Boston. Las Vegas, San Diego, and San Francisco–San Jose are also denser.[14] Greater Boston has been less dense because its population has grown slowly, and communities have zoned land for large lots, which maintain the rural character. With low-density growth, New England has been adding urbanized land at a faster rate than it has been adding population.

Although the low-density development pattern gobbles up open space, local residents have favored it because it seems to maintain the community's traditional "small town" character. According to a 2004 survey, Hopkinton residents continue to value its "rural nature," "wooded quiet acres that are nice for those who walk," "country atmosphere," and "small town feel." The survey found that a major concern of residents is to "slow down residential growth." This is just the sentiment that undergirds country suburbs across the region. Residents fear that rampant development is "destroying the environment" and that additional housing is increasing school costs.[15]

TABLE 10.3
Population of growing suburbs on the I-495 corridor

Municipality	1970	1980	1990	2000	2010
Franklin	17,830	18,217	22,095	29,560	31,635
Hopkinton	5,981	7,114	9,191	13,349	14,925
Mansfield	9,939	13,453	16,568	22,414	23,184
Norfolk	4,656	6,363	9,270	10,460	11,227
Raynham	6,705	9,085	9,867	11,739	13,383

Note: Some of the fastest growing I-495 suburbs have been located on the southern arc of the beltway, below the Massachusetts Turnpike.
Source: US Census Bureau.

FIGURE 10.1
Minuteman Park, Andover. This business park (1997), located off I-93, exemplifies suburban office parks across the region.
Source: © 2012 Alex S. MacLean/Landslides, http://www.alexmaclean.com.

Their concern about rising taxes is not unfounded. The taxes to pay for local education, water supply, sewerage treatment, waste disposal, public safety, libraries, and other public services increased substantially, as Hopkinton evolved from a farm town to a middle-class suburb.

Some I-495 communities have responded to growth pressures by excluding businesses that might compromise their rural qualities, while others have welcomed companies that expand the commercial tax base. Boxborough, for instance, allowed the Silicon Valley telecom giant Cisco Systems to build an office campus and established a Tax Increment Financing special district to provide the infrastructure for Cisco Systems. Meanwhile, neighboring Littleton and Harvard rejected the company.[16] Communities like Marlborough and Franklin have encouraged strip retail through so-called "fiscal zoning" to enlarge their tax base, while Holliston and Hopkinton have curbed retail sprawl to preserve their community character.[17]

McMansions on the Suburban Frontier

The I-495 corridor attracted middle- and upper-middle-class families seeking to trade up in the housing market. It became the land of McMansions, a nickname for pretentious, outsized houses of no distinct architectural style, mass produced in subdivisions for an upper-middle-class market. McMansions, which have also been called "tract mansions" or "starter castles," range in size from at least 3,000 square feet to 9,000 square feet and more.[18] The McMansion has become the expression of an era of growing income inequality in which the affluent seek to show off their material wealth.

Residential development, in particular McMansions along the I-495 beltway, has consumed a great deal of open space. Median house sizes across the country grew from 800 square feet in 1950 to 1,300 square feet in 1970, to 1,900 square feet in 1990, to 2,400 square feet in 2006. In 1970 new houses with four or more bedrooms made up 21 percent of all homes; today, 40 percent of all new homes have at least four bedrooms. Meanwhile, the average American household size declined from 3.1 people in 1974 to 2.6 people in 2004.[19]

New single-family homes in Greater Boston consume twice as much land as older single-family homes, averaging one acre per house lot—one acre (43,560 square feet) is about the size of a football field (48,000 square feet, not including end zones). The large house lots reflect a desire for rural living as well as misplaced belief that

FIGURE 10.2
The Estates at Walpole, Endean Drive, Walpole. This cul-de-sac subdivision of McMansions was started in 2005 by the Toll Brothers. The houses, designed in the Colonial Revival style, go up to 4,000 square feet in size.
Source: Andrew McFarland.

expansive land parcels conserve open space, while they actually fragment wildlife habitats. Low-density land-use patterns also help maintain the social status quo by protecting privacy and restricting access to housing in the community by those of lower economic strata.

The McMansion has its pejorative connotation because it is often mass-produced and looks oversized on its lot. These super-sized houses are found either in large-lot subdivisions on the metropolitan perimeter or are wedged into existing neighborhoods on "teardown" lots. "Teardowns" are a name for demolishing an older, smaller house, often a ranch or split-level from the 1950s or 1960s, and replacing it with a much larger structure whose architecture is out of context and scale with the existing neighborhood. The awkward pastiche McMansions are usually spec-built by developers seeking to appeal to a wide range of tastes and lifestyles, although often appealing to

FIGURE 10.3
Cranberry Cove Subdivision, Westcott Drive, Hopkinton. The McMansions in Cranberry Cove range in size from 6,000 to 10,000 square feet.
Source: © 2012 Alex S. MacLean/Landslides, http://www.alexmaclean.com.

no one in particular. The more tasteful, stylistically coherent large houses are often designed for a specific family. Many are skillful updates of historic styles, particularly Victorian houses, which lend themselves to elaborate porches, dormers, turrets, and other striking architectural features.[20]

Large houses became more affordable because building costs declined due to pre-fabricated materials and shortened construction time. Developers built these large homes because the prosperous upper-income groups generated a demand for houses larger and more lavishly appointed than the Capes and split-levels in postwar subdivisions. Observers explain the taste for McMansions as an expression of the "democratization of luxury" of recent decades. Some people are willing to trade an hours-long commute every day for the opportunity to live in an up-to-date, large house that they can afford. The phrase used to describe this phenomenon is: "Drive until you qualify

INTERSTATES, EXURBS, AND SPRAWL

[for an affordable mortgage]."[21] The demand for McMansions may be declining in the wake of the recent real-estate meltdown, especially as baby boomers downsize and workers seek to reduce commuting costs.

Retailing and "Category Killers"

Perhaps the most visible expression of the sprawl era has been the commercial strip and big box stores. The completion of the Interstate Highway System spurred considerable new retail development adjacent to highways and off-ramps. Fast food outlets, gas stations, motels, and convenience retail were pioneers, and large retailers followed. During the 1980s, retail witnessed a proliferation of specialized market niches and the emergence of large, well-capitalized national corporations seeking to dominate those niches. These companies became known as "category killers" for their ability to kill off weaker competitors. Large versions of these category killers ensconced in stand-alone generic warehouses became known as "big boxes."[22] This trend gained traction in the Sunbelt and moved to New England in the 1990s.

The world's largest big box company, Walmart, started in Bentonville, Arkansas, in 1962. Walmart grew from 125 US stores in 1975 to 1,198 stores in 1987 to 3,600 by 2011. Few Americans live more than sixty miles from a Walmart store. Its relentless drive to cut costs and dominate the full range of shopping services has made it the nation's leading retailer. The chain's power to suck retail out of smaller downtowns across the country is well known.[23]

Walmart did not reach New England until the opening of four stores in Southern New Hampshire in 1991. Two years later, the chain opened its first Massachusetts store, in Fairhaven, and quickly followed with stores along the I-495 corridor, in Bellingham, Westborough, and Hudson. That year, Walmart proposed a 120,000 square-foot big box store in the Western Massachusetts town of Greenfield. The store would have taken up sixty acres, an area larger than Greenfield's downtown. A battle ensued, as it had in Burlington, Vermont. A citizenry mobilized by Al Norman and the Sprawl-Busters organization turned the town against approving the project.[24] Yet in many communities with commercial strips, Walmart was able to fit in without too much opposition. On Cape Cod, where the Cape Cod Commission blocked a Walmart seeking to locate in Hyannis just off the Mid-Cape Highway, Walmart eventually located in the empty Falmouth Mall, where adequate parking and traffic infrastructure were already in place.

As of 2011, there were twenty Walmarts within thirty-three miles of downtown Boston. The majority of these Walmarts are arrayed in the outer suburbs. They are relatively rare inside the Route 128 beltway because they have not yet accommodated themselves to the smaller development footprints available in densely built communities. The Walmart discount stores built in the 1990s are approximately 100,000 square feet, while the newer supercenters meet the national average of 197,000 square feet.[25] The corporation is gradually phasing out the smaller stores, leaving them empty and available for redevelopment, except by competing retail organizations. The market saturation strategy has worked for Walmart, driving out of business most of the competition. In any case, big box construction is a nominal investment and can be easily vacated or demolished.

Along with Walmart, warehouse club stores epitomize the new retail strip. The warehouse clubs sell products in large quantities and levy a nominal membership fee. Warehouse clubs make even less of a visual pretense than Walmart, locating in windowless cinderblock boxes of at least 120,000 square feet. The barebones atmosphere is designed to make customers feel as if they are getting a bargain. Costco has five stores within twenty miles of Boston. The most ubiquitous club is BJ's Wholesale Club. Zayre established the first BJ's in 1984 on the Medford/Malden line (it's still there). There are ten BJ's clubs within twenty-five miles of Boston. Walmart's Sam's Club has 600 clubs nationally, but none inside I-495.[26]

Comparable in size and ubiquity are the Home Depot and Lowe's home-improvement centers. The Home Depot, which entered Massachusetts in 1992 with stores at Danvers and Seekonk, has twenty enormous stores (about 125,000 square feet) serving contractors and the general public inside I-495. Several have been fit into urban neighborhoods like South Boston, West Roxbury, and Watertown. Lowe's, with twenty stores in Greater Boston, has most of its locations on the region's periphery, particularly in Southeastern Massachusetts.[27]

As Walmart, warehouse clubs, and the national home-improvement stores moved into Massachusetts, they drove out competition, as they had across the country. New England-based discounters Ames, Bradlees, Caldor, and Zayre went out of business. In 1999, Caldor closed 145 stores in ten states. Two years later, Bradlees, which had been owned by Stop & Shop, shuttered its 105 stores. Ames, which had absorbed the Zayre discount chain in 1989, went belly up in 2002, after being the nation's fourth largest retailer only four years earlier. Each failed discounter had smaller stores than Walmart and had difficulty competing in the face of wider selections and lower prices.[28]

The local victims of the home-improvement category killers have been countless Main Street hardware stores and the locally owned Grossman's Lumber chain, which had sixty stores in the Northeast when it was forced into bankruptcy in 1996. The Grossman's stores, which were at least one-third smaller than the Home Depot and Lowe's, could not match their selection. The company has reorganized as a smaller Grossman's Bargain Outlet chain. In consumer electronics, Tweeter, which was founded in Boston in 1972, had over 100 stores scattered across the East Coast. Lechmere, which built its first modern store in Cambridge in 1963, grew to twenty-three stores in New England and New York. Lechmere went bankrupt in 1997, and Tweeter closed in 2008. The only specialty consumer electronics and computer remaining on the scene is the national chain Best Buy.

The strategy of category killers is to saturate the market. That is certainly the strategy of more ubiquitous category killers like Dunkin' Donuts and Starbucks. For example, as of 2010, there were 717 Dunkin' Donuts and 120 Starbuck's inside the I-495 beltway. Capital and aggressive marketing are key factors.[29]

The big box discounters, warehouse clubs, and home-improvement centers have, for the most part, located in the in the marginal warehouse districts of cities or on retail strips near highways because of the heavy traffic and the need for a sea of parking. In some places, big box stores have congregated in shopping centers of their own, often called "power centers." A good example is Framingham's Shoppers' World, which was established as an elegant regional shopping mall in the 1950s. In 1994, the developers demolished it and built a 778,000-square foot power center for discount big boxes in its place. Big box stores depend on a large market area in which consumers drive great distances to shop. Suburbs and exurbs have become better known for sprawling retail strips than for the leafy family-oriented neighborhoods that many consider to be the essence of suburbia.

The Darwinian struggle of chain stores is played out across the regional landscape. It is evident in the constant construction of new, bigger retail outlets, which means that there will always be losers in the competitive game. According to urban designer Seth Harry, "A shopping center cannot *generate new business or create new buying power* . . . rather they attract customers from *existing* (shopping) districts or capture a portion of new purchasing power from a growing area."[30] In the meantime, competition from big boxes has devastated traditional downtowns, which lack large land parcels and ample free parking. Regional malls started undermining retail shopping in the downtowns of Lowell, New Bedford, and Worcester in the 1960s, and category-killer chains on the suburban strip virtually finished them off in the 1990s. The shopping district is now almost exclusively on the strip. This retail landscape is shaped almost entirely by national corporations, and it looks the same from city to city.

The boom period prior to the 2008 economic meltdown witnessed billions of dollars being poured into excessive building of commercial real estate. This trend was more pronounced in the Sunbelt than in Greater Boston, where developing inexpensive "greenfields," namely undeveloped open land, has seldom been feasible.[31] In the wake of the recent real-estate bubble, retail vacancy rates have risen and retail rents have dropped. The crisis in commercial real estate means that changes in the retail landscape should occur at a slower pace in the coming years and that the trend toward redevelopment may grow.[32]

FIGURE 10.4
IKEA Store, off Route 24, Stoughton. The IKEA store is part of a cluster of "big boxes" off of Route 24.
Source: Andrew McFarland.

Metropolis Edges into Southern New Hampshire

The growth of Southern New Hampshire demonstrates how Boston's metropolitan population spread out in the late twentieth century. Southern New Hampshire, particularly the traditional mill towns of Nashua, Manchester, and Concord, have fed off of growth south of the state line. In the nineteenth century, these mill towns developed along the Merrimack River, just as Lowell, Lawrence, and Haverhill had done. Manchester's Amoskeag Mill became the largest textile mill in the world. During the nineteenth century, textiles dominated, and shoes replaced them in importance during the first half of the twentieth century.

As highways were built after World War II, suburban development sprouted in the borderlands of the Granite State. Much of this development was spillover from the Merrimack Valley. The majority of New Hampshire in-migrants hailed from the Bay State. Some came to escape state income and sales taxes (although there are very high property taxes). Others simply sought to live in a verdant setting near good job opportunities. From Southern New Hampshire, it has been only a fifteen-to-twenty-minute drive to I-495 and a half-hour drive to Route 128.

Southern New Hampshire's growth in the postwar era was spurred by the construction of highways that linked it to Greater Boston. In 1955, New Hampshire started to construct the Everett Turnpike, which ran from the Massachusetts border through Manchester to Concord. The other significant highway linking New Hampshire and Massachusetts was I-93, which runs parallel to the Everett Turnpike about a dozen miles to the east. Massachusetts built the "Northern Expressway" (later called I-93) between 1956 and 1964, and New Hampshire started building its stretch of I-93 in 1961. This highway connected to Route 128 and I-495. A third significant highway was the New Hampshire Turnpike (subsequently I-95), which connected Massachusetts and the Maine Turnpike in 1950. Each of these highways played an important role in spurring low-density, auto-oriented development in Southern New Hampshire.

The growth of Southern New Hampshire is evident in Hillsborough and Rockingham Counties, located along the Massachusetts border. Hillsborough, home of Manchester and Nashua, grew from 135,512 in 1950 to 400,721 in 2010. Rockingham, where Portsmouth and Derry are located, grew from 70,059 in 1950 to 295,223 in 2010. The area is often called the "Golden Triangle," with Nashua, Manchester, and Portsmouth as the three corners. Communities on the Massachusetts border experienced the most growth. Salem boomed from 4,805 in 1950 to 20,124 in 1970.

Nashua, "The Gateway City," grew from 34,669 in 1950 to 67,865 in 1980 to 86,494 in 2010.

New Hampshire's low taxes helped attract business. Developers Gerry Nash and Sam Tamposi Sr. built industrial parks and lured many companies, particularly from Route 128. They opened their first industrial park in 1960 and, by 1979, they owned nine industrial parks and more than fifty industrial buildings. Nash and Tamposi recruited Anheuser-Busch, Digital Equipment, Raytheon, and Sylvania to their parks.[33] The largest Nashua company was Sanders Associates, which manufactured missile guidance systems, microwave components, and computer circuits and employed 7,000 in the mid-1970s. The rise of the electronics industry, after the decline of textiles and shoes, boosted the economy and wages of New Hampshire workers. In 1988, *Inc. Magazine* ranked Nashua-Manchester as the metropolitan area with the highest proportion of "fast-growing" companies in the country. Because of its strong economy and tax rate, *Money Magazine* named Nashua number one in its "Best Places to Live in America" both in 1987 and 1997.

Just as factories and offices opened in Nashua, shopping malls also proliferated, partly to attract nearby Massachusetts shoppers who wanted to avoid paying sales tax. The first malls were the Nashua Mall (1970) and Southgate Plaza (1970). These malls and smaller shopping centers drained retail activity from downtown Nashua. During the real-estate boom of the 1980s, ten new shopping centers opened along a five-mile stretch of Route 101A north of Nashua. The largest shopping center was the Pheasant Lane Mall (1986), which opened one million square feet of retail space almost directly on the Massachusetts border. Traffic became unbearable and the city was compelled to curb development. In 1984, commercial realtor Heidi Mocek commented: "As far as the golden triangle between Salem, Manchester and Nashua goes, land is getting tight."[34]

The impact of suburbanization can be appreciated by looking at a former mill town such a Milford, which is about 10 miles from both Nashua and the Massachusetts border. Milford's population tripled from 4,159 in 1950 to 15,115 in 2010. A town history, *The Granite Town: Milford, New Hampshire, 1901/1978*, reported that Milford functioned as a "bedroom community for Nashua and Manchester businesses." During the 1970s, the first apartment buildings were erected. The town history lamented: "Additional roads and housing have sprung up in every direction, mostly in the outlying areas. All this has meant a serious loss of the open space that had made Milford such an attractive place in which to live." As for commercial strips, the town history reported: "Extending east and west on Route 101 and Route 101A there were by 1972 an increasing number of small shops, restaurants, and industrial-type buildings on the Nashua-Wilton Road, and there was every indication that Milford was succumbing to what planners describe as urban sprawl."[35]

The US Office of Budget and Management (OMB) recognized how Greater Boston and Southern New Hampshire had merged into a greater metropolitan area in 1980 when it designated a new Boston-Lawrence-Salem, MA-NH Consolidated Metropolitan Statistical Area (CMSA), which included twenty-five communities in Southern New Hampshire, including Nashua. Ten years later, OMB expanded the CMSA to include Manchester and its environs. By 2000, OMB was counting 118 New Hampshire communities in the Boston-Worcester-Manchester, MA-RI-NH Combined Statistical Area (CSA).

New Hampshire politicians and economic development officials tout their state for its superlative growth record and boast how the business climate surpasses Massachusetts, which has a higher tax burden. Yet the real story is captured in a 1988 news story from *Discount Store News* titled "Nashua, N.H.: Chains Seek Sites as Megalopolis Edges North." A Kmart official remarked: "It's not that Nashua is where the goose laid the golden egg. It's the city's proximity to Boston [that is driving economic growth]."[36]

The Spread of Exurbia

The Interstate Highway System spurred development outside metropolitan Boston, which has been termed "exurban." This connotes "small towns" outside traditional suburbs where residents are still connected to the metropolitan core for employment. A 2006 Brookings Institution study of the growth of exurbia defines it as communities with low housing density that have at least 20 percent of their workers commuting to jobs in an urbanized area.[37] Wider availability of services in rural areas, including an advanced telecommunications infrastructure, allowed people to live at a distance from cities and suburbs and still participate in metropolitan life.

Inhabitants of exurbia are a mix of people who have strong ties to the economic and social life of the metropolitan core and people who live and work locally. They are retirees, second-homeowners, home-business telecommuters, and long-distance commuters. Exurbia tends to be less affluent than suburbs nearer the metropolitan core. People move there for the country life or the cheaper cost of housing. In a way, they are creating middle-class versions of the country estates established by wealthy families in the nineteenth century.

According to the Brookings Institution study, New England is much less likely to have exurban growth than the South, where almost half of the nation's 10.8 million exurbanites live. Less than 5 percent of the country's exurbanites live in New England. The South has a large proportion of exurbia because its cities and suburbs have developed more recently than Northeastern cities, and the automobile allows more spread-out development. Boston and other Northeastern metropolitan areas already have established dense suburban communities that can absorb the slow-growing population. Greater Boston ranks seventy-fifth of eighty-eight metropolitan areas in having an exurban population. Only 3 percent of its population lives in exurbs, mainly in Southern New Hampshire and west of I-495 in Worcester County (ironically, Worcester County has 19.9 percent of its population living in exurban census tracts).[38]

Because of the slow pace of growth, most exurban residential development in New England is small-scale and fits into existing communities. Much exurban growth is unplanned and incremental, built one house or a small cluster at a time in farm country or the woods. House lots can have numerous acres—farms without raising produce or livestock. Exurban development maintains the rural character by resisting the construction of sidewalks and street lights.

Though not considered actual exurbia under the Brookings Institution definition, some New England resort areas have exurban characteristics because they serve as second homes for Boston residents. These areas have undergone such development that can no longer be considered truly rural. Lake Sebago and the southern coast in Maine, Lake Winnipesaukee and North Conway in New Hampshire, and the Killington and Okemo ski resorts in Vermont have experienced significant growth in vacation homes and commercial nodes. They have experienced scattered individual development as well as some large-scale master-planned projects.

A prime example of exurban resort development that has become suburban in scale is Cape Cod. Cape Cod's year-round population tripled between 1960 and 2000, from 70,279 to 227,230. Route 3, which connected Boston to the Cape, was completed in 1963, and I-495/Route 25 made the Cape easily accessible to drivers from the west by the mid-1980s. The Cape evolved from a rural seaside resort to a suburban landscape chock-a-block with subdivisions and commercial strips on Route 28 and on Route 132 in Hyannis. Although remaining a distinct region, Cape Cod became sucked into the Greater Boston vortex, since the Cape Cod Canal is located only an hour from downtown Boston. The Cape's landscape became suburbanized, while, in contrast, the shores of Maine's Penobscot Bay, a resort area that is a four-hour drive north of Boston, have maintained their rural character.

Until the 1970s, most seaside resorts were active between Memorial Day and Labor Day and were abandoned the rest of the year. In recent decades, growth has been driven by retirees, second-home owners, and commuters to off-Cape employment who live there much or all of the year or visit weekends year-round. Many second-home owners ultimately retire to their summer homes. Growing dramatically since World War II, the Cape's population has essentially leveled off since 2000. The easiest building sites were built on, and the cost of developing remaining parcels increased. With the explosion in Cape housing prices between 2000 and 2006, it became much more expensive to buy property on Cape Cod and the flood of in-migrants slowed to a trickle.[39]

In nearby Plymouth, the Pinehills is New England's largest planned second-home and retirement community. The Pinehills, which was started in 1999, is located on 3,000 acres which were once intended for use by the Digital Equipment Corporation. Seventy percent of the land is conserved as open space, and the 3,000 homes (partly developed) and 150,000 square feet of commercial space are clustered around nine "villages" and three golf courses. The developer and residents prefer to think of the Pinehills as a rural community because of the extensive amount of open space and the avoidance of cookie-cutter subdivision house lots. This reflects a recent upper-middle-class predilection for creating more common space. The Pinehills pays homage to the idea of a traditional New England community by providing a village green surrounded by shops and offices and offering free concerts during the summer.

The Pinehills is a leading Greater Boston example of the master-planned community land-use form. As former Boston Redevelopment Authority planner Brenda Case Scheer has pointed out, this land-use form, which is also used for office and industrial parks, is usually under a single developer's total control.[40] Residents of this type of community must adhere to strict guidelines laid down by the developer. For instance, the management has required that about one-third of the homes are to be age-restricted to fifty-five and above. In the case of the Pinehills, however, the developer has not built gates to limit public access, as is widely practiced at gated communities in the Sunbelt. The Pinehills project is unlikely to be repeated in Greater Boston, since it has utilized a 3,000-acre parcel, which is scarce. Yet, the individual Pinehills "village" model is being replicated in clustered high-end housing projects being developed elsewhere at the metropolitan edges.

Going forward, exurban development in New England is likely to continue at a slow, piecemeal pace. There will always be demand for rural living and living a simpler life. Conflict over the character of the exurban landscape should continue, focusing on the potential loss of farmland, adverse impacts on wildlife habitats and watersheds, and the depletion of natural scenery. The key determinant of growth will probably be the cost of gasoline. If it is relatively affordable, exurban development could continue apace. If gasoline becomes prohibitively expensive, long-distance driving will be constrained and exurban growth could slow.

Exploring Exurbia and Sprawl

Hopkinton Highlands and The Estates at Highland Ridge, Everett Circle, Greenwood Road, Overlook Road, Summit Way, and Adjoining Roads

This two-phase subdivision of McMansions was started in 1999. It is a development of Toll Brothers, one of the nation's largest builders of luxury houses. Located close to the junction of the Massachusetts Turnpike and I-495, Hopkinton Highlands and The Estates at Highland Ridge are comparable to a range of large-lot developments that have cropped up around the region's perimeter.

Big Box Stores, Exit 19, Route 24, Avon and Stoughton

Big box stores are sprinkled all over Greater Boston. They are creatures of the highway system. One of the most prominent concentrations of big box stores is off Route 24 near Brockton. Behemoth stores such as Jordan's Furniture, Ikea, the Home Depot, Costco, Petco, and the Christmas Tree Shops are arrayed up Stockwell Drive, off Harrison Boulevard at Exit 19.

Gillette Stadium and Patriot Place, Route 1, Foxborough

The stadium of the NFL's New England Patriots and Major League Soccer's New England Revolution is a state-of-the-art facility. Next to the stadium, owner Robert Kraft has built Patriot Place as a shopping-entertainment venue that includes the Patriots Hall of Fame. Arranged along a pedestrian street, Patriot Place attempts to serve as a community center for the area. An outdoor skating rink is open in winter.

Wrentham Village Premium Outlets, Exit 15, I-495, Wrentham

Outlet stores originated in mills where products were manufactured. Fall River was an early center for outlet stores. Gradually, outlet stores became off-price retailers in more conventional shopping centers. The Wrentham Outlets represent the corporate flowering of outlet malls. Situated along I-495, near the intersection with I-95, the Wrentham Outlets (1997) have grown from seventy to 170 stores. Developed by the Chelsea Property Group, which has built similar outlet malls in twenty-five other states.

The Pinehills, Clark Road, Exit 3 off Route 3, Plymouth

The Pinehills started development in the 1990s and continue filling out. The management welcomes visitors and is eager to show model homes. The Village Green offers shops and a café. You are free to explore this 3,000-acre planned development, the largest in New England. Plymouth has plenty of room for development, with almost 100 square miles, making it the largest municipality in the state.

The Smart Growth Era (1990–2012)

Dukakis Takes on Sprawl

As auto-dependent development spread across Southern New England, people became alarmed at how it consumed broad swaths of farmland and forests. Cookie-cutter subdivisions multiplied. The proliferation of commercial strips, with attendant traffic congestion, troubled residents desirous of preserving the small-town qualities of their communities.

As a national phenomenon, William H. Whyte dubbed this condition "urban sprawl" in *The Exploding Metropolis* in 1958. One of the first responses to sprawl occurred during mid-1960s, when Lady Bird Johnson addressed the shabby state of the nation's strips and roadsides. At the time, billboards, junkyards, and litter lined the nation's highways. The First Lady brought attention to the problem and helped spur the environmental movement by appealing to people's desire for scenic places. She championed the Highway Beautification Act (1965), which promoted the banning of billboards, the removal or screening of junkyards, and the beautification of roadways with wildflowers and other plantings.

Dissatisfaction with sprawl grew as low-density suburbs spread into the countryside. Historian Robert Fishman argued that this discomfort stemmed from the feeling that the classic suburban balance between the city and the country was being destroyed. By the 1980s, the "bourgeois utopia"—where everyone can live in a single-family house in a verdant setting—was fading.[1] Traffic multiplied. Endless commercial strips lined with chain stores and restaurants diminished the sense of place and alienated citizens from their local communities.

Greater Boston communities had been trying to constrain growth with restrictive zoning and land conservation since before World War II. These efforts gained intensity by the 1970s, as exclusionary NIMBY zoning tactics gained in usage. Meanwhile, planners sought to create a balanced strategic approach, most frequently called the "smart growth" movement, which conserved natural areas, regulated the impacts of new projects, built denser development, and encouraged public transit, walking, and biking as alternatives to the automobile. The crisis of the suburban ideal forced a reimagining of Boston's metropolitan landscape.

The first concerted strategy for pursuing "smart growth" (a decade before the term was coined at UMass–Amherst) was spearheaded by Governor Michael Dukakis (1975–1979, 1983–1991). This was the Mike Dukakis, who, during his 1988 presidential campaign, admitted to reading a book on Swedish land-use planning for pleasure.

When Dukakis took over the Governor's office in 1975, the Massachusetts unemployment rate was 11.2 percent and the economy was in a tailspin. Aging industrial cities were in dire straits. Dukakis believed that a coordinated statewide planning approach was needed to turn the economy around, so he established the Office of State Planning (1975–1979) under the leadership of Lowell planner Frank Keefe. Working with the legislature's Commission on the Effect of Growth Patterns on the Quality of Life in Massachusetts (Wetmore Commission), Keefe organized an unprecedented grassroots planning process to develop a vision of what communities needed to thrive.

In their Local Growth Policy Statements, 14 communities expressed an interest in achieving higher growth; 19 communities desired about the same amount of growth as in the recent past; 103 municipalities wanted slower growth; 55 wanted no growth; and 83 could not decide or did not indicate a preference. Most of Boston's inner suburbs desired slow or no growth because they lacked open space to accommodate new development. Keefe's report observed: "This desire to preserve and protect the distinctive character of communities and regions is expressed consistently and compellingly in growth policy statements. Villages don't want to be suburbs; suburbs don't want to be cities; and cities don't want to be wastelands."[2]

The Dukakis administration keyed on the fading industrial cities and shaped a revitalization strategy that invested in downtown infrastructure. State government would play a major partnership role with the cities and local businesses. The state provided financing for parking garages in such cities as Lowell, New Bedford, and Springfield and for streetscape improvements like brick sidewalks and historic period streetlights. Seeking to promote community pride, tourism, and an anchor for cultural activities, the state established Heritage State Parks in Fall River, Gardner, Holyoke, Lawrence, Lowell, and Lynn. The Dukakis administration also encouraged suburban and rural towns to accommodate more growth in their centers so that "the identity of these communities will remain separate and distinct from their neighbors and the role of their centers in the life of the community will be enhanced."[3]

The Dukakis administration was concerned about the abandonment of historic nineteenth-century buildings and the declining image of urban communities. A 1975 policy paper on "Adaptive Reuse of Vacant Mill Buildings" argued that postwar suburbanization seduced Massachusetts into neglecting a valuable inventory of older buildings: "What was once thought to be an endless supply of land and other resources, has seemingly discouraged any sustained interest in adaptively reusing old—but sound—structures as a means by which to satisfy contemporary economic development needs." The report went on to say: "Recent economic and social trends have made the adaptive reuse of existing physical resources an increasingly promising alternative to new construction, as well as a cost effective alternative to enhance and promote economic development in the Commonwealth."[4] Across the state, developers were picking up on the idea and were rehabilitating historic mill buildings for stores, offices, housing, and museums.

To incentivize companies to invest in cities and reuse old buildings, the Dukakis administration created several quasi-public financing agencies: the Massachusetts Industrial Finance Agency, Massachusetts Capital Resource Fund, and the Massachusetts Housing Finance Agency, each of which made low-interest financing available to projects revitalizing downtowns. The Massachusetts Capital Resource Fund, for example, provided a construction loan for Wang Laboratories to build its headquarters in Lowell. Combined with federal financing programs and tax incentives, the Dukakis-era programs spurred the recycling of a host of aging industrial and commercial buildings in city and town centers, a legacy that survives.

As he grappled with the decline of downtowns, Governor Dukakis recognized that, to revive urban centers, commercial sprawl in greenfield locations should be curbed. New suburban development had reduced the number of farms from 35,000 in 1945 to only 6,000 in 1977. The state had lost 1.3 million acres of farmland.[5] This environmental damage convinced the Dukakis administration to curb the

proliferation of shopping malls, which were gobbling up open space, producing traffic jams, and draining downtowns of business.

Frank Keefe issued a study on suburban malls that documented their adverse environmental, economic, and social impacts. He concluded that the state should use its
environmental and infrastructure review to force commercial developments into urban
settings.[6] The administration used environmental regulations to force developers to
improve their shopping center projects, minimizing environmental damage and
making traffic improvements, but it was unsuccessful in directing retail development
back into downtowns. Market forces were trending too strongly toward suburban
development. The biggest battles were over two shopping mall proposals for the environs of Pittsfield. Dukakis successfully steered a mall proposed for Route 7 in Lenox
into downtown Pittsfield, but the state was unable to thwart construction of the Berkshire Mall in rural Lanesborough, an event that hastened Pittsfield's retail decline.

Although Dukakis enjoyed urban support for efforts to constrain suburban commercial development, businesspeople objected. Real-estate developer George E. Slye,
of the Spaulding and Slye Corporation, resigned from Dukakis's Shopping Center
Task Force with these words: "From a philosophical point of view I must state that I
am opposed to any further involvement by the various levels of government in private business affairs including the right of private property." William Connaughton,
President of Algonquin Properties, argued that the Governor's downtown emphasis
was a mistake: "Businessmen are ringing our phones off the hook with plans to evacu-
ate the City of Boston. . . . It is incumbent upon your administration to get in step
with the market rather than attempting to create one where one does not exist."[7] This
reflected the perspective of many executives who sought more of a pro-business
approach, with lower taxes and construction of infrastructure wherever business
needed it, not just in cities.[8]

Governor Dukakis suffered for his perceived anti-business bias and the "Taxachusetts" reputation, losing the 1978 Democratic primary to Massport Executive
Director Edward King.[9] Once in office, King abolished the Office of State Planning
and supported a laissez-faire business approach. He advocated cuts in taxes, social
spending, and business regulation. King promoted high technology with his "Make
It in Massachusetts" marketing and business recruitment campaign.

When Dukakis regained the governor's office in 1982, he did not revive the
Office of State Planning. Nevertheless, he pursued urban revitalization and anti-
sprawl initiatives under other agencies and continued to provide beleaguered central
cities financial assistance for parking garages, street improvements, and rehabilitation

of historic buildings. The result was attractive vibrant downtowns in Lowell, Springfield, and Northampton, helping him to earn national plaudits for the "Massachusetts Miracle" and win the 1988 Democratic Presidential nomination.

After Dukakis left office, in 1991, however, his successors dropped the state's focus on urban revitalization. During the 1990s, the exodus of retail activity from most cities and towns accelerated. Some cities, including Lowell, New Bedford, and Worcester, were able to achieve revitalization with a combination of health care, higher education, cultural activities, sports, and restaurants. Nevertheless, planners believe that urban centers are an underutilized resource where new development can be most efficiently accommodated.

Grappling with "Buildout"

In managing sprawl, the Commonwealth of Massachusetts recognized that urban revitalization should be complemented by preserving rural open space. The spread of low-density development and the rise of ecological awareness spurred a movement to preserve forest and farm lands before they could be built upon. In 1971, the state had 17 percent of its land mass developed. By 1999, 24 percent had been developed, according to the Massachusetts Audubon Society. Massachusetts lost forty acres of open space per day to development between 1985 and 1999 (since 2000, the state has lost twenty-two acres per day to development). The unnoticed impacts of roads and runoff areas added another forty acres of open space lost each day. In eliminating all this green space, spread-out development also threatened wetlands and biodiversity.[10]

To counter the loss of critical natural areas, Massachusetts aggressively pursued land conservation. During the 1950s, local land trusts started to protect undeveloped open space in such communities as Concord, Lincoln, Sudbury, and Wayland. By the 1970s, the state initiated a long-term conservation strategy, which has led to government and nonprofit organizations to preserve permanently about 20 percent of the state's land area. This amounts to 1.2 million acres out of six million acres. Not only has this provided the ecological benefits of protecting species habitats and water supply and managing rainwater runoff, it has maintained the rural character in many suburbs.

Governor Francis Sargent, in 1972, signed the state's first open-space bond bill for purchasing new parkland since World War II. Governor Michael Dukakis continued to make open-space acquisition a major initiative. In 1984, he approved an open-space bond bill for $162 million, and three years later, at the height of the "Massachusetts Miracle," the state passed a $500 million environmental bond bill, most of which was targeted toward preserving open land. Open-space bond bills were also passed under the William Weld and Deval Patrick administrations. Efforts to promote land conservation have been given a strategic focus by the Statewide Land Conservation Plan (2003), which is a long-range plan to conserve 1.5 million acres over a twenty-year period. This would insure that a total of 30 percent of the state would be protected land, including the most valuable areas for protecting water supplies and wildlife habitat.[11]

Besides pursuing open-space conservation outright, planners also realized it was necessary to locate new development so that it minimized land consumption. At the University of Massachusetts–Amherst, the Center for Rural Massachusetts popularized the technique of clustering development in rural areas to preserve agricultural and forest land. During the late 1980s, the center, which was under the direction of notable planners Randall Arendt and Robert Yaro, termed its approach to concentrating development in growth centers: "growing smart." This sounded more development-friendly than the reigning term—"growth management." The American Planning Association soon adopted UMass–Amherst term, which morphed into the popular tagline "smart growth."[12]

The era's most notable battle about over-development and the need for smart growth was on Cape Cod, where construction boomed during the 1970s and 1980s. The population doubled in those years from 96,656 to 186,605. Towns had difficulty controlling the development of houses and commercial buildings. Cape Codders saw their groundwater and coastal embayments degraded by nitrogen runoff from septic waste and lawn fertilizer. At the Massachusetts Military Reservation, toxic materials infiltrated some of the water supply.

There was a widespread feeling that Cape Cod needed to impose strong controls on development. A *Boston Globe* article "The Rape of the Cape" reported that Cape Cod was "in danger of becoming a cheap, glass trinket. . . . Its natural resources are being obliterated, its roads are congested and its land is being swallowed up by development. Cape Cod, as we know it, is being ruined."[13] A broad coalition of interests called for establishing a regional planning commission with strong regulatory powers similar to the Martha's Vineyard Commission (1974). In 1990, Cape Codders voted by referendum to establish the Cape Cod Commission, with Governor Dukakis and the state legislature approving the enabling legislation.

The Cape Cod Commission developed a Regional Policy Plan, which set out regional development guidelines that actually had teeth. The Commission's key feature has been its authority to regulate Developments of Regional Impact (DRIs), which have essentially been commercial developments of more than 10,000 square feet and residential developments of more than thirty units. The Cape set out to control development by requiring new projects to mitigate their impacts—namely, pay for traffic improvements, preserve a specified amount of open space, avoid the storage of large quantities of hazardous materials in groundwater supply protection areas, and employ architectural designs that do not detract from the region's traditional character. The Cape Cod Commission's regulatory approach has been most effective in checking retail strip sprawl and the proliferation of big box stores.

Still, Cape Codders recognized that regional development regulations were insufficient to stem the rapid consumption of open space by housing construction. Cape towns started to purchase privately owned open space and placed it under permanent conservation protection. As Cape Cod added 36,000 people in the 1990s, residents decided that something more dramatic had to be done to preserve the rapidly dwindling open space. In 1998, voters passed the Cape Cod Land Bank, which levied a 3 percent surcharge on real-estate taxes to be used for purchasing undeveloped land, as well as for building affordable housing and preserving historic structures.

The Cape Cod Land Bank became the model for the statewide Community Preservation Act (2000), which allows individual communities to vote a property surtax to be devoted to the same purposes as the Cape Cod Land Bank. As of 2012, 148 Massachusetts communities had adopted the Community Preservation Act. The program has led to the protection of over 14,900 acres of open space, support for 5,080 units of affordable housing, and appropriations for 2,480 historic preservation projects.[14] It should be noted that the most affluent communities, particularly on the North and South Shores and west of Boston, have tended to adopt the Community Preservation Act to protect their quality of life, while less prosperous places have not approved an additional real-estate tax for community preservation projects.

All across the state, communities have grappled with sprawl. The areas of Massachusetts developing at the fastest rate have been referred to as the "sprawl frontier" by the Massachusetts Audubon Society. One "sprawl frontier" is concentrated in the Blackstone River watershed just west of I-495. It includes Grafton, Hopedale, Hopkinton, Northbridge, and Upton. A second high-growth area is in the Ten Mile and Narragansett Bay watersheds of Southeastern Massachusetts, which include Berkley, Rehoboth, Seekonk, Somerset, and Swansea. Many of these towns have large-lot zoning, the sort of development that can destroy habitat of flora and fauna and negatively impact water quality, agricultural production, and rural character.

According to the Massachusetts Audubon Society, there is also a "sprawl danger zone," which includes communities that are experiencing increased growth rates, even though they are not as great as the "sprawl frontier." Towns in this zone, which are near the Quabbin Reservoir and the Upper Connecticut River, have substantial areas of unprotected natural land. These exurban communities, which contain some of the state's largest forests and most fertile farms, usually lack the planning staff and the infrastructure to accommodate the development heading their way.[15]

The problems of sprawl have been exacerbated by state zoning and subdivision control laws, which undermine local planning by laying down a minefield of exemptions, prohibitions, and zoning freezes. The state's current Zoning Act (1975) and the Subdivision Control Act (1953) were passed when low-density suburban development was desirable. They have not been updated for the "smart growth" age. The American Planning Association rates Massachusetts state zoning laws among the most outmoded in the country.

Massachusetts requires a two-thirds vote of either a city/town council or town meeting to pass zone changes. This is a higher hurdle for changing zoning and promoting smart growth than most states, which require only a simple majority. Another predicament is posed by excessive "grandfathering" rights, which can stymie the updating of land-use regulations. A property owner can "freeze" existing zoning for eight years simply by submitting a preliminary subdivision plan for development under existing zoning, without any intention of ever building according to that subdivision plan. Such legal provisions have entrenched current zoning and subverted smart growth efforts. In response, a coalition of planners, municipal officials, environmentalists, and affordable-housing advocates has been promoting comprehensive zoning reform legislation.[16]

In order to obtain a clearer picture of exactly how much new development can be built under existing zoning, state and local officials have tried to measure the possible "buildout" for each city and town. To ascertain this potential, the Massachusetts Environmental Affairs Secretary Robert Durand issued a study in 2002 that projected the buildout potential under existing zoning laws of virtually every community. According to the state's study, the I-495 corridor has some of the greatest development potential—36 percent growth and 60,453 new housing units. Meanwhile, the buildout of forty-five communities in the region's inner core (not including Boston) would be only 11 percent. The conclusion is there is little open developable land left inside or along the I-495 beltway.

TABLE 11.1
Eastern Massachusetts buildout projections under existing zoning (2002)

Sub-Region	Number of Municipalities	Potential Additional Population	Existing Housing Units (2000)	Potential Additional Housing Units	Potential Unit Growth (%)	Potential Additional Commercial-Industrial Space/ Square Feet
Greater Boston	45 (not including Boston)	150,904	588,966	61,763	10.5	129,740,906
I-495 Corridor	27	162,581	167,906	60,453	36	194,832,460
Northeast	41	213,423	548,133	86,011	15.7	235,610,488
Southeast	52	724,346	596,826	259,792	43.5	117,964,732
Cape Cod	15	52,347	147,083	21,517	14.6	9,019,568
Total	180	1,303,601	2,048,914	489,536	23.9%	687,168,154

Source: Massachusetts Executive Office of Environmental Affairs, *The State of Our Environment: A Special Report on Community Preservation and the Future of Our Commonwealth* (Boston: Commonwealth of Massachusetts, 2002).

The limits of buildout are evident along the I-495 corridor, where the towns with the greatest buildout potential are Hopkinton (43 percent growth), Bolton (118 percent), and Berlin (150 percent). At the other end of growth potential are Chelmsford (8 percent), Framingham (12 percent), and Maynard (12 percent). These projections indicate the limited amount of new development that can take place under the current low-density zoning. If future growth is to be accommodated, more compact development patterns seem necessary.[17]

The findings about buildout are buttressed by the Metropolitan Area Planning Council's (MAPC) *MetroFuture* Plan (2008), which organizes the region's cities and towns into four categories related to their character and potential for future development: (1) "inner core"; (2) "regional urban centers"; (3) "maturing suburbs"; (4) "developing suburbs." Of 164 municipalities in Eastern Massachusetts, MAPC categorizes thirty-seven communities as "inner core" or "regional urban centers." These communities are either within Route 128 or are smaller cities and dense suburbs, such as Brockton, Framingham, Norwood, and Salem. They are essentially built out, so growth there must come from redevelopment. There are fifty "maturing suburbs," located mainly along Route 128 and south of Boston. "Maturing suburbs," which include Concord, Duxbury, and Southborough, are built out predominantly with single-family homes on large lots. MAPC has identified seventy-seven "developing suburbs," which are located along I-495 and on the North and South Shores. These communities, typified by Boxford, Lakeville, Medway, and Stow, still have rural qualities and have ample developable land. They represent the sprawl frontier.[18]

With these findings, it is apparent that open land for new development in Greater Boston is limited. The options for future development are either building on open space in the far suburbs or redeveloping areas in settled areas.

Reinvigoration of Public Transit and Compact Development

The most widely experienced consequence of sprawl is traffic congestion, which has grown dramatically. Between 1970 and 2000, while metropolitan Boston's population increased 10 percent, the annual "Vehicle Miles Traveled" for all vehicles using the Eastern Massachusetts highway system increased by 286 percent. ("Vehicle Miles Traveled" [VMT] tracks the total amount of miles of either a given vehicle or the aggregate of all the region's vehicles travel in a specific period.) People are driving a lot more, especially as residences, workplaces, shopping, and entertainment have spread farther apart. The average Greater Boston family now drives forty-nine miles a day, with families in the more distant suburbs averaging almost seventy-five miles per day.[19]

As the public has become more concerned with climate change and rising energy costs, they recognize the need to reduce gasoline consumption. Many believe that more fuel-efficient cars are the solution, but that is not enough. It is also necessary to create compact land use patterns that support public transit and allow people to walk or bike to more destinations. This sort of development goes by many names, depending upon the particular emphasis: smart growth, transit-oriented development, New Urbanism, walkable urbanism.

Boston has a distinct advantage over most American cities with its subway system, numerous bus lines, and a network of commuter rail lines. Boston's transit network, managed by the Massachusetts Bay Transportation Authority (MBTA), is second to New York City in per capita transit trips, though less than 9 percent of all Greater Boston commuter trips are on the MBTA.[20] Despite its aging rolling stock, somewhat unreliable service, and a heavy bond debt, the transit infrastructure provides a competitive advantage that Sunbelt cities wish they could replicate. Boston

Driving Patterns—Location Matters

Average Metro Boston household drives 49 miles per day

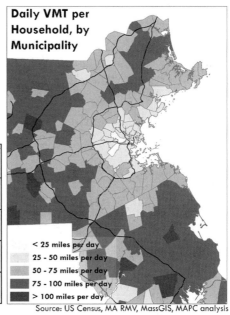

Daily VMT per Household, by Municipality

< 25 miles per day
25 - 50 miles per day
50 - 75 miles per day
75 - 100 miles per day
> 100 miles per day

Source: US Census, MA RMV, MassGIS, MAPC analysis

Community Type	% of Region's Households	% of region's VMT	Average VMT per Household
Inner Core	34%	20%	29
Regional Urban Centers	25%	24%	48
Maturing Suburbs	22%	28%	61
Developing Suburbs	19%	27%	73

FIGURE 11.1

Map of daily vehicle miles traveled per household, by municipality, 2010. One of the most telling indicators of sprawl is the amount of "Vehicle Miles Traveled" (VMT) by the region's vehicles. The least driving is done by households in the urban core, while the most driving is done by households on I-495 and the South Shore.

Source: Metropolitan Area Planning Council, *Metropolitan Area Planning Council 2010 Calendar* (2010).

never completely abandoned the commuter rail lines that have fed into the city since the 1830s, although it came close. During the 1950s and 1960s, several passenger lines were eliminated and service was cut back on the remainder. In 1973, the MBTA bought up the remaining bankrupt commuter lines, which had once been operated by the Boston & Maine, the New York Central, and the New Haven Railroads.

By the 1980s and the revival of the downtown Boston office sector, use of the commuter lines increased. Under Governor Dukakis, the state remodeled South Station, which had almost been demolished in the 1970s, into a handsome terminal that also serves Amtrak.[21] A new North Station was opened in 1995 with the construction of the TD Garden. These station improvements anticipated the expansion of the MBTA commuter rail system. The most important factor in expanding commuter rail service was the 1990 environmental settlement that accompanied the Big Dig burial of the Central Artery. The Conservation Law Foundation brought a lawsuit over the environmental impacts (mainly auto air pollution) of the Big Dig, seeking to balance the highway project with expanded transit service. The lawsuit led to restoration of commuter rail service on the Worcester Line (1994), Kingston-Plymouth Line (1997), Middleborough Line (1997), Newburyport Line (1998), and Greenbush/South Shore Line (2007). With approximately 130,000 passengers per weekday, ridership on Boston's commuter rail system is surpassed by only New York and Chicago.

As for subway/streetcar service, the MBTA rerouted the Orange Line along the land cleared for the Inner Beltway in Roxbury and Jamaica Plain. The transit agency extended the Red Line to Alewife Station in the north and Braintree in the south after Governor Sargent vetoed the Inner Beltway plan in 1970 and received approval to use federal transportation funds for transit projects. The Silver Line, a bus rapid transit line, has operated since 2002 on dedicated travel lanes on city streets and in tunnels between South Station and Logan Airport. The MBTA plans to open a $375 million extension of the Green Line north of the Charles River through Somerville to West Medford by 2018 and is increasing the frequency of service on the Fairmount commuter rail line (also referred to as the Indigo Line) within the city of Boston.

In tandem with public transit improvements, communities are striving to become more walkable and bikeable to provide a true alternative to the automobile. The inner-ring suburbs and town centers, which developed prior to the ascendancy of the automobile, are well served with sidewalks, though postwar suburbs and strips tend to have fewer sidewalks. Accommodating bicycle travel has been problematic. Greater Boston's crowded roadways can be unwelcoming to cyclists. The region has been building separate bicycle paths and creating bicycle lanes on major arteries. The most notable bike paths are the Minuteman Bikeway (Bedford, Lexington, Arlington, Cambridge), Charles River Bike Path (Boston, Cambridge, Watertown), and Southwest Corridor Park (Boston). Perhaps the biggest break-through for biking has been the establishment in Boston of the Hubway bike rental program. In 2011, Boston emulated bike-sharing programs around the globe and opened sixty Hubway rental stations, with expansion of service to Brookline, Cambridge, and Somerville in 2012. Boston, which *Bicycling Magazine* once called "one of the worst cities for cycling," has been rated America's twenty-sixth most bike-friendly city because of its recent improvements.[22]

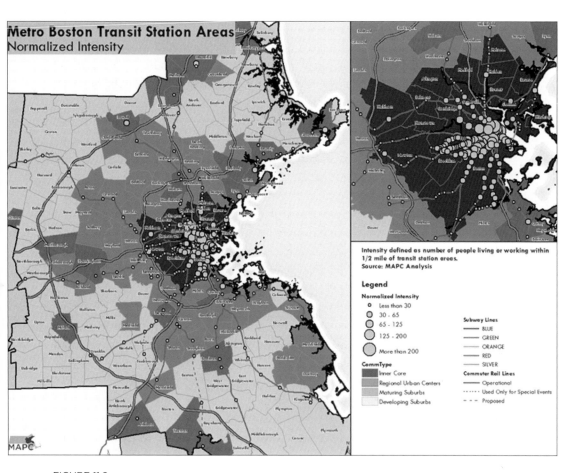

FIGURE 11.2
Metro Boston transit-oriented development map. This map indicates the development intensity
around the stations of the MBTA's commuter rail and subway/streetcar networks.
Source: Metropolitan Area Planning Council, "Transit-Oriented Development Goals for Metro
Boston, 2010–2035," Powerpoint presentation, March 14, 2012.

As non-automobile transportation has gained traction, growth in compact mixed-use development located near transit service has gathered momentum. The vast MBTA transit system offers many opportunities at approximately 130 railroad stations and more than 130 subway and trolley stops, not to mention hundreds of bus stops. This infrastructure, which dates back more than 150 years, encourages transit-oriented development (TOD). Development that is walkable, compact, and has mixed-uses also is called New Urbanism, after the movement to promote a rediscovery of urban forms that was started by architects Andrés Duany and Elizabeth Plater-Zyberk in the 1980s. Around many Greater Boston stations, in a radius of one-quarter to one-half mile, are late nineteenth- and early twentieth-century neighborhoods that already have the compactness and mixed uses that are sought by the smart growth and New Urbanist movements. A report published by the National Academy of Sciences—*Driving the Built Environment* (2009)—estimated that doubling residential density in a given area could reduce Vehicle Miles Traveled (VMT) by as much as 25 percent if public transit improvements and concentrated work opportunities were in place.[23]

There has been an increasing amount of development around transit stations in recent years. In 2006, the State Office of Commonwealth Development estimated that there were over ninety transit-oriented projects that were built or were being built in Eastern Massachusetts. These projects (each of which has at least fifty housing units) have over 25,000 total units, with an additional 4.5 million square feet of retail and 10.5 million square feet of office space.[24]

An important factor in promoting transit-oriented development has been rezoning. Until recently, Greater Boston communities were not zoned for this type of development. During the latter twentieth century, the planning ideal was to separate housing from commercial uses and single-family homes from multifamily dwellings. This made it very difficult to promote transit-oriented development because housing was kept out of town centers. Canton, which is located off Route 128 and I-95, started a trend in 2000, when it set out to revitalize its fading town center by permitting housing to be built above retail space. This placed housing within walking distance of the Canton commuter rail station. With this incentive, Canton attracted several new mixed-use developments, including the Village at Forge Pond, Grover Estates, Washington Place, and several other comparable projects. Residents appreciated living near shops and restaurants.

Framingham also rezoned its center. In 1972, the town prohibited multifamily dwellings after a spate of mid-rise apartments on Route 9 near the Massachusetts

FIGURE 11.3
Aerial view of transit-oriented development, Waltham. This view shows an early example of
contemporary transit-oriented development (TOD). The Waltham MBTA commuter rail station is
located above the Charles River. Below the river is Cronin's Landing (1998), a residential and retail
development on the site of the shuttered Grover Cronin department store. The factory complex in
the upper right includes the country's first vertically integrated cotton mill, opened by Francis Cabot
Lowell in 1814. It is currently used for housing.
Source: © 2012 Alex S. MacLean/Landslides, http://www.alexmaclean.com.

FIGURE 11.4
Station Landing, Medford. The Transit-Oriented Development (TOD) of Station Landing (2007) is
located near the Wellington MBTA station. It is one of the region's most effective New Urbanist attempts
at building residences above retail uses.
Source: Author's collection.

Turnpike upset local citizens. It was only after 2002, when the ordinance was changed, that apartments could be built downtown, which might take advantage of the commuter rail station. The new Framingham zoning sought to encourage denser mixed-use development, which has occurred in several rehabilitated commercial and industrial buildings. Since 2000, similar rezoning efforts for mixed uses have been undertaken in Attleboro, Franklin, Gloucester, Natick, Norwood, and Wilmington. Both national and local development companies have built housing complexes near transit stations and in downtown settings, including Woodland Station in Newton and Station Landing in Medford (Arborpoint); Hingham (Avalon); Waltham, Watertown, and downtown Boston (Archstone); Abington (Beacon Properties); and Salem (JPI). A notable project is Medford's Station Landing (National Development), which has actual blocks and streets resembling a townscape; and it is located adjacent to the Orange Line Wellington station.

State government has provided financial incentives for the creation of dense housing in order to promote transit use and create more affordable units. The Chapter 40R program, initiated under Governor Mitt Romney, has provided incentive grants to communities that zone smart growth housing districts (eight to twenty units per acre with twenty percent of the units considered "affordable"). The Massachusetts Chapter 40R program has provided funds to thirty-three districts, which have zoned districts for 12,350 new housing units in such in such communities as Kingston, Lakeville, Reading, and Sharon.[25]

The leading candidates for redevelopment are medium-sized cities. Lowell has used the Lowell National Historical Park, UMass–Lowell, and minor league sports to boost revitalization efforts. In Worcester, the University of Massachusetts Medical School, Massachusetts College of Pharmacy and Health Sciences, and a new downtown Worcester Medical Center have created a vital medical science center. Smaller cities, like Salem, Newburyport, and Portsmouth, New Hampshire, have made comebacks based on the appeal of their historic architecture and vibrant restaurant and nightlife.

The most ambitious redevelopment plans currently underway are in Quincy, which is seeking to create a thriving downtown eight miles from Boston. Quincy is pursuing a $1.6 billion project that would intensify development in an already active downtown. Developers Street-Works Development and the Beal Companies plan to add 1,200 new housing units, two hotels, office space, stores and restaurants, higher education, and health service to a twenty-block area. The developers would rehabilitate some existing buildings and construct up to a dozen new ones.[26] The key element is the MBTA's Red Line and commuter rail service that feeds into Boston.

Less advantaged older "gateway cities," such cities as Brockton, Fitchburg, Haverhill, Lawrence, and Lynn, are having greater difficulty with revitalization. Although they have the physical infrastructure to support additional development, including commuter rail service, they have been plagued by poverty, disinvestment, and the flight of retail activity to suburban strips. Gateway cities have enjoyed some revitalization achievements, but they are struggling to be magnets for redevelopment.

The lessons of urbanism are spreading to the commercial strip. Developers have started retrofitting aging shopping centers to introduce more density, walkability, and a mix of uses. Imitating old town centers has been a response to the decline of enclosed regional malls. The standardization and impersonality of malls began to pall on consumers. Standard & Poor's reported that, during the 1990s, mall trips declined by 50 percent and the number of stores visited on a typical mall visit declined by 67 percent.[27] What had been modern in the 1960s and 1970s became tiresome. Obsolete shopping centers were termed "greyfields" because they are prime sites for redevelopment.[28]

In response to the distaste for regional malls, developers have created "lifestyle centers," open-air pseudo-townscapes with a New Urbanist scale and themed architecture. They found that the easiest place to redevelop is the commercial strip, with all its disposable, unloved construction. Lifestyle centers have sought to resuscitate the sociability of street life and incorporate entertainment into the shopping experience. They have also rearranged parking so that it is located behind the stores, sometimes even in a concealed garage. Lifestyle centers can seem formulaic because most of them are owned by large shopping center management corporations, which are funneling Wall Street money through real estate investment trusts (REITs), which are seeking predictable returns on investment.

Mashpee Commons, on Cape Cod, could be considered the prototype for lifestyle centers in New England. In 1988, developer Cornish Associates, of Providence, hired the pioneer New Urbanist architects Andrés Duany and Elizabeth Plater-Zyberk to create a master plan for retrofitting an obsolete shopping plaza into a pedestrian-oriented townscape. Their blueprint included stores, cinemas, and restaurants with offices and apartments on the upper floors. Mashpee Commons even incorporated a post office, Catholic church, and the town library. It is notable that 80 percent of commercial tenants in Mashpee Commons are independently owned local businesses, whereas the national average for independents in regional shopping malls is only 10 percent.[29]

FIGURE 11.5

Mashpee Commons, Mashpee. Mashpee Commons, on Cape Cod, is the New Urbanist prototype for lifestyle centers in New England. In 1988, developer Cornish Associates hired the architects Andrés Duany and Elizabeth Plater-Zyberk to create a master plan for retrofitting an obsolete shopping plaza into a pedestrian-oriented townscape.

Source: Mashpee Commons. *Photograph:* Elton Pope-Lance.

Bay State Commons (2007), adjacent to downtown Westborough and an MBTA commuter rail station, might come closest to combining a lifestyle center with a transit orientation. The development has 350,000 square feet of retail space and fifty condominiums. There are eleven buildings laid out on streets adjacent to a common. Located on a former industrial site, this project earns extra points for being "green." Hingham Shipyard (2008), built near downtown Hingham on the site of a World

War II shipbuilding facility, is a mixed-use project that combines housing, offices, stores, restaurants, cinema, and a marina. The entire development resembles a New Urbanist project with compact blocks, streets, and brick facades. The largest and most recent lifestyle center is Dedham's Legacy Place (2009), which was built on the site of an obsolete shopping center.

The rise of lifestyle centers and transit-oriented developments is particularly apparent along the Route 128/I-95 and I-495 beltways. At major interchanges, developers have built or are planning lifestyle retail centers. When the Derby Street Shoppes (2004) opened in Hingham, lifestyle centers seemed like a novelty. Now that the formula has been repeated at major highway interchanges, lifestyle centers seem like refined shopping centers, not mixed-use New Urbanist developments. These lifestyle centers are essentially reformatted shopping centers full of national retail chains, with virtually no offices, housing, or local services. Since the lifestyle center is still a shopping mall, it has no public space for meetings, protests, or spontaneous public activities. In the words of *Boston Globe* architectural critic Robert Campbell, a lifestyle center is "a theatrical representation of town life."[30]

Even Patriot Place (2007), the shopping-entertainment center New England Patriots owner Robert Kraft has built next to Gillette Stadium in Foxborough, is arranged along a pedestrian street. Patriot Place incorporates national fashion retailers with the Patriots Hall of Fame, CBS sports restaurant, cinemas, an outdoor skating rink, and an outpatient health care center run by Brigham & Women's and Massachusetts General Hospitals. It serves as a little downtown for the Foxborough area and an activity node for sports fans. The Natick Mall has added a different wrinkle to shopping centers by building 215 luxury condos, named "Nouvelle at Natick."[31] This is the first project in Greater Boston where housing has been integrated into an enclosed suburban mall. These projects point to new opportunities for redevelopment on the commercial strip, where it is crowded, visually unattractive, and malleable.

Smart Growth and NIMBYism

Transit-oriented development and New Urbanism have become popular over the past decade because they meet a market demand. Christopher Leinberger explains in *The Option of Urbanism: Investing in a New American Dream* (2007) that America's knowledge economy and evolving demographics are generating a demand for more varied housing and job location options. Leinberger calls the compact development template that allows people to walk from their houses to stores and transit "walkable urbanism." It contrasts with the one-size-fits-all "drivable suburbanism" and detached single-family homes that prevailed in the latter twentieth century. The template for "walkable urbanism" includes townhouses and low- to mid-rise apartment buildings intermixed with shops, restaurants, and offices. Waltham's Moody Street and Cronin's Landing apartments, located near a commuter rail station, are an illustrative example.

Leinberger cites a market survey showing that 40 percent of those responding in Greater Boston desire "walkable urbanism," while 30 percent prefer "drivable suburbanism" and 30 percent would accept either. Leinberger estimates that, with 25 percent of Boston housing located in walkable neighborhoods, there is a significant unmet demand.[32] He also believes that 60 to 70 percent of all demand for walkable urbanism will be met in suburbs, implying a pent-up need for suburban redevelopment. The largest markets for walkable and transit-oriented development are among young professionals and empty-nesters. Families, meanwhile, will probably continue to prefer single-family homes with ample yards.

The large demand for walkable urbanism is demonstrated by high real-estate prices in attractive walkable neighborhoods, such as Beacon Hill, Back Bay, South, End, Charlestown, Cambridge, and Brookline. Housing units that have best held their value during the recent economic downturn have been in walkable neighborhoods and the houses that have lost the most value have been located on the suburban periphery near I-495 and beyond. Urban gentrification has occurred when there are not enough walkable housing units to meet demand, and the less affluent get squeezed out.

The taste for urban living has been stoked by the experience of millions of Americans traveling to Europe and seeking to recreate the experience of lively city and town centers in this country. The market segments that appreciate urban neighborhoods are attracted by "third places," which are the pubs, cafés, restaurants, libraries, cinemas, gyms, and similar hangouts where they can congregate in society.[33] Besides the urban neighborhoods of Boston, Cambridge, and Somerville, many suburban town centers have been redeveloped as concentrations of "third places" in recent years. Towns with lively restaurants, coffee shops, nightlife, and shopping include, from north to south, Salem, Melrose, Arlington, Lexington, Concord, Waltham's Moody Street, Newton Centre, Wellesley, Needham, Norwood, and Hingham.

"Creative class" economic development theorist Richard Florida puts the coming housing shift into another perspective. He argues that the shift is part of a "great reset" of the economy, which is transitioning from enormous investments in suburban housing and automobiles to cheaper, more compact housing and the use of public transportation. Florida argues that "our overwhelming reliance on suburban-style single-family home ownership is an experiment that has outlived its usefulness," since that is what produced the 2008 economic downturn. He explains that by anchoring Americans to specific geographic locations, home ownership makes it more difficult to move to areas with job opportunities. Florida advocates renting for many people, maintaining that the housing system should be "more in tune with the knowledge-driven economy's need for flexibility and labor mobility."[34]

In Greater Boston, the trend toward transit-oriented development and walkable urbanism has been achieving a growing regional consensus. Boston's Metropolitan Area Planning Council (MAPC), the quasi-governmental regional planning agency representing in Greater Boston's 101 cities and towns, has articulated this vision through the *MetroFuture* Plan. Under the leadership of Executive Director Marc Draisen, MAPC estimated that the region's population would grow by 465,000 people by 2030 and sought to identify where these new residents would be best accommodated. An extensive multiyear planning process engaged several thousand citizens in examining three potential development scenarios. Under existing trends, growth would flow to communities with open land on the metropolitan periphery. Restrictive large-lot zoning in outer towns would contribute to the loss of 150,000 acres of open space. Continued dispersal of housing and jobs would maintain dependency on the automobile, increase traffic jams, and limit opportunities to use the transit system. The planning process determined these trends would be unsustainable.

MetroFuture proposed a scenario that would consume only 28,000 acres of open land and build 65 percent of new housing in existing urban neighborhoods and town centers. This approach would employ smart growth strategies like clustering residential zoning and transit-oriented development. Since MAPC is strictly an advisory body that provides technical planning assistance, it is up to municipalities to provide the appropriate zoning and infrastructure, the state to provide funding and program support, and individuals and businesses to do the actual building.[35]

Progress toward transit-oriented development and walkable urbanism has been fitful. Urbanized communities tend to support redevelopment, while residential suburbs are nervous about new infill projects. Suburbanites are concerned with protecting

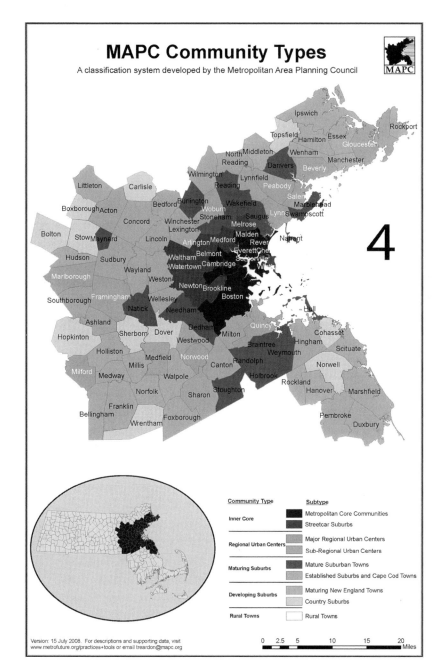

FIGURE 11.6
Metropolitan Area Planning Council map of community types, 2008. The Metropolitan Area Planning Council has designated eight categories of development for the region's 101 cities and towns.
Source: Metropolitan Area Planning Council.

the investment in their house and their emotional attachment to a particular type of community. They often oppose dense development, especially multifamily housing or below-market "affordable" housing. On a fiscal level, many citizens are concerned that residential growth will increase town budgets, especially for schools. In inner-city Boston, some neighborhoods are suspicious of gentrification brought on by redevelopment.

The communities most opposed to development are the affluent, low-density places like Carlisle, Lincoln, Sherborn, and Weston, whose residents treasure the exclusive community character and have the resources to resist changes to that character. In Weston, neighbors have mounted a successful challenge to the efforts of Regis College to build an academic village oriented to seniors. Westonites have even blocked efforts to build a bike trail along an abandoned rail line out of fear of potential crimes by interlopers. *Boston Globe* columnist Tom Keane has observed of the Massachusetts localism: "Be it a skyscraper downtown, transit-oriented developments in suburbia or windmills in Nantucket Sound, there are always voices raised in opposition. Sometimes they come in the clothes of environmentalism, preservation, or tradition. Other times, more nakedly, they are simply opposition to any change whatsoever."[36] NIMBYism is a real problem for a region seeking to grow its economy, whether building houses or businesses.

Opponents of new development often argue that their community is "built out." This is more of a mindset than an actual limit to construction. A critic of this thinking is Harvard economics professor Edward Glaeser, who argues that communities do not have to be locked into current zoning. Zoning can be changed and taller buildings can be constructed if there is political will. Glaeser believes that denser development in urban neighborhoods and town centers is essential for Greater Boston's economic growth. Both Glaeser and Northeastern University labor economist Barry Bluestone maintain that the region's high cost of housing is a drag on the local economy. More college graduates would stay in Boston and more workers would move here if the housing supply were expanding and units were less costly.[37] They argue that zoning must be changed to allow additional housing and more incentives for denser housing must be put in place.

In addition to the political obstacles posed by NIMBYism, it is logistically difficult to build infill development. Redevelopment requires considerable planning, investment, public infrastructure, and local support. Because redevelopment is more costly and complicated than building on open land, opportunities for small-scale investors are limited. The historic development patterns of the streetcar suburbs relied on an army of small investors to build three-deckers. On the postwar commercial strips, a small businessman could erect a gas station, a fast food outlet, or a small shopping plaza. Since the redevelopment paradigm has to be customized to a location and developers have to be skillful, building compact, mixed-use projects will not be a cookie-cutter exercise. Transit-oriented residential and commercial projects as well as lifestyle centers have been built by corporations using significant capital investments. The complexity and cost of such developments should prove an impediment to their construction.

Smart growth will require smart planning to convince the public of the need for compact mixed-use development. Perhaps enlightened self-interest will prevail in suburbs, which are struggling to maintain the quality of life its residents are seeking. Joel Kotkin, an advocate of what he terms the "New Suburbanism," argues that this is a watershed moment for suburbs:

> In historic terms, we may consider the amenity limited traditional housing tract, the formula mall and even strip centers as a stage in suburban development from which we are now—slowly but inexorably—passing, in some measure due to pointed critiques by new urbanists. New Suburbanism looks to the next stage of suburban development, where often ignored values of community, family and nature are being reasserted. It is as if suburbia is moving from its rough "Deadwood" phase to a more hospitable form.[38]

Exploring Smart Growth Development

Commuter Rail Lines, Departing from North Station and South Station

Excursions on metropolitan Boston's twelve commuter railroad lines provide a glimpse of the skeleton of almost two centuries of suburban development. The traveler can both visit the nineteenth-century bedroom communities and mill towns and view twenty-first-century transit-oriented developments.

The magnificently restored South Station, with its spacious waiting room and varied food court, serves the Fairmount, Framingham/Worcester, Franklin, Greenbush, Kingston/Plymouth, Middleboro/Lakeville, Needham, and Providence/Stoughton lines. North Station is the jumping-off point for the Fitchburg, Haverhill, Lowell, and Newburyport/Rockport routes. There are 133 commuter stations in the MBTA's commuter rail system.

Following each train line, which was originally built by such railroads as the Boston & Albany, Boston & Maine, and the Old Colony, you get a sense of how the metropolis grew. The passenger is struck by the dense urban landscape that stretches as far as Route 128. As soon as the train passes Route 128, the landscape changes to become a checkerboard of low-density development and open spaces. The most arresting natural areas are the cranberry bogs of Southeastern Massachusetts along the Kingston/Plymouth and Middleboro/Lakeville lines and the placid marshlands traveling north to Newburyport.

Most suburban centers developed around railroad stations. The architecture is full of character, and walking opportunities abound. Town centers offer a wide array of independently owned shops and restaurants, coffeehouses, art cinemas, ethnic groceries, antiques shops, art galleries, and other one-of-a-kind places. Many suburbs sport new transit-oriented developments. These downtowns are still the primary place that people think of when they imagine Melrose, Needham, Wakefield, or Winchester.

Lively commercial districts range from West Newton and Newtonville to Natick and Waltham. Ethnic eateries and shops abound in Framingham (Brazilian) and Lynn (Latin American of all nationalities). Comfortable middle-class suburban downtowns can be explored in Andover, Belmont, and Hingham. The upscale shopping scene can be found in Wellesley, Concord, and Manchester-by-the-Sea. Historic maritime cities that have reinvented themselves include Salem and Newburyport. The fishing towns of Gloucester and Rockport have become tourist meccas.

Most of the rail lines take about one hour to traverse, with Needham (forty minutes), Worcester (one-and-one-quarter hours) and Fitchburg (one-and-one-half hours) being the exceptions. It is easy to get off at one station, explore, and catch the next train to a further destination.

Station Landing, Intersection of Route 28 and Route 16, Medford

Many new housing developments have been built near transit stations over the past decade, but few of them have successfully incorporated retail uses on the ground floor. Station Landing (2006), which is located at the MBTA Orange Line station at Wellington, may be the most complete example of building transit-oriented development (TOD) from scratch. It has shops, services, and eateries beneath the housing, just like an old-fashioned neighborhood. Though it seems like a no-brainer, this sort of development has proven complicated to pull off because of having to mix residences and retail space.

Canton transit-oriented development at The Village at Forge Pond, Washington Street
at Forge Pond, and Washington Place, 717 Washington Street, Canton

Since 2000, many Massachusetts communities have rezoned their upper floors in
commercial buildings to allow housing. These communities have included Attleboro,
Canton, Framingham, Franklin, Gloucester, Hyannis, Norwood, and Wilmington.
The first of these communities to strategically rezone for residential over retail was
Canton. Canton wanted to revitalize its fading town center, which had lost much
business to strip shopping centers. Town meeting adopted zoning that encouraged a
mix of dense housing and new retail in the town center. One of the major draws has
been proximity to the commuter rail station. Canton has attracted several new developments with housing above retail space near the station, including Village at Forge
Pond and Washington Place. It does not seem like a revolutionary idea, but allowing
residential over retail space was a discovery at the turn of the millennium.

Mashpee Commons, Intersection of Route 28 and Route 151, Mashpee

Mashpee Commons (1988) is considered a New Urbanism pioneer in New England
because of its master plan by Andrés Duany and Elizabeth Plater-Zyberk. It has created a town center on the site of an obsolete shopping center. The architectural style
sets out to recapture the brick and shingle buildings of a traditional New England
town. There are many shops and restaurants and a scattering of apartments. The projected single-family houses are still in the development phase. Mashpee Commons
prefigured lifestyle shopping centers, such as Bay State Commons (Westborough),
Hingham Shipyard, Derby Street Shoppes (Hingham), Legacy Place (Dedham), and
Patriot Place (Foxborough).

Postscript: The Coming Era

The Digital Revolution and Metropolitan Development

Two trends that could dramatically affect the region's landscape loom ahead: the ongoing digital revolution and climate change. The effects from digital technology will be significant, although they are still under the radar. Digital data are providing feedback for managing metropolitan life, such as improving the flow of vehicular traffic or allowing transit riders to track the real-time availability of buses and trains with hand-held devices.

The plethora of applications introduced by smartphones demonstrates the advent of the "smart city," as smart people at MIT like to call it. One of the world's leading think tanks for creating smart cities is MIT's SENSEable City Laboratory, which is affiliated with the famed Media Lab. It was established in 2004 to undertake projects that use digital technology to study and manage life in cities. SENSEable City Laboratory researchers are analyzing vast amounts of data from sensors implanted in the urban infrastructure, vehicles, and hand-held devices to describe and understand how actual cities work. IBM, Cisco Systems, and other leading technology firms are currently making investments in wiring cities, advancing computational power, and developing programs to manage life in the city. IBM, for example, has developed software to track crimes and predict where they might occur next. One gets the flavor of what may lie ahead from a report issued by the Institute for the Future—*When*

Everything Is Programmable (2009). Dramatic advances in digital technology's ability to manage cities are being brought about by smart personal devices, increased broadband connectivity, cloud computing, availability of real-time data, and ubiquitous public interfaces.[1]

The City of Boston has established the Mayor's Office of New Urban Mechanics (2010), in coordination with Liberty Mutual and InnoCentive, to develop digital applications to improve life in the city. One project is Street Bump, which uses a sensor in a cell phone and a GPS (global positioning system) to detect when a driver hits a pothole. The information is relayed to City Hall for an appropriate response. The Office of New Urban Mechanics also is using sensors to improve the trash collection system. Boston's Spot Tag Program (2012) is placing 2D tags (like bar codes) on street furniture, public building, or public art. By scanning these 2D tags, citizens with a smartphone will be able to leave a comment that a trash can is overflowing or that they like a piece of public art. They will be able to receive information about open hours at a public library or recreational facility.[2]

One of the most promising areas for digital technology is for improving traffic flow. Once again MIT is involved, with the CarTel project, which is developing computer algorithms to help traffic flow more efficiently. The big idea is to use every motor vehicle as a sensor transmitting data about traffic conditions. The information gathered from vehicles could make traffic lights work more efficiently, work with GPS to provide autos directions for taking the most efficient routes, and charge tolls for those riding in HOT (high-occupancy toll) highway lanes to avoid congestion. Some traffic engineers even foresee the day when digital technology essentially guides all vehicle traffic.[3]

Each metropolitan area, city, and neighborhood will have its own digital interface. Increasingly sophisticated technology will favor customization over standardization. Because Boston is highly advanced in the employment of digital technology and has vigorous higher-education and technology sectors, it promises to be a leader in developing smart cities. At this point, the development pattern of compact mixed-use development should increase in popularity as digital connections make urban areas safer and more engaging. More sophisticated programming could produce more efficient functioning of transportation, electric power, telecommunications, water supply, wastewater treatment, environmental protection, and other public services. There seems to be little evidence that providing a digital interface to communities would encourage sprawl.

The ultimate impact of digital technologies will be decided by the system of governance. Will it be controlled through democratic means or will proprietary corporations shape the future? Will the programmable metropolitan area mark a significant improvement over the current situation or could it be dystopian, where digital surveillance eliminates privacy and curbs free association and expression? One hopes that the new programmable metropolitan infrastructure is as beneficial as the water supply, sewer, park, and transportation systems that have preceded it.

Coping with Climate Change and Expensive Oil

Greater Boston could suffer far more radical impacts from climate change, which should shape the next era of metropolitan development. Some of the most knowledgeable environmental scientists predict damaging environmental, social, and economic effects to Boston during the next century. A 2007 report by the Union of Concerned Scientists, *Confronting Climate Change in the US Northeast: Science Impacts, and Solutions*, posits scenarios for both "high carbon emissions" (continued heavy reliance on fossil fuels) and "low emissions" (widespread adoption of alternative energy). Under the "high emissions" scenario, the region could experience up to sixty-three days a year above ninety degrees and twenty-four days over 100 degrees (New England recently has experienced an average of nine days per summer above ninety degrees). Under the low-emissions scenario, Boston summers would feel like current summers around Washington, DC; under the high-emissions scenario, summers would feel like South Carolina's.[4]

The greatest risk to Northeast seaboard cities over the next century is posed by melting of the Greenland Ice Sheet. A report issued in 2009 by the Allianz insurance company, of Germany, and the World Wide Fund for Nature (former World Wildlife Fund) estimates that sea levels could rise twenty to twenty-six inches by 2050 (sea levels rose by ten inches during the entire twentieth century). Boston would have the fourth highest risk exposure from flooding of any coastal American city, after Miami, New York–Newark, and New Orleans. The World Wide Fund for Nature-Allianz report argues that the effects of sea-level rise may be compounded by hurricanes, which could occur with greater force and frequency. For example, flooding and wind damage from a 10-year storm could have the intensity of today's 100-year storm, and the 100-year storm could have the impact of today's 500-year storm.[5]

According the Union of Concerned Scientists study, current 100-year coastal floods could occur every two to four years by midcentury and every year by 2100. Flooding could reach across the Rose Kennedy Greenway to Quincy Market and North Station. In the Back Bay, the Charles River could flood all the streets and the Public Garden. Parts of South Boston, East Boston, Cambridge, and the communities along the North and South Shores could be prey to heavy flooding. Excessive damage could result from flooding of Boston's thirty miles of highway and subway tunnels. The low-lying coast will be vulnerable to flooding from the North Shore all the way around to Cape Cod. Over the long term, there could be pressure to move important economic and institutional functions farther inland.

The City of Boston and local architects, engineers, and planners have been examining potential scenarios and solutions to cope with the rising sea level. Massport is strategizing how to protect Logan Airport, located on the harbor in East Boston, against flooding and how to keep the shipping port operating in the midst of rising sea levels. The Boston Water and Sewer Commission is studying how to drain the city in the wake of a massive storm surge. Planners are discussing potential building code changes that would flood-proof structures.[6]

Architects Antonio Di Mambro and Hubert Murray, who was chief architect for the Central Artery Project, have proposed building a barrier at the mouth of Boston Harbor to protect against storm surges. Di Mambro originally conceived this project, called the Sea Belt, in 1988. The barrier would link Deer Island, Long Island, and the Squantum area of Quincy, and fifteen-foot-high gates would close to protect the harbor against storm surges.[7] The Di Mambro and Murray proposal is only a concept. It would take at least a generation to design and build such a project; neither the state nor the city is even considering it yet. The threat of serious flooding seems decades away and such a multi-billion-dollar project, exceeding the Big Dig in scope, poses a monumental fiscal challenge.

Yet other cities have built storm surge barriers. During the mid-1960s, the US Army Corps of Engineers built storm surge barriers to protect the harbors of New Bedford, Massachusetts; Providence, Rhode Island; and Stamford, Connecticut. The movable gates at each barrier have successfully protected the harbors on several occasions. London has constructed the Thames Barrier (1984) to protect against flooding, and the Netherlands has the Dutch Delta Works (1997) to protect the Rhine-Meuse-Scheldt estuary against storm-force tides. The Italian government is building the $6 billion MOSE Project to protect Venice (2014), one of the cities most endangered by sea-level rise. To cope with flood tides, three sets of boxlike gates will rise from the water to block the mouth of the Venetian Lagoon.

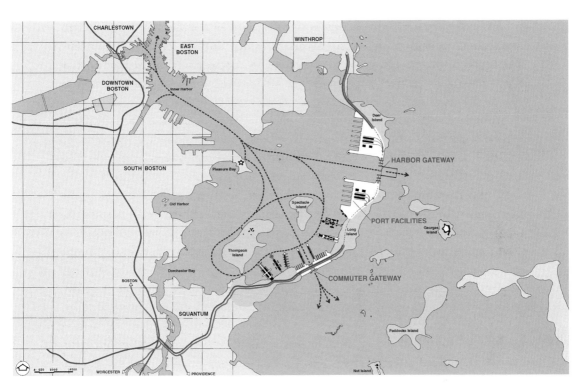

FIGURE 12.1

"Sea Belt" schematic for protecting Boston Harbor against sea-level rise, 1988. Architects Antonio Di Mambro and Hubert Murray have proposed building a barrier at the mouth of Boston Harbor to protect against sea-level rise. Fifteen-foot-high gates would close to protect the harbor against storm surges triggered by climate change.

Source: Antonio Di Mambro + Associates, Inc.

To foster sustainable development in the face of climate change, Massachusetts and the City of Boston are promoting measures that help reduce carbon emissions. They include bicycle and walking improvements, transit investments near existing commercial and residential development, and planting trees and roof gardens to absorb carbon gasses. Under Governor Deval Patrick, Massachusetts has made a major commitment to energy efficiency with the Green Communities Act (2008). With this legislation, the state is projected to reduce electricity use by 2.4 percent and natural gas by 1.5 percent between 2009 and 2012, conservation targets that have been rated the most aggressive in the country.

These measures complement the state's efforts to reduce greenhouse gases from power plants as part of the Regional Greenhouse Gas Initiative. This coalition of nine Northeastern states is the nation's first mandatory, market-based program to reduce emissions of carbon dioxide at power plants. The nine states have committed to reducing carbon dioxide emissions 10 percent by 2018 through a mix of energy efficiency and renewable energy. Massachusetts has committed to carbon-emission reductions in the Global Warming Solutions Act (2008).[8]

Climate change is not the only factor affecting consumption patterns of fossil fuels. Increasing global demand and fluctuating oil prices are causing economic dislocations, forcing energy conservation and a search for alternatives. Four dollar-a-gallon gasoline seems to be a trip wire for motorists that effects how much they drive and consume gasoline. Even with the discovery of extensive oil reserves in the Arctic, Western Canada, and Plains and Rocky Mountain states, it is unclear how long-term gasoline prices will be affected. It is uncertain how much of the oil is recoverable and what the costs (both economic and environmental) would be of hydraulic fracturing ("fracking") and other environmentally risky extraction methods. Volatile oil prices and consequent socioeconomic dislocations, together with a desire for greater transportation efficiency, are stoking interest in vehicles powered by biofuels, hydrogen, electric batteries, hybrids, "smart" electronic-directed vehicles, and more robust public transportation.

It is difficult to predict how effectively regions like metropolitan Boston will adapt to changes in the world's climate, oil supplies, and transportation technology. Progress is slow because of climate-change skepticism and resistance to policies that may increase energy costs in the short term, such as a carbon tax. Yet, Boston seems better prepared to make the transition than most American cities because of the strong presence of compact urbanism and public transportation. According to Sustainlane.com, Boston ranks sixth among America's largest fifty cities in a composite rating of infrastructure, building, and planning factors relating to sustainability.[9] Just as Greater Boston was ahead of the curve in developing country estates, railroad and streetcar suburbs, suburban beltways, edge cities, and revitalized central cities, it is positioned to be a leader in forging solutions to the challenges posed by climate change and rising oil prices.

Exploring the Metropolitan Landscape: Recommended Sites by Community

---

Andover

Shawsheen Heights, William and Kensington Streets

Shawsheen Village, Argyll and Arundel Streets

Ward Reservation (Bay Circuit Trail), off Prospect Street

Avon/Stoughton

Jordan's Furniture, Ikea, the Home Depot, Costco, Petco, and the Christmas Tree Shops, Stockwell Drive, off Harrison Boulevard, Exit 19, Route 24

Belmont

Beaver Brook Metropolitan Reservation/Waverly Oaks, Mill Street

Modernist houses, Snake Hill Road

Beverly

Endicott College, 376 Hale Street (Route 127)

Boston

Boston City Hall, City Hall Plaza

Faneuil Hall Marketplace/Quincy Market, Faneuil Hall Square

Fenway-Riverway-Jamaicaway-Arborway-VFW Parkway, Emerald Necklace Parks

HarborWalk, along Boston's forty-seven-mile harbor front

Prudential Center, 800 Boylston Street

Rose Fitzgerald Kennedy Greenway, above I-93, between South Station and North Station

Brighton

Brighton Cattle Market, Market and Washington Streets

Dorchester

Victorian houses at Melville Avenue, Ocean Street, Welles Avenue, Wellesley Park, and parts of Ashmont and Jones Hills.

Jamaica Plain

Victorian houses at Elm Street, Parley Vale, and Robinwood Avenue

North End

Prince Macaroni Building, 45–69 Atlantic Avenue

Roxbury

Shirley-Eustis House, 33 Shirley Street

Brookline

Beacon Street, Park Drive to Cleveland Circle

Cottage Farm, bounded by Amory, Dummer, St. Mary's, and Freeman Streets

Fisher Hill Historic District, bounded by Clinton and Sumner Roads, Boylston Street, and Chestnut Hill Avenue

Frederick Law Olmsted National Historic Site/Fairsted, 99 Warren Street

Hancock Village, Gerry Road, Independence Drive, Sherman Road, and Thornton Road

John Fitzgerald Kennedy National Historic Site, 83 Beals Street

Larz Anderson Auto Museum, 15 Newton Street

Linden Park, Linden Place

Longwood, bounded by Kent, Chapel, St. Mary's, and Monmouth Streets

---

Cambridge

Kendall Square, Broadway and Main Street

Massachusetts Institute of Technology, Massachusetts Avenue and Memorial Drive

Memorial Drive/Charles River Basin

North Cambridge Cattle Market, Porter Square, 1815, Massachusetts Avenue

Three-decker houses at Alberta Terrace, Marie Avenue, Cambridge Terrace

---

Canton

Transit-oriented development, Village at Forge Pond, Washington Street at Forge Pond, and Washington Place, 717 Washington Street

---

Foxborough

Gillette Stadium and Patriot Place, Patriot Place and Route 1

Framingham

Shoppers' World site, Shoppers' World Drive and Route 9
Campanelli Brothers subdivision, Pinewood Drive, Griffin Road, and adjoining streets

Hopkinton

Hopkinton Highlands and The Estates at Highland Ridge, Everett Circle, Greenwood Road, Overlook Road, Summit Way, and adjacent streets

Ipswich

Crane Estate at Castle Hill, 290 Argilla Road

Kingston

Cranberry Watershed Preserve (Bay Circuit Trail), behind Silver Lake Regional High School

Lawrence

Lawrence Heritage State Park, 1 Jackson Street

Lexington

Cape Cod and Colonial Revival houses, Wellington Estates, Constitution Road, Revolutionary Road, Paul Revere Road

Lexington Green, Massachusetts Avenue in Lexington Center

Modernist Houses, Six Moon Hill, Moon Hill Road

Lincoln

Battle Road Farm, Old Bedford Road

Gropius House, 68 Baker Bridge Road

Lowell

The Boott Cotton Mills Museum, Lowell National Historical Park, 115 John Street

Manchester, New Hampshire

Isadore and Lucille Zimmerman House, 223 Heather Street

Mashpee

Mashpee Commons, Route 28 and Route 151

Maynard

Digital Equipment Corporation, Main Street (Route 62) and Great Road (Route 117)

Medford

Station Landing, intersection of Route 28 and Route 16

Medford/Malden/Melrose/Stoneham/Winchester

Middlesex Fells Reservation and Fellsway

Milton

Captain Forbes House, 215 Adams Street

Milton/Quincy/Randolph/ Canton

Blue Hills Reservation and Blue Hills Parkway

Natick

Natick Mall, Speen Street and Route 9

Needham

New England Industrial Park, Highland Street at Exit 19A, Route 128

Newton

Commonwealth Avenue

Jackson Homestead, 527 Washington Street

Kenrick Park, between Church and Franklin Streets

Newton Centre Green Line MBTA Station, 70 Union Street

Oak Hill Park, Wiswall and Spiers Roads

Quincy

Quincy Shore Reservation and Drive

Plymouth

The Pinehills, Clark Road, Exit 3, Route 3

Reading

Reading Common, Main Street at Lowell and Salem Streets

Saugus

Commercial Strip, Route 1

Sharon

Moose Hill Farm Massachusetts Audubon Sanctuary (Bay Circuit Trail), 396 Moose Hill Street

Sudbury

Tippling Rock (Bay Circuit Trail), in Nobscot Boy Scout Reservation, top of Brimstone Lane, off Route 20

Waltham

Boston Manufacturing Company Mills, 144–154 Moody Street

Gore Place, 52 Gore Street

Stonehurst/Robert Treat Paine House, 577 Beaver Street

The Vale/Lyman Estate, 185 Lyman Street

Waltham Business Parks, Winter Street, Exit 27, Route 128

Wellesley

Hunnewell Estate, 845 Washington Street

Wenham

Gordon College, 255 Grapevine Road

Weston

Glen House Hotel, 247 Glen Road

Henderson House, 99 Westcliff Road

Weston Town Green, Boston Post Road at School and Church Streets

Winchester

Rangeley Park, Rangeley Road

Wrentham

Wrentham Village Premium Outlets, Exit 15, I-495

Notes

Preface

1. Dolores Hayden, *Building Suburbia: Green Fields and Urban Growth, 1820–2000* (New York: Pantheon Books, 2003). Dolores Hayden categorizes American suburbs into seven types: Borderlands (1820–); Picturesque Enclaves (1850–); Streetcar Buildouts (1870–); Mail-Order and Self-Made Suburbs (1900–); Sitcom Suburbs (1940–); Edge Nodes (1960–); and Rural Fringes (1980–). Each type of suburb is represented in metropolitan Boston, although their timing and prevalence may differ from other parts of the country. The National Park Service has published a useful report providing a somewhat different categorization of American suburbs: Railroad and Horsecar Suburbs (1830–1890); Streetcar Suburbs (1888–1928); Early Automobile Suburbs (1908–1945); and Post–World War II and Early Freeway Suburbs (1945–1960). The periodization does not continue later because the National Register of Historic Places set out to categorize only structures that are at least fifty years old. David L. Ames and Linda Flint McClelland, *National Register Bulletin: Historic Residential Suburbs: Guidelines for Evaluation and Documentation for the National Register of Historic Places* (Washington, D.C.: National Park Service, 2002), http://www.nps.gov/nr/publications/bulletins/suburbs/index.htm.

Chapter 1

1. "City Mayors Statistics," City Mayors website, http://www.citymayors.com/statistics/largest-cities-area-125.html. Of the world's twelve largest metropolitan cities by area, eleven are in the United States.

2. Olmsted, Vaux & Co., "Preliminary Report upon the Proposed Suburban Village at Riverside, near Chicago," in *Civilizing American Cities: A Selection of Frederick Law Olmsted's Writings on Cityscapes*, ed. S. B. Sutton (Cambridge, Mass.: MIT Press, 1971), p. 295.

3. *A Handbook of New England* (Boston: Porter E. Sargent, 1917), p. 404. The US Census Bureau first recognized the existence of metropolitan areas with the 1910 census. It backdated metropolitan population figures to 1900.

4. Robert Fishman, *Bourgeois Utopias: The Rise and Fall of Suburbia* (New York: Basic Books, 1987), p. 189.

5. The following regional planning agencies border the Metropolitan Area Planning Council service area. Many of their communities may be considered part of Greater Boston, depending upon what issues are being considered: Central Massachusetts Regional Planning Commission—forty communities of Greater Worcester; Merrimack Valley Planning Commission—fifteen communities between Lawrence and Newburyport; Montachusett Regional Planning Commission—twenty-three communities stretching west from I-495 on the northern tier of Massachusetts, including Fitchburg and Leominster; North Middlesex Council of Governments—nine communities focused on Greater Lowell; Old Colony Planning Council—fifteen communities stretching from Brockton to Plymouth; Southeastern Regional Planning and Economic Development District—twenty-seven cities and towns in Southeastern Massachusetts, including Fall River, New Bedford, and Taunton.

Chapter 2

1. John R. Stilgoe, *Common Landscape of America, 1580 to 1845* (New Haven, Conn.: Yale University Press, 1982), p. 48.

2. Joseph S. Wood, *The New England Village* (Baltimore: Johns Hopkins University Press, 1997), p. 70.

3. Ibid., p. 103.

4. Henry C. Binford, *The First Suburbs: Residential Communities on the Boston Periphery, 1815–1860* (Chicago: University of Chicago Press, 1985), pp. 5–6.

5. John R. Stilgoe, *Borderland: Origins of the American Suburb, 1820–1939* (New Haven, Conn.: Yale University Press, 1988), p. 89; Timothy Dwight, *Travels in New England and New York*, Vol. III, ed. Barbara Miller Solomon (1822; Cambridge, Mass.: Harvard University Press, 1969), p. 80.

6. John Hayward, "Boston/Boston Harbor," *The New England Gazetteer*, 7th edition (Boston: John Hayward, 1839).

7. Keith N. Morgan, Naomi Miller, Richard Candee, and Roger Reed, *Buildings of Massachusetts: Metropolitan Boston* (Charlottesville: University of Virginia Press, 2009), p. 442.

Chapter 3

1. Alexander von Hoffman, *Local Attachments: The Making of an Urban Neighborhood, 1850 to 1920* (Baltimore: Johns Hopkins University Press, 1994), p. 66.

2. "Discover Historic Chestnut Hill" (Newton, Mass.: Newton Planning and Development Department, 2002), p. 1.

3. John P. Marquand, *The Late George Apley* (Boston: Little, Brown, 1936), p. 33.

4. Sam Bass Warner, Jr., *Streetcar Suburbs: The Process of Growth in Boston, 1870–1900* (Cambridge, Mass.: Harvard University Press, 1962), pp. 53, 63.

5. John Stilgoe, *Borderland: Origins of the American Suburb, 1820–1939* (New Haven, Conn.: Yale University Press, 1988), pp. 9–13.

6. Michael Rawson, *Eden on the Charles: The Making of Boston* (Cambridge, Mass.: Harvard University Press, 2010), pp. 137, 164.

7. Stilgoe, *Borderland,* pp. 9–13.

8. Ibid., p. 49.

9. Thomas P. Sileo, *Historical Guide to Open Space in Lexington* (Lexington, Mass.: Thomas P. Sileo, 1995), p. 283.

10. Robert Morris Copeland, *Country Life: A Handbook of Agriculture, Horticulture, and Landscape Gardening* (Boston: J. P. Jewett and Company, 1859), p. 774.

11. Leslie Crumbaker, *The Baker Estate or Ridge Hill Farms of Needham* (Wellesley, Mass.: Wellesley Historical Society, 1975), p. 9.

12. Cleveland Amory, *The Proper Bostonians* (New York: E. P. Dutton, , 1947), p. 196.

13. Andrew Jackson Downing, *A Treatise on the Theory and Practice of Landscape Gardening, Adapted to North America* (New York: Wiley and Putnam, 1841), p. 56. With his brother Charles, Downing wrote *Fruits and Fruit Trees of America* (1845), which strongly influenced the love of horticulture among antebellum gentlemen.

14. Ibid., pp. 259, 272.

15. Andrew Jackson Downing, *The Architecture of Country Houses* (New York: D. Appleton, 1850), p. 257. Cottage houses can be found in parts of Roxbury, Cambridge, and Newton.

16. Diana Muir, *Reflections in Bullough's Pond: Economy and Ecosystem in New England* (Hanover, N.H.: University Press of New England, 2000), p. 245.

17. "Spring Real Estate Supplement," *Boston Evening Transcript,* April 5, 1913.

18. "Weston Has Become the Lenox of the East: One Town without a Trolley Line; Sylvan Retreat for Busy Boston Men," *Boston Sunday Herald,* May 11, 1902. This article profiled more than a dozen of the town's leading estates.

19. Quoted from the *Boston Herald* in Pamela W. Fox with Sarah B. Gilman, *Farm Town to Suburb: The History of Weston, Massachusetts, 1830–1980* (Portsmouth, N.H.: Peter E. Randall, 2002), p. 407.

20. Wood, *The New England Village,* p. 6.

21. Arthur Shurtleff, "Autobiography of Arthur A. Shurtleff" (unpublished manuscript, Loeb Library, Harvard University Design School, 1943–1947).

22. Wood, *The New England Village,* pp. 46, 67.

23. Ibid., p. 91.

24. John C. MacLean, *A Rich Harvest: The History, People, and Buildings of Lincoln, Massachusetts* (Lincoln, Mass.: Lincoln Historical Society, 1987), p. 554.

25. Paul Brooks, *The View from Lincoln Hill: Man and the Land in a New England Town* (Boston: Houghton Mifflin, 1976), p. 224.

26. Ibid., p. 529.

27. "A Town That Doesn't Desire to be Up-to-Date," *Boston Herald,* May 18, 1902, quoted in MacLean, *A Rich Harvest,* p. 530.

28. Brooks, *The View from Lincoln Hill,* p. 222.

29. Ibid., p. 141.

30. Fox, *Farm Town to Suburb*, pp. 515, 457, 586.

31. Ibid., pp. 181–182.

32. Dorothy M. Anderson, *The Era of the Summer Estates: Swampscott, Massachusetts, 1870/1940* (Canaan, N.H.: Phoenix Publishing, 1985), p. 124.

33. Pamela W. Fox, *North Shore Boston: Houses of Essex County, 1865–1930* (New York: Acanthus Press, 2005), p. 173.

34. *The WPA Guide to Massachusetts: The Federal Writers' Project Guide to 1930s Massachusetts* (1937; New York: Pantheon Books, 1983), p. 274.

35. "Castle Hill on the Crane Estate," The Trustees of Reservation website, http://www.thetrustees .org/places-to-visit/northeast-ma/castle-hill-on-the-crane.html.

36. Ibid., pp. 40, 116–119.

37. Joseph E. Garland, *The North Shore: A Social History of Summers among the Noteworthy, Fashionable, Rich, Eccentric, and Ordinary on Boston's Gold Coast, 1823–1929* (Beverly, Mass.: Commonwealth Editions, 1998), pp. 353–355.

38. Elizabeth Coatsworth, *South Shore Town* (New York: Macmillan, 1948), p. vii.

39. M. F. Sweetser, *King's Handbook of Newton, Massachusetts* (Boston: Moses King Corporation, 1889), p. 205.

Chapter 4

1. Henry C. Binford, *The First Suburbs: Residential Communities on the Boston Periphery, 1815–1860* (Chicago: University of Chicago Press, 1985), p. 95.

2. Kenneth T. Jackson, *The Crabgrass Frontier: The Suburbanization of the United States* (New York: Oxford University Press, 1985), pp. 37–38; Binford, *The First Suburbs*, pp. 129, 149.

3. John Stilgoe, *Borderland: Origins of the American Suburb, 1820–1939* (New Haven, Conn.: Yale University Press, 1988), pp. 204, 122.

4. Oscar Handlin, *Boston's Immigrants: A Study in Acculturation*, revised edition (New York: Atheneum, 1972), p. 91.

5. Thomas J. Humphrey and Norton D. Clark, *Boston's Commuter Rail: The First 150 Years* (Cambridge: Boston Street Railway Association, Inc., 1985), p. 9.

6. "Discover Historic Auburndale" (Newton, Mass.: Newton Planning and Development Department, 2002), p. 1.

7. Stacey A. Bancroft Neustadt, "The Impact of the Massachusetts Turnpike Extension on the Citizens of the City of Newton" (master's thesis, Harvard University, 1994), p. 8.

8. M. F. Sweetser, *King's Handbook of Newton, Massachusetts* (Boston: Moses King Corporation, 1889), p. 192.

9. Ibid., p. 132.

10. Ibid., p. 275.

11. Sweetser, *King's Handbook to Newton*, p. 40.

12. Newton Tricentennial Corporation, *Newton, Massachusetts, 1688–1988, A Celebration of Three Hundred Years* (Newton, Mass.: Newton Tricentennial Corporation, 1988), p. 37.

13. Ibid., p. 161.

14. John Gould Curtis, *History of the Town of Brookline, Massachusetts* (Boston: Houghton Mifflin, 1933), p. 283.

15. Michael Rawson, *Eden on the Charles: The Making of Boston* (Cambridge, Mass.: Harvard University Press, 2010), p. 165.

16. Ibid., p. 149.

17. Peter Bernstein, *All the Money in the World* (New York: Random House, 2007), p. 280.

18. Olmsted, Vaux & Co., "Preliminary Report upon the Proposed Suburban Village at Riverside, near Chicago," in *Civilizing American Cities: A Selection of Frederick Law Olmsted's Writings on Cityscapes*, ed. S. B. Sutton (Cambridge, Mass.: MIT Press, 1971), p. 295.

19. *Boston Evening Transcript*, February 15, 1907, quoted in Gerald Gamm, *Urban Exodus: Why the Jews Left Boston and the Catholics Stayed* (Cambridge, Mass.: Harvard University Press, 1999), p. 192.

20. Frederick Law Olmsted, "Public Parks and the Enlargement of Towns," in *Civilizing American Cities*, ed. Sutton, pp. 68–69.

21. Olmsted, "Report upon Riverside," pp. 294–295.

22. Ibid., pp. 293, 294, 295.

23. Steven Johnson, *The Ghost Map: The Story of London's Most Terrifying Epidemic—and How It Changed Science, Cities, and the Modern World* (New York: Riverhead Books, 2006), p. 69.

24. Olmsted, "Report upon Riverside," pp. 294–295.

25. Robert Fishman, *Bourgeois Utopias: The Rise and Fall of Suburbia* (New York: Basic Books, 1987), pp. 146–147.

26. *The [Brookline] Chronicle*, March 2, 1889, quoted in Keith N. Morgan, Elizabeth Hope Cushing, and Roger Reed, *Community by Design: The Role of the Frederick Law Olmsted Office in the Suburbanization of Brookline, Massachusetts, 1880–1936* (Brookline, Mass.: Frederick Law Olmsted National Historic Site, 2010), p. 355.

27. Alexander Garvin, *The American City: What Works, What Doesn't*, 2nd ed. (New York: McGraw-Hill, 2002), p. 263.

28. Morgan, et al., *Community by Design*, pp. 415–416.

29. Ibid., p. 113.

30. Gwendolyn Wright, *Building the Dream: A Social History of Housing in America* (Cambridge, Mass.: MIT Press), pp. 111–112.

31. Arthur J. Krim, *Survey of Architectural History in Cambridge, Report Five: Northwest Cambridge* (Cambridge, Mass.: Cambridge Historical Commission, 1977), p. 42.

32. Ibid., pp. 38, 42.

33. Arlington Historic Commission, *Northwest Arlington, Massachusetts: An Architectural and Historical Study* (Arlington, Mass.: Arlington Historic Commission, 1995), pp. 17, 20–21.

34. Richard B. Betts, Victoria Haase, Norma A. Marsh, and Alfred Shea, *Belmont* (Charleston, S.C.: Arcadia Publishing, 2000), p. 60.

35. Henry Smith Chapman, *History of Winchester, Massachusetts*, Vol. I (Winchester, Mass.: Town of Winchester, Mass., 1975), p. 304.

36. Kevin Stevens, *Winchester, Massachusetts: The Architectural Heritage of a Victorian Town* (Winchester, Mass.: Winchester Historical Society, 1988), pp. 47–49, 34.

37. Ibid., p. 34. Chapman, *History of Winchester,* p. 267.

38. Chapman, *History of Winchester,,* p. 357.

39. "Charms of Rural Life," *Boston Globe*, May 4, 1890.

40. Ibid.

41. Thomas P. Sileo, *Historical Guide to Open Space in Lexington* (Lexington, Mass.: Thomas P. Sileo, 1995), pp. 59–60.

42. Henry David Thoreau, *Walden* (New York: The Library of America, 1985), p. 414.

43. Robert Gross, "Transcendentalism and Urbanism: Concord, Boston, and the Wider World," *Journal of American Studies* (1984): 361–381.

Chapter 5

1. Sam Bass Warner, Jr., *Streetcar Suburbs: The Process of Growth in Boston, 1870–1900* (Cambridge, Mass.: Harvard University Press, 1962), p. 22.

2. Ibid., p. 53.

3. *The WPA Guide to Massachusetts: The Federal Writers' Project Guide to 1930s Massachusetts* (1937; New York: Pantheon Books, 1983), p. 179.

4. Charles Mulford Robinson, *Modern Civic Art; or, The City Made Beautiful* (New York: G. P. Putnam's Sons, 1904), p. 209.

5. Stephen Puleo, *A City So Grand: The Rise of an American Metropolis, Boston, 1850–1900* (Boston: Beacon Press, 2010), p. 215.

6. Susan E. Maycock, *East Cambridge: Survey of Architectural History in Cambridge, Revised* (Cambridge, Mass.: MIT Press, 1988), p. 76. In 1890, 70 percent of American street railways used horses, but 97 percent were using electricity by 1902. Gunther Barth, *City People: The Rise of Modern City Culture in Nineteenth-Century America* (New York: Oxford University Press, 1980), p. 55.

7. Ibid., p. 22.

8. Warner, *Streetcar Suburbs*, p. 26. Henry Whitney's West End Land Company and West End Street Railway Company included such partners as department store magnate Eben Jordan, Sr., *Boston Journal* editor W. W. Clapp, and bicycle manufacturer Albert Pope. The West End Street Railway Company was the largest street railway system in the world, the first consolidated street railway company in America, and the first big city electrified system in the country—all originating from a scheme to promote suburban development in Brookline. Charles W. Cheape, *Moving the Masses: Urban Public Transit in New York, Boston, and Philadelphia, 1880–1912* (Cambridge, Mass.: Harvard University Press, 1980), pp. 115–116. It should be noted that Henry Whitney's career in public transportation was brief. He

started the West End Land Company in 1886, bought up the city's horsecar lines in 1887, and left the business in 1893 over an impasse related to building either a subway or an elevated transit line to alleviate congestion downtown. He went on to pursue interests in coal mining and gas production.

9. "Brookline in Transit," *Boston Evening Transcript*, April 5, 1913.

10. Ibid. A luxury development along Beacon Street was built at Aspinwall Hill, located southwest of Beacon and Washington Streets. Developed by Eugene Knapp around 1890, it included Beaconsfield Terrace, turreted condominiums at Gordon, Bernard, and Parkman Terraces, and an apartment hotel on Beacon Street.

11. John Gould Curtis, *History of the Town of Brookline, Massachusetts* (Boston: Houghton Mifflin, 1933), p. 316.

12. *The WPA Guide to Massachusetts*, p. 179.

13. Greer Hardwicke and Roger Reed, *Brookline* (Charleston, S.C.: Arcadia Publishing, 1998), p. 79.

14. "Action on Parks, *Boston Globe*, December 31, 1902.

15. *The WPA Guide to Massachusetts,* p. 270.

16. Edward S. Mason, *The Street Railway in Massachusetts: The Rise and Decline of an Industry* (Cambridge, Mass.: Harvard University Press, 1932), p. 9.

17. Ibid., p. xvi.

18. Robert Fogelson, *Downtown: Its Rise and Fall, 1880–1950* (New Haven, Conn.: Yale University Press), p. 199.

19. Mason, *Street Railway*, p. 12.

20. Henry K. Rowe, *Tercentenary History of Newton, 1630–1930* (Newton, Mass.: City of Newton, 1930), pp. 278–297. Planner Charles Mulford Robinson wrote of Commonwealth Avenue: "From Boston, too, we may draw one example that is justly becoming widely known. This is in the long extension of Commonwealth Avenue, now stretching its sinuous length many miles into the country. But aside from the sinuosity of the street, a succession of lovely curves applied to an avenue of stately width and exceptionally long and elaborate surface development, this highway might well demand attention." Robinson, *Modern Civic Art*, p. 201.

21. Ibid., p. 172.

22. Robert A. Woods and Albert J. Kennedy, *The Zone of Emergence: Observations of the Lower Middle and Upper Working Class Communities of Boston, 1905–1914*, 2nd edition, ed. Sam Bass Warner, Jr. (Cambridge, Mass.: MIT Press, 1969), pp. 36, 39.

23. Ibid., p. 34.

24. Arthur J. Krim, *Survey of Architectural History in Cambridge, Report Five: Northwest Cambridge* (Cambridge, Mass.: Cambridge Historical Commission, 1977), p. 70. Boston introduced a municipal water supply in 1848, Cambridge followed suit in 1865, as did Newton in 1876. The Cambridge Gas Light Company was established 1852, and a gas company initiated service in Newton in 1855.

25. Douglas Shand-Tucci, *Built in Boston: City and Suburb, 1800–2000* (Amherst: University of Massachusetts Press, 1999), p. 120.

26. Woods and Kennedy, *The Zone of Emergence*, p. 152.

27. Arthur J. Krim, *The Three-Deckers of Dorchester: An Architectural Historical Survey* (Boston: Boston Landmarks Commission, 1977), p. viii.

28. Keith N. Morgan, Naomi Miller, Richard Candee, and Roger Reed, *Buildings of Massachusetts: Metropolitan Boston* (Charlottesville: University of Virginia Press, 2009), pp. 22–23.

29. Krim, *Northwest Cambridge*, p. 142.

30. *The WPA Guide to Massachusetts,* p. 444.

31. Brian Donahue, *Reclaiming the Commons: Community Farms and Forests in a New England Town* (New Haven, Conn.: Yale University Press, 1999), p. 63; Arlington Historical Commission, *Mill Brook Valley: A Historical and Architectural Survey* (Arlington, Mass.: Arlington Historical Commission, 1976), p. 7; Arlington Bicentennial Planning Committee, *Arlington Celebrates the Growing Years: 1875–1975* (Arlington, Mass.: Arlington Heritage Trust, 1977), p. 49; Richard A. Duffy, *Arlington* (Dover, N.H.: Arcadia Publishing, 1997), p. 109.

32. Duffy, *Arlington*, p. 109.

33. Richard B. Betts, Victoria Haase, Norma A. Marsh, and Alfred Shea, *Belmont* (Charleston, S.C.: Arcadia Publishing, 2000), p. 42.

34. Ibid., p. 33.

35. "The Tenement House Act," *Boston Evening Transcript*, April 5, 1913.

36. The Metropolitan District communities with planning boards in 1922 were Arlington, Belmont, Boston, Braintree, Brookline, Cambridge, Dedham, Everett, Lexington, Malden, Melrose, Newton, Quincy, Reading, Somerville, Stoneham, Wakefield, Waltham, Watertown, Wellesley, Winchester, Winthrop, and Woburn.

37. Arlington Bicentennial Committee, *Arlington Celebrates the Growing Years*, p. 59; Arlington Historical Commission, *Mill Brook Valley*, p. 7; Alexander von Hoffman, "Creating an Anti-Growth Regulatory Regime: A Case from Greater Boston," (Cambridge, Mass.: Rappaport Institute for Greater Boston, Kennedy School of Government, Harvard University, February, 2006); Henry Smith Chapman, *History of Winchester, Massachusetts*, Vol. I (Winchester, Mass.: Town of Winchester, Mass., 1975), p. 337; Elizabeth M. Hinchcliffe, *Five Pounds Currency, Three Pounds Corn: Wellesley's Centennial Story* (Wellesley, Mass: Town of Wellesley, 1981), p. 82.

Chapter 6

1. Carol R. Goldberg Seminar, *The Greening of Boston: An Action Agenda: A Report for the Boston Foundation* (Boston: Boston Foundation, 1987), p. 48.

2. Ibid., p. 44. Charles Eliot, Arthur Shurcliff, and other landscape architects working on Boston's Metropolitan Park System spent their formative years with the Olmsted firm, which dominated the profession.

3. Ibid., p. 318.

4. Metropolitan Park Commissioners, *Report of the Metropolitan Park Commissioners* (Boston: Commonwealth of Massachusetts, 1893).

5. Charles W. Eliot, Sr., *Charles Eliot, Landscape Architect* (Amherst: University of Massachusetts Press, 1999), p. 402.

6. Karl Haglund, *Inventing the Charles River* (Cambridge, Mass.: MIT Press, 2003), p. 149.

7. Laura Wood Roper, *FLO: A Biography of Frederick Law Olmsted* (Baltimore: Johns Hopkins University Press, 1973), p. 453.

8. Sylvester Baxter, "25 Years of the Premier Park System of the World—in Boston," *Boston Evening Transcript*, July 13, 1918.

9. H. G. Wells, "The Future of America: A Search after Realities," *Harper's Weekly* 50, 1906, p. 1018.

10. Lawrence W. Kennedy, *Planning the City upon a Hill: Boston since 1630* (Amherst: University of Massachusetts Press, 1992), pp. 122–123.

11. Mel Scott, *American City Planning since 1890* (Berkeley, Calif.: University of California Press, 1971), p. 116.

12. Kennedy, *Planning the City upon a Hill*, p. 152.

13. Scott, *American City Planning since 1890*, p. 435.

14. Suburbs are reluctant to grant more political control to urban centers or "new layers of bureaucracy." Regionalism has been a progressive "good government" issue that appeals to policy wonks and connected activists. In 1997, when the state's Regionalization Commission polled voters, they opposed creating a new "regional government" and became fairly negative if they thought it might threaten local autonomy. Those surveyed favored "cooperative action" between municipalities in delivering services if it were done voluntarily. The Regionalization Commission survey also found that most voters think their town governments are doing well at delivering services. Regionalization Commission, *Regionalization Commission Final Report* (Boston: Commonwealth of Massachusetts, 1997), pp. 23–24.

15. Eliot, *Charles Eliot*, pp. 537–538.

16. The parkways connecting Fresh Pond and Lynn were Fresh Pond Parkway, Mystic Valley Parkway, Lynn Fells Parkway, Revere Beach Parkway, Winthrop Parkway, and the Lynnway.

17. Frederick Law Olmsted recognized the urban planning aspect of parkways in an 1886 letter to the Minneapolis Park Commissioners, in which he wrote that parkways "are likely to become the stems of systems of streets which will be the framework of the permanent residence quarters of our cities of the future." August Heckscher, *Open Spaces: The Life of American Cities* (New York: Harper & Row, 1977), p. 195.

18. Planners made a distinction between the avenue or boulevard and the parkway. The avenue or boulevard traversed urbanized areas. They were wide and liberally planted with grass and trees, creating appealing addresses for wealthy people. The parkway either linked the city with outlying parks, linked parks, or created its own linear park. It maintained a park-like appearance. City planner Charles Mulford Robinson explained the distinctions: "Considered closely, however, the parkway may have a development that belongs to neither boulevard nor avenue and that justifies its separate discussion. In speaking of the former thoroughfares, it was noted that the first requirement was that they should afford ease of communication and that the second was that they should have a certain "dignified and stately" beauty. When we come to parkways, there is no restriction as to the kind of beauty that may be given. It may be as picturesque, gentle, and softly winning as we please." Charles Mulford Robinson, *Modern Civic Art or The City Made Beautiful* (New York: G. P. Putnam's Sons, 1904), p. 308. The Bronx River Parkway, completed in 1923, was the first truly limited-access parkway, becoming the progenitor of the limited-access freeway.

19. Metropolitan Park Commissioners, *Report of the Board of the Metropolitan Park Commissioners, December, 1911* (Boston: Metropolitan Planning Commission, 1912), p. 23. In 1957, the *Christian Science Monitor* recognized that "Without this step [establishment of the metropolitan park system in 1893], Boston and its immediate suburbs today might be a completely unrelieved congestion of wood, brick and cement." "Suburbs Sprawl Outward in Bay State," *Christian Science Monitor*, May 18, 1957.

20. "Tree Bordered Roads of Parks Assets of City," *Christian Science Monitor*, July 28, 1915.

21. "Great Parkway to the Fells," *Boston Globe*, December 3, 1896.

22. Clay McShane, *Down the Asphalt Path: The Automobile and the American City* (New York: Columbia University Press, 1994), p. 220.

23. *A Handbook of New England* (Boston: Porter E. Sargent, 1917), p. 507. Commonwealth Avenue later served as the connector between the Massachusetts Turnpike exit at Weston and Route 128 between 1957 and 1965, before the Turnpike Extension was completed into downtown.

24. Arlington Historic Commission, *Northwest Arlington, Massachusetts: An Architectural and Historical Study* (Arlington, Mass.: Arlington Historic Commission, 1995), p. 26.

25. Haglund, *Inventing the Charles River*, p. 222.

26. Elmer Osgood Cappers, *Centennial History of The Country Club* (Brookline, MA: Country Club, 1981), p. 23. During the early twentieth century, The Country Club installed squash courts and even sponsored automobile races on the racetrack.

27. Golf even overtook Boston's Franklin Park (1888), which Frederick Law Olmsted had designed to be a "country park." He intended the long rolling meadow for families to stroll and picnic. In 1896, however, sporting goods manufacturer George Wright set up a golf course, against the wishes of Olmsted's firm. Within a decade, the golf course became a permanent feature of the park. It was the country's second public course and helped democratize the sport.

28. Richard J. Moss, *Golf and the American Country Club* (Urbana, Ill.: University of Illinois Press, 2001), p. 15.

29. James M. Mayo. *The American Country Club: Its Origins and Development* (New Brunswick, N.J.: Rutgers University Press, 1998), p. 193.

30. Moss, *Golf*, p. 114.

31. Ibid., p. 91.

32. Oliver Gillham, *The Limitless City: A Primer on the Urban Sprawl Debate* (Washington, D.C.: Island Press, 2002), p. 30.

33. "Real Estate Development Speeds Exodus from City," *Christian Science Monitor*, November 18, 1925.

34. *Handbook of New England*, p. 66.

35. Ibid., p. 152.

36. Ibid., pp. 152–153.

37. John E. Fogelberg, *Burlington: Part of a Greater Chronicle* (Burlington, Mass.: Burlington Historical Commission, 1976), p. 326.

38. The Massachusetts Department of Public Works developed a comprehensive system of interstate and intrastate highway routes, which were marked with directional signs in 1926. Massachusetts Department of Public Works, *Annual Report of the Department of Public Works for the Year Ending November 30, 1925*, No. 54 (Boston: Commonwealth of Massachusetts, 1925).

39. Yanni Tsipis and David Kruh, *Building Route 128* (Charleston, S.C.: Arcadia Publishing, 2003), p. 7.

40. G. H. Delano, "Frederick Calhoun Pillsbury," *Transactions of the American Society of Civil Engineers* 103 (1938): 1862.

41. *The WPA Guide to Massachusetts: The Federal Writers' Project Guide to 1930s Massachusetts* (1937; New York: Pantheon Books, 1983), p. 290.

42. Lloyd Rodwin, *Housing and Economic Progress: A Study of the Housing Experience of Boston's Middle-Income Families* (Cambridge, Mass.: Harvard University Press and Technology Press, 1961), p. 39.

43. Alan Gowans, *The Comfortable House: North American Suburban Architecture, 1890–1930* (Cambridge, Mass.: MIT Press, 1986), p. 28.

44. Ibid., p. 208.

45. Gwendolyn Wright, *Building the Dream: A Social History of Housing in America* (Cambridge, Mass.: MIT Press, 1981), p. 171.

46. Gowans, *The Comfortable House*, pp. 17, 33, 213, 224; Candace M. Volz, "The Modern Look of the Early-Twentieth-Century House: A Mirror of Changing Lifestyles," in *American Home Life, 1880–1930*, eds. Jessica H. Foy and Thomas J. Schlereth (Knoxville, Tenn.: University of Tennessee Press, 1992), p. 27.

Chapter 7

1. Carole Zellie, *Beyond the Neck: The Architecture and Development of Somerville* (Somerville, Mass.: City of Somerville, 1982), pp. 40, 58, 60, 67; "Beauty or Business: Shall We Have Parks or Factories," *Somerville Journal*, March 13, 1896.

2. Metropolitan Park Commission, *Report of the Metropolitan Park Commissioners* (Boston: Commonwealth of Massachusetts, 1893), p. 71.

3. "Spring Real Estate Supplement," *Boston Evening Transcript*, April 4, 1913.

4. Quincy-built ships that saw combat in World War II included the battleships USS *Massachusetts* and USS *Nevada* and aircraft carriers USS *Lexington*, USS *Hancock*, and USS *Bunker Hill*.

5. The "Lowell System" was preceded by the "Rhode Island System" of manufacture, which had spun off from Samuel Slater's mill in Pawtucket, Rhode Island (1793), which was the nation's first water-powered factory manufacturing cotton thread. According to a National Park Service study on the Blackstone River Valley, the "Rhode Island System," which prevailed in the Blackstone River Valley of Rhode Island and Massachusetts, was characterized by "its relatively small-scale mills, ownership by individuals, or partnerships rather than corporations, use of families as the labor force, location in multiple detached villages in a rural setting, and a symbiotic relationship with agriculture." In contrast, the "Lowell System" was based on large-scale integrated factories where raw cotton was converted into finished fabric. This system entailed urban sites, large workforces, intricate machinery, and significant corporate investment. National Park Service, *Blackstone River Valley Special Resource Study Report 2011* (Boston: National Park Service Northeast Region, 2011), p. 24.

6. *A Handbook of New England* (Boston: Porter E. Sargent, 1917), pp. 455, 603.

7. Federal Writers' Project, Works Progress Administration, *Massachusetts: A Guide to Its Places and People* (Boston: Houghton Mifflin, 1937), p. 252.

8. Cathy Stanton, *The Lowell Experiment: Public History in a Postindustrial City* (Amherst: University of Massachusetts Press, 2006), p. 103; Constance Williams, "Re-Employment Programs in Four Massachusetts Textile Cities, 1928–40" (PhD dissertation, University of Chicago, 1942), p. 7; "Amoskeag Manufacturing Company," Wikipedia, http://en.wikipedia.org/wiki/Amoskeag_Manufacturing_Company.

9. Jonathan Harr, *A Civil Action* (New York: Vintage Books, 1995), p. 12.

10. Patricia J. Fanning, *Norwood, A History* (Charleston, S.C.: Arcadia Publishing, 2002), p. 94.

11. John Nolen, *New Towns for Old: Achievements in Civic Improvement in Some American Small Towns and Neighborhoods* (1927; Amherst: University of Massachusetts Press in association with the Library of American Landscape History, 2005), pp. lxii–lxiii.

12. Ibid., pp. 39, 49.

13. Margaret, Crawford, *Building the Workingman's Paradise: The Design of American Company Towns* (New York: Verso, 1995), p. 76.

14. Robert Campbell, "Forgotten Utopias," *Boston Sunday Globe*, May 21, 1995.

15. Shawsheen Renaissance Project website, http://beautifulshawsheen.com/shawsheen.asp.

16. Dolores Hayden, *Building Suburbia: Green Fields and Urban Growth, 1820–2000* (New York: Pantheon Books, 2003), p. 119. Hayden argues that "self-built" suburbs started in the early twentieth century and were oriented to the automobile. They tended to be built one house or two at a time. They were not mass-built in a subdivision.

17. "The Exodus of the Home-Seeker," "Spring Real Estate Supplement," *Boston Evening Transcript*, April 5, 1913. Landscape Research, *Stoneham, Massachusetts: A Shoe Town* (Stoneham, Mass.: Stoneham Historical Commission, 1981), pp. 68–69.

18. Marc Scott Miller, *The Irony of Victory: World War II and Lowell, Massachusetts* (Urbana: University of Illinois Press, 1988), p. 89.

19. Ibid., p. 208.

20. Quoted in Stanton, *The Lowell Experiment*, p. 108.

21. Historian Jesse Lemisch coined this term in the early 1960s. Timothy Coogan, "History from the Bottom Up," LaGuardia Community College website, http://www.lagcc.cuny.edu/maus/bottomup.htm.

22. Miller, *The Irony of Victory*, p. 213.

23. Mark Muro, John Schneider, David Warren, Eric McLean-Shinaman, Rebecca Sohmer, Benjamin Forman, with David Ansel and Greg Leierson, *Reconnecting Massachusetts Gateway Cities: Lessons Learned and an Agenda for Renewal* (Boston: The Massachusetts Institute for a New Commonwealth and The Brookings Institution Metropolitan Policy Program, 2007).

Chapter 8

1. John Cheever, *The Wapshot Chronicle* (New York: Ballantine Books, 1957), p. 3; John P. Marquand, *Point of No Return* (Boston: Little, Brown, 1949); John P. Marquand, *Sincerely, Willis Wayde* (Boston: Little, Brown, 1955).

2. Peter G. Rowe, *Making a Middle Landscape* (Cambridge, Mass.: MIT Press, 1991), p. 16.

3. Carolyn Shank, "History of Route 128," Investigating Lexington's History, 1998 (unpublished manuscript, Lexington History Room, Lexington, Mass. Library, 1998), p. 9.

4. Stephen H. Herring, *Framingham: An American Town* (Framingham, Mass.: Framingham Historical Society and Framingham Tercentennial Commission, 2000), pp. 313-322; Betsy Friedberg, "Postwar Housing Comes of Age" [Massachusetts Historical Commission] *Preservation Advocate*, Spring 2003, pp. 1, 6–7.

5. Ibid., p. 313.

6. Ralph Bodek, *How and Why People Buy Houses: A Study of Subconscious Home Buying Motives* (Philadelphia: Municipal Publications, Inc., 1958), p. 24. Parks historian Jere Stuart French argues that large numbers of Americans during the postwar era did not value public parks because they could enjoy their private yard. Jere Stuart French, *Urban Green: City Parks of the Western World* (Dubuque, Iowa: Kendall/Hunt Publishing, 1973), p. 4.

7. James E. Vance, "Democratic Utopias and the American Landscape," in *The Making of the American Landscape*, ed. Michael P. Conzen (Boston: Unwin Hyman, 1990), p. 217.

8. Donald L. Elliott, *A Better Way to Zone: Ten Principles to Create More Livable Cities* (Washington, D.C.: Island Press, 2008), pp. 72–73.

9. J. Anthony Lukas, *Common Ground: A Turbulent Decade in the Lives of Three American Families* (New York: Alfred A. Knopf, 1985), p. 648.

10. Sam Bass Warner, Jr., *The Private City: Philadelphia in Three Periods of Its Growth* (Philadelphia: University of Pennsylvania Press, 1968), p. x.

11. Gerald Gamm, *Urban Exodus: Why the Jews Left Boston and the Catholics Stayed* (Cambridge, Mass.: Harvard University Press, 1999), pp. 193, 226.

12. Ibid., pp. 273, 241, 242–243.

13. Lizabeth Cohen, *A Consumer's Republic: The Politics of Mass Consumption in Postwar America* (New York: Knopf, 2003), p. 204; Dolores Hayden, *Building Suburbia: Green Fields and Urban Growth, 1820–2000* (New York: Pantheon Books, 2003), p. 151.

14. *Discover Historic Oak Hill Park*, (Newton, Mass.: Newton Planning and Development Department, 2002).

15. "Route 128 Timeline" website, http://www.route128history.org/id8.html.

16. David Fixler, "Hipsters in the Woods," *Architecture Boston*, Spring 2009, p. 28.

17. "Spruce Hill Road Area," Weston Historical Commission website, http://westhistcomm.org/?page_id=529.

18. Ibid. The Architects' Collaborative (TAC) also designed another Lexington neighborhood, Five Fields (1951–1957), which included approximately sixty homes. TAC's goal was to keep prices

moderate, so the firm provided three standard designs, with some opportunity for customization. Other Lexington Modernist subdivisions included Peacock Farms (1951–60), where MIT-trained architects Danforth Compton and Walter Pierce designed sixty-eight split-levels and single-floor homes. Working with developers Harmon White and Edward Green, they also developed Lexington subdivisions at Upper Turning Mill Road (1957–1961), Rumford Road (1959), Glen at Countryside (1960–1962), and the Grove (1962–1964), as well as similar subdivisions in Newton and Wayland.

19. Giorgio Ciucci, Francesco Dal Co, Mario Manieri-Elia, and Manfredo Tafuri, *The American City: From the Civil War to the New Deal* (Cambridge, Mass.: MIT Press, 1979), p.294.

20. Bodek, *How and Why People Buy Houses*, p. 46.

21. "Eight Houses for Modern Living," *Life*, September 26, 1938, pp. 44–67; "Royal Barry Wills," *Life*, August 26, 1946, pp. 67–72.

22. Ibid., pp. 31–36. According to the study, families still living in an urban row house were considered "unprogressive," "lazy," "shiftless," or "low income."

23. Witold Rybczynski, *Last Harvest: How a Cornfield Became New Daleville: Real Estate Development in America from George Washington to the Builders of the Twenty-First Century, and Why We Live in Houses Anyway* (New York: Scribner, 2007), p. 209.

24. Tony Hill, "The Man Who Drove Hard to Build Roads," *Boston Sunday Globe*, August 25, 2002; Massachusetts Department of Public Works, *The Massachusetts Highway Story, 1949–1956* (Boston: Commonwealth of Massachusetts, 1956), pp. 2–3. The Commonwealth bonded for $522 million in highway investments between 1949 and 1956.

25. Yanni Tsipis and David Kruh, *Building Route 128* (Charleston, S.C.: Arcadia Publishing, 2003), pp. 27, 117.

26. "Route 128 Historical Overview," The Roads of Metro Boston website, http://www.bostonroads.com/roads/MA-128/; Christopher Rand, *Cambridge, U.S.A.: Hub of a New World* (New York: Oxford University Press, 1964), p. 8.

27. Gerald Blakely has been a significant real-estate developer in Greater Boston. Besides his involvement with business parks at Cabot, Cabot & Forbes, he owned the Ritz-Carlton Hotel between 1964 and 1983 and developed the 60 State Street office tower.

28. Elizabeth Hardwick, "Boston," *A View of My Own: Essays in Literature and Society* (New York: Farrar, Straus and Cudahy, 1962), p. 149.

29. Rand, *Cambridge, U.S.A.*, p. 9.

30. Tsipis and Kruh, *Building Route 128*, p. 117; Robert Fishman, *Bourgeois Utopias: The Rise and Fall of Suburbia* (New York: Basic Books, 1987), p. 196.

31. Annalee Saxenian, *Regional Advantage: Culture and Competition in Silicon Valley and Route 128* (Cambridge, Mass.: Harvard University Press, 1994), pp. 16–17.

32. Ibid., p. 100.

33. Ibid., p. 103.

34. Ibid., pp. 61, 99.

35. Quoted in "Microsoft Sees 'Fantastic' Opportunities," *Boston Globe*, February 26, 2009.

36. Richard Florida, *The Rise of the Creative Class: And How It's Transforming Work, Leisure, Community, and Everyday Life* (New York: Basic Books, 2002), p. 249.

37. John R. Stilgoe, *Borderland: Origins of the American Suburb, 1820–1939* (New Haven, Conn.: Yale University Press, 1988), p. 213; Robert Fogelson, *Downtown: Its Rise and Fall, 1880–1950* (New Haven, Conn.: Yale University Press), p. 199.

38. Herring, *Framingham*, p. 324.

39. Benton MacKaye, "The Cape Cod Region: The Basic Need—A Main Road Plan" (paper presented at Cape Cod Chamber of Commerce, December, 1927), p. 3. MacKaye's broader theories of regional planning were published in *The New Exploration: A Philosophy of Regional Planning* (New York: Harcourt, Brace, 1928).

40. Eric Schlosser, *Fast Food Nation* (Boston: Houghton Mifflin, 2001), pp. P.S.-3, 3.

41. Edward Relph, *The Modern Urban Landscape* (Baltimore: Johns Hopkins University Press, 1987), p. 181.

42. Municipal Finance Task Force, *Local Communities at Risk: Revisiting the Fiscal Partnership between the Commonwealth and Cities and Towns* (Boston: Metro Mayors Coalition, 2005), p. 15.

43. Brenda Case Scheer, "Shape of the City," *Planning*, July, 2007, pp. 30–33.

44. Metropolitan Area Planning Council, "Retail Parking Requirements" (December), *Metropolitan Area Planning Council 2009 Calendar* (2009). This formula assumes that each parking space requires at least 300 feet of pavement (including lanes and driveways), so there are 3.3 parking spaces per 1,000 gross square feet of retail.

45. Keith N. Morgan, Naomi Miller, Richard Candee, and Roger Reed, *Buildings of Massachusetts: Metropolitan Boston* (Charlottesville: University of Virginia Press, 2009), p. 385.

46. Cohen, *A Consumer's Republic*, p. 202.

47. "Met. Dist. Area Extension Hit," *Boston Herald*, March 26, 1941.

48. "Would Expand MDC Parks Area," August 25, 1961, unidentified Boston newspaper, *Boston Herald* clippings file, Beebe Communications Library, Boston University; "White Asks End of MDC," *Boston Herald-Traveler*, March 26, 1970.

49. The 1950 density of the thirty-nine MDC communities was high, with 5,418 persons per mile, compared with all of Greater Boston's sixty-five municipalities at 3,078 persons per square mile. The New York metropolitan area had 3,278 persons per square mile, and Greater Chicago had 1,519 per square mile. Metropolitan District Commission, Parks Division, *Study and Recommended Programs of the Development of Parks and Reservations and Recreational Facilities of the Metropolitan Parks District, 1956* (Boston: Metropolitan District Commission, 1956), p. 76.

50. Commonwealth of Massachusetts: Metropolitan Area Planning Council in cooperation with the Metropolitan District Commission and Massachusetts Department of Natural Resources, *Open Space and Recreation Program for Metropolitan Boston*, Vol. I (Boston: Commonwealth of Massachusetts, 1969), p. 7.

51. Twenty-six percent of roadways, mainly in the urban core, have sidewalks on both sides of the street, while 16 percent of streets have sidewalks on one side of the street. Metropolitan Area Planning Council (September), *Metropolitan Area Planning Council 2008 Calendar* (2008).

52. Metropolitan District Commission, *Study 1956*, pp. 34, 80.

53. Ibid., pp. 1, 76.

54. Ibid., p. 4.

55. Green Ribbon Commission, *Enhancing the Future of the Metropolitan Park System: Final Report and Recommendations of the Green Ribbon Commission* (Boston: Commonwealth of Massachusetts, 1996), p. 19.

56. Sam Bass Warner, Jr., *The Urban Wilderness: A History of the American City* (New York: Harper & Row, 1972), p. 41. In 1924, the top speed an average American automobile could reach was forty-seven mph. By 1937, the average top speed increased to seventy-two mph. Highway engineers started designing highways that allowed vehicles to drive fifty mph in the city and seventy mph in open country. The highways provided gentle curves, moderate grades, and long, clear lines of vision to accommodate high speeds. Median strips and breakdown lanes increased safety. All this required a 200–300-foot right-of-way.

57. Norman T. Newton, *Design on the Land: The Development of Landscape Architecture* (Cambridge, Mass.: Belknap Press of Harvard University Press, 1971), p. 333.

58. Trustees of Public Reservations of Massachusetts, *The Bay Circuit* (Boston: The Trustees of Public Reservations of Massachusetts, 1937), p. 11.

59. Ibid., pp. 11, 14.

60. The Bay Circuit parkway was regarded as the linchpin for expanding the MDC. The *Christian Science Monitor* reported: "If the Metropolitan Parks District should be enlarged and a way found for the Bay Circuit to become a public parkway under metropolitan administration it is entirely possible that more lands adjacent to the circuit might be donated. This would extend still further the protection of the rural countryside, insuring, as fast as can be seen, future beautiful drives for all Greater Boston." "Public Service Group Backs 'Bay Circuit,'" *Christian Science Monitor*, November 16, 1940.

61. "Suburbs Sprawl Outward in Bay State," *Christian Science Monitor*, May 18, 1957.

62. Sam Nejame, "For the Fearless, an Outer Necklace," *Boston Sunday Globe*, April 3, 2005.

63. Walter Muir Whitehill, *Boston in the Age of John Fitzgerald Kennedy* (Norman: University of Oklahoma Press, 1966), pp. 44–45.

64. *Lexington Minuteman*, December 24, 1953, quoted in Carolyn Shank, "History of Route 128," p. 1.

65. Weston Town Records, 1951, Board of Selectmen, p. 16, quoted in Alexander von Hoffman, *To Preserve and Protect: Land Use Regulations in Weston, Massachusetts* (Cambridge, Mass.: Rappaport Institute for Greater Boston, Kennedy School of Government, and Joint Center for Housing Studies, Harvard University, 2010), p. 15.

66. Ibid., pp. 12–16.

67. Herring, *Framingham,* p. 315.

68. "Wayland Planning Report Annual Report, 1945," quoted in George Lewis, *Sudbury Valley Trustees: Fifty Years of Conservation* (Sudbury, Mass.: Sudbury Valley Trustees, 2004), pp. 8–9, 41.

69. Sam Bass Warner, *The Way We Really Live: Social Change in Metropolitan Boston since 1920* (Boston: Trustees of the Public Library of the City of Boston, 1977), p. 72.

70. *Lexington: The Ideal Community of Home Owners* (Lexington, Mass.: n.p., 1938). This promotional pamphlet related that "Modern houses are appropriately built to fit this colonial setting" and showed illustrative examples of Colonial Revival, Dutch Revival, and Cape Cod houses.

71. Boston National Historic Sites Commission, *The Lexington-Concord Battle Road: Interim Report of the Boston National Historic Sites Commission to the Congress of the United States* (Washington, D.C.: Boston National Historic Sites Commission, 1958), p. 35.

72. John C. MacLean, *A Rich Harvest: The History, People, and Buildings of Lincoln, Massachusetts* (Lincoln, Mass.: Lincoln Historical Society, 1987), p. 597.

73. Paul Brooks, *The View from Lincoln Hill: Man and the Land in a New England Town* (Boston: Houghton Mifflin, 1976), p. 229.

74. "40B Zoning Law Is Not about Snobbery, but Smart Growth," editorial, *Boston Globe*, September 19, 2010.

75. "Chapter 40B," Citizens Housing and Planning Association website, http://www.chapa .org/?q=chapter40B. Besides the fifty-plus Massachusetts communities that currently have at least 10 percent of their housing deemed "affordable" by the state, approximately forty other communities have housing stock that is between 8 and 10 percent "affordable."

76. Fixler, "Hipsters in the Woods," p. 26.

Chapter 9

1. Charles H. Trout, *Boston: The Great Depression and the New Deal* (New York: Oxford University Press, 1977), pp. 5–7.

2. Jane Jacobs, *Cities and the Wealth of Nations* (New York: Random House, 1984), p. 228.

3. Lloyd Rodwin, *Housing and Economic Progress: A Study of the Housing Experience of Boston's Middle-Income Families* (Cambridge, Mass.: Harvard University Press and Technology Press, 1961), p. 93.

4. Robert C. Wood, *Suburbia: Its People and Their Politics* (Boston: Houghton Mifflin, 1958), p. 72.

5. Elizabeth Hardwick, "Boston," *A View of My Own: Essays in Literature and Society* (New York: Farrar, Straus and Cudahy, 1962), pp. 148, 156, 158.

6. Herbert J. Gans, The *Urban Villagers: Group and Class in the Life of Italian-Americans* (New York: The Free Press, 1962), p. 285, 16.

7. Fred L. Standley and Louis H. Platt, eds., *Conversations with James Baldwin* (Jackson: University Press of Mississippi, 1989), p. 42. James Baldwin coined the term "Negro removal" to characterize urban renewal in an interview with Kenneth B. Clark in 1963.

8. Lawrence W. Kennedy, *Planning the City upon a Hill: Boston since 1630* (Amherst: University of Massachusetts Press, 1992), p. 159.

9. Walter Muir Whitehill, *Boston in the Age of John Fitzgerald Kennedy* (Norman: University of Oklahoma Press, 1966), p. 46.

10. In 1958, the City of Boston painted the red line that still guides visitors along the Freedom Trail from the Boston Common through the historic streets to the Bunker Hill Monument. Today twenty million tourists visit Boston each year, and the Freedom Trail forms the core of Boston's historical image.

11. Katherine Bradbury, Anthony Downs, and Kenneth Small, *Urban Decline and the Future of American Cities* (Washington, D.C.: Brookings Institution, 1982), p. 52.

12. Quoted in Frank Colcord, Edmund P. Fowler, and Alan Lupo, *Rites of Way: The Politics of Transportation in Boston and the US City* (Boston: Little, Brown, 1971), p. 106.

13. As of 2005, there were 350 parking lots and garages in the downtown area. In 1993, the EPA imposed a freeze on park-and-fly spaces and rental car spaces around Logan Airport in East Boston and the following year imposed similar limits in South Boston and the developing Seaport District.

14. Charles E. Claffey, "Celebration of Cities Opens," *Boston Globe*, Sept. 23, 1980. An intriguing conference session featured a debate between Quincy Market developer James Rouse and urban activist Jane Jacobs over the merits of strong central planning versus grass roots incrementalism. Rouse declared that "Big plans can take in the multitude of inter-related human needs and enable 'the building of community.' Jacobs countered that powerful bureaucratic planners, as exemplified by the Boston Redevelopment Authority, were "'stiflers, smotherers, routinizers.'" She praised the type of revitalization brought about by urban pioneers who rehabbed old houses and industrial lofts and who opened small neighborhood businesses and restaurants. "Big Plans, or Little by Little," *Boston Globe*, September 26, 1980.

15. Barry Bluestone and Mary Huff Stevenson, *The Boston Renaissance: Race, Space, and Economic Change in an American Metropolis* (New York: Russell Foundation Publications, 2002), p. 4.

16. Ibid., p. 8.

17. Saskia Sassen, *The Global City: New York, London, Tokyo* (Princeton, N.J.: Princeton University Press, 1991), pp. 3–4.

18. "The Global Cities Index 2010," *Foreign Policy*, http://www.foreignpolicy.com/node/373401; "Global Power City Index 2010," Institute for Urban Strategies, The Mori Memorial Foundation, http://www.mori-m-foundation.or.jp/english/research/project/6/pdf/GPCI2010_English.pdf; 2thinknow, "2thinknow Innovation Cities Global 256 Index," http://www.innovation-cities .com/2thinknow-innovation-cities-global-256-index.

19. PricewaterhouseCoopers, "The 150 Richest Cities in the World by GDP in 2005," http://www .citymayors.com/statistics/richest-cities-2005.html.

20. Peter Temin, "The Transition from a Mill-Based to a Knowledge-Based Economy, 1940–2000," *Engines of Enterprise: An Economic History of New England*, ed. Peter Temin (Cambridge, Mass.: Harvard University Press, 2000), p. 239.

21. Richard Florida, *The Great Reset: How New Ways of Living and Working Drive Post-Crash Prosperity* (New York: Harper, 2010), p. 152.

22. Richard Florida, *The Rise of the Creative Class: And How It's Transforming Work, Leisure, Community, and Everyday Life* (New York: Basic Books, 2002), p. 249.

23. Ibid., p. 246.

24. Stephen V. Ward, *Selling Places: The Marketing and Promotion of Towns and Cities, 1850–2000* (New York: Routledge, 1998), p. 234.

25. Karl E. Case, "A Dream House after All," *New York Times*, September 2, 2010; Joint Center for Housing Studies of Harvard University, *The State of the Nation's Housing, 2011* (Cambridge, Mass., 2011), p. 40.

26. Greg Torres and Andrew Sum, "The Income Gap: The Middle Class, and Middle Ground, Is Disappearing," *Boston Globe*, October 6, 2010.

27. The minority concentrations are located in the Roxbury, Dorchester, and East Boston neighborhoods of Boston and in the traditional immigrant/industrial cities of Brockton, Chelsea, Lawrence, Lowell, and Lynn. Boston alone has 38.8 percent (2000) of the Boston MSA's total number of individuals living in poverty. Boston has 62.9 percent of the metropolitan area's African Americans and 37.9 percent of Latinos. This social and economic segregation intensifies the difficulties of disadvantaged persons in seeking to better their condition.

28. Bluestone and Stevenson, *The Boston Renaissance*, pp. 370, 377, 15.

Chapter 10

1. Alan Berube, Audrey Singer, Jill H. Wilson, and William H. Frey, *Finding Exurbia: America's Fast-Growing Communities at the Metropolitan Fringe* (Washington, DC: Brookings Institution, 2006), p. 6. The term "exurban" was coined by Auguste Comte Spectorsky, *The Exurbanites* (Philadelphia: Lippincott, 1955) to differentiate low-density country commuter communities from the denser suburbs.

2. William H. Whyte, "Urban Sprawl," in *The Exploding Metropolis*, ed. William H. Whyte (Berkeley: University of California Press, 1993; originally published 1958), pp. 133–134. Whyte coined the term "urban sprawl" in *Fortune* in 1958.

3. Christopher B. Leinberger, *The Option of Urbanism: Investing in a New American Dream* (Washington, D.C.: Island Press, 2007), p. 32.

4. Joel Garreau, *Edge City: Life on the New Frontier* (New York: Doubleday, 1991), pp. 89, 425.

5. Peter G. Rowe, *Making a Middle Landscape* (Cambridge, Mass.: MIT Press, 1991), p. 16.

6. Garreau, *Edge City*, p. 84. Joel Garreau wrote that edge cities required five qualities to grow—insurmountability (physically being able to expand), affordability, mobility, accessibility, and maintaining attractiveness. Greater Boston's growth became limited by physical insurmountability and affordability. Garreau, *Edge City*, p. 81.

7. The Boston-Providence-Manchester, MA–RI–NH Combined Statistical Area (CSA) comprises Boston-Cambridge-Quincy, MA–NH Metropolitan Statistical Area (MSA), Providence-Fall River-New Bedford, MA–RI MSA, Worcester, MA MSA, Concord, NH Micropolitan Statistical Area, and Laconia, NH Micropolitan Statistical Area. Note that the Office of Management and Budget (OMB) has made many changes to the terms and definitions related to metropolitan areas in recent years. These are the current terms. In the recent past, the terms Standard Metropolitan Statistical Area, Primary Metropolitan Statistical Area, and Consolidated Metropolitan Statistical Area were used and discarded.

8. The U.S. Department of Labor, Bureau of Labor Statistics defines "labor market areas" as "an economically integrated geographic area within which individuals can reside and find employment within a reasonable distance or can readily change employment without changing their place of residence." US Department of Labor, Bureau of Labor Statistics, *Labor Market Areas, 2011* (March 2011), p. iii. "Retail trade areas," or "trade areas," are considered to be the geographic area where businesses draw their customers from. *Rand McNally Commercial Atlas & Marketing Guide 2010* (Chicago: Rand McNally, 2010) provides detailed maps of the nation's trade areas.

9. Jean Gottmann, *Megalopolis: The Urbanized Northeastern Seaboard of the United States* (New York: Twentieth Century Fund, 1961); Richard Florida, *The Great Reset: How New Ways of Living and Working Drive Post-Crash Prosperity* (New York: Harper, 2010), p. 142.

10. Joel Garreau, *The Nine Nations of North America* (Boston: Houghton Mifflin, 1981) provided an early description of the country's emerging megaregions. Catherine L. Ross, *Megaregions: Planning for Global Competitiveness* (Washington, D.C.: Island Press, 2009) makes a strong case that America's megaregions will have to plan transportation and other infrastructure elements on a megaregional basis if they are to compete globally. The infrastructure advocacy organization America 2050 delineates eleven megaregions in the United States:

• Northeast: Southern Maine to Norfolk, Virginia

• Piedmont Atlantic: Inland North Carolina, South Carolina, Georgia, and Alabama; from Raleigh, North Carolina to Montgomery, Alabama

• Great Lakes/Midwest: Pittsburgh to Green Bay, Wisconsin

• Florida: Orlando to Miami

• Gulf Coast: Mexican border to Pensacola, Florida

• Texas Triangle: Dallas-San Antonio-Austin-Houston

• Northern California

• Southern California

• Cascadia: Pacific Northwest

• Arizona Sun Corridor

• Front Range: Albuquerque to Denver-Boulder (America 2050 website, http://www.america2050.org/megaregions.html).

11. Dolores Hayden, *Building Suburbia: Green Fields and Urban Growth, 1820–2000* (New York: Pantheon Books, 2003), p. 174.

12. Peter Canellos, "Aerotropolis: The Rise of a New Kind of City—and How Massachusetts Missed a Chance to Have One," *Boston Globe*, October 31, 2010.

13. Amy Dain, *Housing and Land Use Policy in Massachusetts: Reforms for Affordability, Sustainability, and Superior Design*, No. 37 (Boston: Pioneer Institute for Public Policy Research, 2007), p. 16.

14. Reid Ewing, Rolf Pendall, Don Chen, "Measuring Sprawl and Its Impact," 2002, Smart Growth America website, http://www.smartgrowthamerica.org/research/measuring-sprawl-and-its-impact/MeasuringSprawl.PDF. MIT Center for Real Estate, "Housing Affordability—Land Use Research Findings," January 31, 2006, http://web.mit.edu/cre/research/hai/land-use.html.

15. Town of Hopkinton, MA, Planning Board, *Master Plan Update Survey* (2004).

16. Christina Rosan and Lawrence Susskind, *Land-Use Planning in the Doldrums: Growth Management in Massachusetts' I-495 Region* (Cambridge, Mass.: Rappaport Institute for Greater Boston, Kennedy School of Government, Harvard University, 2007), p. 7.

17. Donald L. Elliott, *A Better Way to Zone: Ten Principles to Create More Livable Cities* (Washington, D.C.: Island Press, 2008), p. 72.

18. The term "McMansion" dates from the early 1980s. "McMansion," Wikipedia, http://en.wikipedia .org/wiki/McMansion; Dolores Hayden, *A Field Guide to Sprawl* (New York: W. W. Norton, 2004), pp. 94, 110.

19. Massachusetts Executive Office of Environmental Affairs, *The State of Our Environment: A Special Report on Community Preservation and the Future of Our Commonwealth* (Boston: Commonwealth of Massachusetts, 2002), p. 35; Cathleen McGuigan, "The McMansion Next Door: Why the American House Needs a Makeover," *Newsweek*, October 27, 2003, p. 85; Witold Rybczynski, *Last Harvest: How a Cornfield Became New Daleville: Real Estate Development in America from George Washington to the Builders of the Twenty-First Century, and Why We Live in Houses Anyway* (New York: Scribner, 2007), p. 209.

20. Kris Frieswick, "The March of the McMansions," *Boston Globe*, July 18, 2010.

21. Leinberger, *The Option of Urbanism*, p. 65.

22. Hayden, *Field Guide to Sprawl*, p. 30; Robert Spector, *Category Killers: The Retail Revolution and Its Impact on Consumer Culture* (Boston: Harvard Business Review Press, 2005), p. xii. According to Spector, "category killers" "use everyday low prices and wide and deep inventories . . . to kill competition— whether it be mom-and-pop stores, smaller regional chains, or general merchandise stores that cannot compete on price and/or selection."

23. Matthew Zook and Mark Graham, "Wal-Mart Nation: Mapping the Reach of a Retail Colossus," in *Wal-Mart World: The World's Biggest Corporation in the Global Economy*, ed. Stanley D. Brunn (New York: Routledge, 2006), pp. 15–25; *Walmart Annual Report 2011*, http://walmartstores.com/sites/ annualreport/2011/financials/Walmart_2011_Annual_Report.pdf.

24. Sophfronia Scott Gregory, Patrick E. Cole, Leslie Whitaker, and Tom Witkowsi, "They're Up Against the Wal," *Time Magazine*, November 1, 1993, pp. 56–57.

25. Walmart website, http://www.walmart.com/storeLocator/ca_storefinder.do.

26. Costco website, http://www.costco.com/Warehouse/locator.aspx; BJ's Club website, http://www .bjs.com/webapp/wcs/stores/servlet/LocatorIndexView?storeId=10201&catalogId=10201&langId=-1; Sam's Club website, http://www3.samsclub.com/clublocator.

27. The Home Depot website, http://www.homedepot.com/; Lowe's website, http://www.lowes.com/ StoreLocatorDisplayView?storeId=10151.

28. "The Last Days of Caldor," *Discount Store News*, February 8, 1999; "Bradlees," Wikipedia, http:// en.wikipedia.org/wiki/Bradlees; "Ames Department Stores Inc., Wikipedia, http://en.wikipedia.org/ wiki/Ames_(discount_stores); Jerry Ackerman, "Grossman's Closing Its 60 Retail Stores," *Boston Globe*, March 29, 1996; "All 27 Lechmere Stores Close; Montgomery Ward Struggling," *Boston Globe*, November 8, 1997; Jenn Abelson, "Tweeter to Shutter Remaining Stores," *Boston Globe*, November 4, 2008.

29. Matt Carroll, "Snapshot: Dunkin' Donuts vs. Starbucks: Where Do You Stand?" *Boston Globe*, June 17, 2010, http://www.boston.com/yourtown/massfacts/snapshot_dunkin_donuts_vs_starbucks_ massachusetts.

30. Seth Harry, "A Short History of Suburban Retail" (Seth Harry and Associates, Inc., February 8, 2004), www.placemakers.com/library/HistoryofSuburbanRetail.doc.

31. Hayden, *Field Guide to Sprawl*, p. 42.

32. Congressional Oversight Panel, *February Oversight Report: Commercial Real Estate Losses and the Risk to Financial Stability* (Washington, D.C.: Congressional Oversight Panel, February 19, 2010), p. 2.

33. Alison Zaya, Steven Butzel, and Linda N. Taggart, *The Nashua Experience: A Three-Decade Upgrade, 1978–2008* (Portsmouth, N.H.: Jetty House, for the Nashua Public Library, 2009), pp. 12–13.

34. "Nashua Puts Brakes on Business Growth Along Jammed Roads," *New England Business*, October 7, 1985; Brad Pokorny, "Commercial/Industrial Real Estate Review: New Hampshire Reporting Huge Expansion," *Boston Globe*, March 13, 1984.

35. Winifred A. Wright, *The Granite Town: Milford, New Hampshire, 1901/1978* (Canaan, N.H.: Phoenix Publishing, for the Town of Milford, 1979), pp. 62, 58–59.

36. "Nashua, N.H.: Chains Seek Sites as Megalopolis Edges North," *Discount Store News*, May 23, 1988.

37. Berube et al., *Finding Exurbia*, p. 6.

38. Ibid., pp. 13, 36–37.

39. James C. O'Connell, *Becoming Cape Cod: Creating a Seaside Resort* (Hanover, N.H.: University Press of New England, 2003), pp. 126–129, 132. Between 2000 and 2010, Cape Cod's population declined from 222,230 to 216,902, the first time the region's population declined since the 1910s.

40. Brenda Case Scheer, "Shape of the City," *Planning*, July, 2007, pp. 30–33.

Chapter 11

1. Robert Fishman, *Bourgeois Utopias: The Rise and Fall of Suburbia* (New York: Basic Books, 1987), p. 207.

2. Massachusetts Office of State Planning, *City and Town Centers, A Program for Growth: The Massachusetts Growth Policy Report* (Boston: Commonwealth of Massachusetts, 1977), pp. ii, 10.

3. Ibid., p. ii.

4. Commonwealth of Massachusetts, "Economic Development Work Program—303D and 308D—Adaptive Reuse of Vacant Mill Buildings," prepared for the U.S. Economic Development Administration (Boston: Commonwealth of Massachusetts, 1975), pp. 1–2.

5. Massachusetts Office of State Planning, *City and Town Centers*, p. i. Between 1950 and 1970, the state's population increased by 21 percent, while urbanized land grew from 8 percent to 15 percent of the state's land mass.

6. "Attached Policy Paper on Shopping Center Development," June 12, 1975, Archives, Massachusetts Office of State Planning, Massachusetts State Archives; Memo, Frank Keefe to Governor Dukakis, May 27, 1975, Archives, Massachusetts Office of State Planning, Massachusetts State Archives.

7. Letter, George E. Slye, Executive VP, Spaulding and Slye Corporation, to Frank Keefe, May 26, 1976; William Connaughton, President, Algonquin Properties, Inc., to Governor Michael Dukakis, December 13, 1976, Massachusetts Office of State Planning Archives, Massachusetts State Archives.

8. Richard Gaines and Michael Segal, *Dukakis and the Reform Impulse* (Boston: Quinlan Press, 1987), p. 145.

9. The earliest mention found in the *Boston Globe* of the nickname "Taxachusetts" was in "The Origin of a Pie," *Boston Globe*, November 18, 1953. The term became particularly popular during the run-up to the Proposition 2½ property tax limit vote in 1980.

10. Kevin Breunig, *Losing Ground: At What Cost?*, 3rd edition (Lincoln, Mass.: Massachusetts Audubon Society, 2003), p. 1; James DeNormandie, *Losing Ground: Beyond the Footprint: Patterns of Development and their Impact on the Nature of Massachusetts,* 4th edition (Lincoln, Mass.: Massachusetts Audubon Society, 2009), p. 2.

11. This strategy has been given even greater salience by a study of the Harvard Forest—David Foster, David Kittredge, Brian Donahue, Glenn Motzkin, David Orwig, Aaron Ellison, Brian Hall, Betsy Colburn, and Anthony D'Amato, *Wildlands & Woodlands: A Vision for the Forests of Massachusetts* (Petersham, MA: Harvard Forest, Harvard University, 2006). The report warns that Massachusetts, which currently has 60 percent of its land area forested, needs at least 50 percent forest land in order to maintain ecological health. The Harvard Forest report calls for protecting an additional 1.25 million acres of "woodland" and 250,000 acres of "wildland" reserves, which would preserve valuable wildlife habitats and the state's remaining "old growth forests."

12. Randall Arendt, Elizabeth A. Brabec, Harry L. Dodson, Christine Reid, and Robert D. Yaro, *Rural by Design: Maintaining Small Town Character* (Chicago: Planners Press American Planning Association, 1994); Randall Arendt, Elizabeth A. Brabec, Harry L. Dodson, and Robert D. Yaro, *Dealing with Change in the Connecticut River Valley: A Design Manual for Conservation and Development* (Cambridge, Mass.: Lincoln Institute of Land Policy, 1988).

13. Theresa M. Hanafin, "The Rape of the Cape," *Boston Globe*, August 30, 1987.

14. "Statewide CPA Statistics," Community Preservation Coalition website, http://www.community preservation.org/pprojects?qid=22&dbid=bca5gqwrk.

15. Massachusetts Audubon Society, *Losing Ground*, 4th edition, pp. 5–6.

16. The most recent zoning reform bill before the legislature is called the Comprehensive Land Use and Partnership Act (CLURPA). "CLURPA—Text and Summary," City Solicitors and Town Counsel Association website, http://www.massmunilaw.org/clurpa-text-and-summaries.

17. Massachusetts Executive Office of Environmental Affairs, *The State of Our Environment: A Special Report on Community Preservation and the Future of Our Commonwealth* (Boston: Commonwealth of Massachusetts, 2002).

18. Metropolitan Area Planning Council, *MetroFuture: Making a Greater Boston Region* (Boston: Metropolitan Area Planning Council, 2008), p. 9.

19. Boston Metropolitan Planning Organization, "Traffic Volumes and Hours of Congestion for Eastern Massachusetts Express Highways," *Boston Metropolitan Planning Organization,* http://www.bostonmpo .org/bostonmpo/3_programs/6_mms/2_roadways/hours_of_congestion.pdf. The number of Vehicle Miles Traveled on Eastern Massachusetts express highways increased from 19.6 million in 1970 to 56.1 million in 2000. Metropolitan Area Planning Council, "Passenger Vehicle Miles Travelled" (September), *Metropolitan Area Planning Council 2010 Calendar* (2010). Residents of the cities of Boston, Cambridge, and Somerville average less than thirty VMTs per day, compared with outer suburbs, which can average around seventy-five miles per day.

20. Office of Planning, Federal Highway Administration, "Chapter 4: Means of Travel to Work," *Journey to Work Trends in the United States and Its Major Metropolitan Areas, 1960–2000* (2003), http://www.fhwa.dot.gov/planning/census_issues/ctpp/data_products/journey_to_work/jtw4.cfm.

21. Although the 1980s restoration of South Station encouraged significant growth in commuter rail ridership, it paled in comparison with the early twentieth century. Opened in 1899, South Station was the busiest railroad station in the world. It served 3,000 trains a day, with the vast majority carrying commuters. South Station had twenty-eight tracks but has only thirteen tracks today. The state is planning to increase the number of tracks to twenty to allow commuter service to expand. Stephen Puleo, *A City So Grand: The Rise of an American Metropolis, Boston, 1850–1900* (Boston: Beacon Press, 2010), p. 255.

22. "America's Top 50 Bike-Friendly Cities," *Bicycling Magazine*, www.bicycling.com/news/advocacy/26-boston-ma.

23. National Academy of Sciences, Committee for the Study on the Relationships among Development Patterns, Vehicle Miles Traveled, and Energy Consumption, *Driving the Built Environment: The Effects of Compact Development on Motorized Travel, Energy Use, and CO2 Emissions—Special Report 298* (Washington, D.C.: National Academies Press, 2009), p. 154.

24. Massachusetts Office of Commonwealth Development, *Transit-Oriented Development Inventory of Sites* (Boston: Massachusetts Office of Commonwealth Development, October 17, 2006).

25. "Chapter 40R," Massachusetts Executive Office of Housing and Economic Development, http://www.mass.gov/hed/docs/dhcd/cd/ch40r/40ractivitysummary.pdf.

26. Steve Adams, "Quincy Center Makeover One of the Most Ambitious in New England," *The Patriot-Ledger*, February 26, 2012.

27. Ann Satterthwaite, *Going Shopping: Consumer Choices and Community Consequences* (New Haven, Conn.: Yale University Press, 2001), p. 187.

28. Peter Calthorpe and William Fulton, *The Regional City: Planning for the End of Sprawl* (Washington, D.C., 2001), pp. 204–208.

29. Sarah Shemkus, "Mashpee Commons: A Community Rises," *Cape Cod Times*, February 27, 2011.

30. Robert Campbell, "Town Center, but No Town," *Boston Globe*, October 18, 2009.

31. When General Properties was redesigning the Natick Mall, the company wanted to drop the term "mall" and just name the shopping center "Natick." This was too much for the local citizenry, whose town had been named "Natick" since 1781. Town meeting vehemently opposed an effort to equate the town with the mall. The developer ended up calling the mall "Natick Collection."

32. Christopher B. Leinberger, *The Option of Urbanism: Investing in a New American Dream* (Washington, D.C.: Island Press, 2007), p. 94.

33. Sociologist Ray Oldenburg wrote in *The Great Good Place: Cafés, Coffee Shops, Community Centers, Beauty Parlors, General Stores, Bars, and Hangouts and How They Get You through the Day* (New York: Paragon Press, 1989) about the importance of "third places." The "first" place is home, the "second" is work, and the "third" is the neutral place where you can get away from it all and live as part of a community. Oldenburg explains: "Though a radically different kind of setting from a home, the third place is remarkably similar to a good home in the psychological comfort and support that it extends. . . . They are the heart of a community's social vitality, the grassroots of democracy. . . . " Some are chains like

Starbuck's, while others are one-of-a-kind-local spots. Americans have become more interested in "third places" after having experienced them in Europe, where they have long been an important part of life—cafés in Paris, pubs in England and Ireland, beer gardens in Germany and the Czech Republic, coffeehouses is Vienna, and tapas bars in Spain.

34. Richard Florida, *The Great Reset: How New Ways of Living and Working Drive Post-Crash Prosperity* (New York: Harper, 2010), p. 179.

35. Metropolitan Area Planning Council, *MetroFuture*. It should be noted that the Metropolitan Area Planning Council introduced the concept of concentrating new growth in "subregional centers" in its 1990 *MetroPlan 2000*. This plan was a conceptual overview rather than the detailed implementation strategy that MAPC produced eighteen years later. Metropolitan Area Planning Council, *MetroPlan 2000: A Plan for Future Growth* (Boston: Metropolitan Area Planning Council, 1990).

36. Tom Keane, "40B in Voters' Backyard," *Boston Globe,* September 27, 2010.

37. Edward Glaeser, *Triumph of the City: How Our Greatest Invention Makes Us Richer, Smarter, Greener, Healthier, and Happier* (New York: Penguin Press, 2011), p. 263; Edward L. Glaeser with Jenny Schuetz and Bryce Ward, *Regulation and the Rise of Housing Prices in Greater Boston* (Cambridge, Mass.: Rappaport Institute for Greater Boston, Kennedy School of Government, Harvard University, 2006), p. 36; Barry Bluestone, Charles Billingham, and Tim Davis, *The Greater Boston Housing Report Card 2008: From Paradigm to Paradox: Understanding Greater Boston's New Housing Market* (Boston: The Center for Urban and Regional Policy, Northeastern University, 2008), p. 12.

38. Joel Kotkin, *The New Suburbanism: A Realist's Guide to the American Future* (Costa Mesa, Calif.: The Planning Center, 2005), p. 2.

Chapter 12

1. Institute for the Future, *When Everything Is Programmable* (2009), http://www.iftf.org/node/3724. Institute for the Future, *A Planet of Civic Laboratories: The Future of Cities, Information, and Inclusion* (December, 2010), http://www.rockefellerfoundation.org/uploads/files/814a5087-542c-4353-9619-60ff913b4589-sr.pdf.

2. Boston Mayor's Office of New Urban Mechanics website, http://www.newurbanmechanics.org.

3. Massachusetts Institute of Technology CarTel Project website, http://cartel.csail.mit.edu/doku.php.

4. Peter C. Frumhoff, James J. McCarthy, Jerry M. Melillo, Susanne C. Moser, Donald J. Wuebbles, *Confronting Climate Change in the US Northeast: Science Impacts, and Solutions* (Cambridge, Mass.: Union of Concerned Scientists, 2007), pp. 6–7. According to the report, average winter temperatures in Massachusetts could rise 8 to 12°F by the end of the twenty-first century, and average summer temperatures are projected to rise 6 to 14°F.

5. Tim Lenton, Anthony Footitt, and Andrew Dlugolecki, *Major Tipping Points in the Earth's Climate System and Consequences for the Insurance Sector* (Gland, Switzerland and Munich, Germany: World Wide Fund for Nature and Allianz, 2009), p. 33.

6. Frumhoff, el at, *Confronting Climate Change,* pp. 20–21. The higher-emissions scenario entails a continued heavy reliance on fossil fuels, which cause heat-trapping gases to increase significantly over the next century. The lower-emissions scenario entails a transition to clean energy technologies, which would induce a reduction of heat-trapping gases by midcentury.

7. Hubert Murray and Antonio Di Mambro, "The High Tide of Opportunity," *Architecture Boston*, Summer 2010, pp. 24–27.

8. "RGGI Fact Sheet," Regional Greenhouse Gas Initiative website, http://www.rggi.org/docs/RGGI_Fact_Sheet.pdf; "Mass. Ranked First in the Nation for Energy Efficiency," Massachusetts Department of Energy Resources website, http://www.mass.gov/governor/pressoffice/pressreleases/2011/111020-energy-efficiency.html.

9. "Boston—2008 US Cities Sustainability Ranking," SustainLane.com, http://www.sustainlane.com/us-city-rankings/cities/boston.

Index

Hamilton, 31, 104

Hammond Pond Reservation, 159

Hancock Village, 141, 176, 263

Handbook of New England, A, 5

Hand-held devices, 253–254

Handlin, Oscar, 44

Hanscom Air Force Base, 153

Hanson, 129

Harbor cleanup, 191

Harbor Point, 138

HarborWalk, 194, 199, 262

Hardwick, Elizabeth, 152, 184

Harr, Jonathan, 125

Harrison, Peter, 37

Harvard, MA, 210

Harvard Forest report, 291n11

Harvard Square subway, 77

Haverhill, 5, 124, 133, 217

Hawthorne, Nathaniel, 64, 172

Hayden, Dolores, x, 129, 140, 206

Hazardous waste sites, 131

Heartbreak Hill, 114

Hemenway, Augustus, 104

Hemlock Gorge, 93

Henderson House, 38, 267

Heritage State Parks, 227

Hewlett-Packard, 154, 156, 206

"Hialewa," 30

Higgins, George V., 188

Higginson, Alexander Henry, 27

Highland Branch commuter rail, 18

High-tech industry, 6, 153–156

Highway Beautification Act of 1965, 225

Highway system, 6–7, 125. *See also* Interstate
    highway system
    and commuters, 202
    and distribution centers, 206
    and edge cities, 201–203
    and entertainment centers, 206–207
    federal and state route designations, 108
    and land-use patterns, 201
    limited-access highways, 150
    and mill towns, 126, 129
    New Hampshire, 217
    and North Shore development, 33–34
    opposition to, 30

and parkland, 167

and postwar suburbs, 135–136, 149, 167

and retail development, 206, 213

and sprawl, 202

and strip development, 108, 160–163

and suburban development, 6–7, 107–108,
    135–136, 148–149

and urban decline, 184, 190, 193

Hillsborough, 217

Hilltop Steak House, 162, 163, 179

Hingham, 34, 241, 244, 245, 250

Hingham Shipyard, 243–244, 251

Hinston, John, 108

"Hipsters in the Woods," 144

Historic preservation, 130–131, 170, 172
    housing, 111
    mill buildings, 227
    and urban renewal, 188

H. M. Pulham, Esquire, 19

Hoar, Samuel, 172

Holbrook, 49, 129

Holbrook, Elisha N., 49

Holl, Steven, 199

Holliston, 210

Holmes, Oliver Wendell, Sr., 77

Holyoke, 227

Home Depot, 214–215, 261

Honeywell, 155, 206

Hopedale, 231

Hopkinton, 208, 209, 210, 212, 231, 233
    Estates, The, 211, 222, 264
    Hopkinton Highlands, 222, 264

Horse-drawn streetcars, 4, 69–70, 72–73

Horse-drawn vehicles, 100

Hotels, resort, 35–36

Household size, 210

Housing. *See also* Lot size; Single-family housing;
    Subdivisions; Zoning
    affordable, 173–174, 177
    amenities, 107, 109–112
    antebellum, 24
    comfortable, 110
    country villas, 23–24
    early twentieth century, 109–110
    family, 245
    and green spaces, 5